against Sharia's remarkable resemblance to both Communism and Nazism, against the concept of 'dialogue' explicitly intended to dupe and delude, against the constant equation of jihad and crusade in spite of the latter's launching in reaction to more than four centuries of the former, against Muhammad's evil perversion of Jesus into the unrecognizable *'Îsâ* of the Koran, against Sharia's mandate to lie known as *taqiya*, against the origins of Islam as a Judeo-Christian heretical sect, and perhaps most of all against His Holiness Pope Francis' error in his attitude towards Islam.

"Let us all take to heart this book's urgent warning, and that of its inspiration, the great Catholic freedom fighter Plinio Corrêa de Oliveira.

"Let us stay the hand of the West before it deals itself a fatal blow. In the name of the Father, the Son, and the Holy Spirit I pray."

— *Christopher C. Hull, Ph.D.*
Executive Vice President, Center for Security Policy

"A concise but comprehensive guide to Islam's threat to the West, this informative book shows how today's terror is linked to Islamic theology and history. *Islam and the Suicide of the West* also tells the story of how the West is naively collaborating in its own demise. Solimeo's eye-opening book contains many useful insights, as well as a novel theory of Islam's origins."

— *William Kilpatrick*
Author of **Christianity, Islam, and**
Atheism: The Struggle for the Soul of the West

ISLAM
AND THE
SUICIDE
OF THE
WEST

ISLAM
AND THE
SUICIDE
OF THE
WEST

THE ORIGIN, DOCTRINE, AND GOALS OF ISLAM

Luiz Sérgio Solimeo

The American Society for the Defense of Tradition, Family, and Property—TFP

Spring Grove, Penn.

Citations for Bible versions other than the Douay-Rheims are designated by their
respective abbreviated prefix. Citations for English Koran quotes other than Abdullah
Yusuf Ali's translation published in *Meaning of the Noble Qu'ran* are identified by their
corresponding abbreviated prefix (see List of Abbreviations). All *hadith* citations are
from Sunnah.com, and the abbreviated prefix for the respective collection is used,
followed by the Arabic *hadith* number. Citations for quotes from Church Fathers are
abbreviated in the footnotes with full source details in the Bibliography. All
translations from cited foreign language sources are the publisher's. Unless otherwise
noted all emphases in quotes are the author's.

ISBN 978-1-877905-58-2
ISBN 978-1-877905-59-9 (ebook)
Library of Congress Catalogue Card No. 2018956888

Printed in the United States of America

To download the e-book version of this book, please visit:
http://www.tfp.org/IslamSuicideWest

DEDICATION

This book is dedicated to
Asia Bibi,
and the innumerable Christians who have
endured hardship, persecution, imprisonment,
and exile at the hands of Islam since the
Hijra (AD 622), but especially to the beloved martyrs
who were slain "because of the witness they bore
to the word of God" (Apoc. 6:9), having refused to
renege on their baptismal vows and deny
Our Lord Jesus Christ,
the Word Incarnate, and our Divine Redeemer;
the Blessed Trinity,
—the Father, the Son, and the Holy Spirit—
One God, in Three Persons;
and Mary, the Immaculate Conception
and Blessed Mother of God.

The International Pilgrim Virgin Statue of Our Lady of Fatima visiting the American TFP's headquarters in Spring Grove, Pennsylvania, in 2002.

"We are in the extreme throes of a struggle . . . that would be mortal if one of the contenders were not immortal. . . .

"Behold . . . the unvarying confidence of the Catholic soul, which kneels but remains firm amid the general convulsion—firm with all the firmness of those who, in the storm, and with a strength of soul even greater than it, continue to affirm from the bottom of their heart: '*Credo in Unam, Sanctam, Catholicam et Apostolicam Ecclesiam*,' that is, 'I believe in the Holy Roman Catholic and Apostolic Church, against which, as promised to Saint Peter, the gates of hell will never prevail.'"

— Plinio Corrêa de Oliveira,
Revolution and Counter-Revolution

Contents

Part One: Islam's Renewed Onslaught

Part Two: Islam's Anti-Christian Doctrines and Origins

Acknowledgments

Firstly, I want to express my gratitude to the late Prof. Plinio Corrêa de Oliveira, founder of the Brazilian Society for the Defense of Tradition, Family, and Property, for the intellectual and spiritual formation I received from him, beginning in 1959. His articles warning of the dangers of a resurgent Islam dating as far back as 1947 and the TFP studies on its advances that he directed from then until his death in 1995 were fundamental for the elaboration of this book.

I am also indebted to Raymond E. Drake, American TFP president, and my brother, Gustavo Antônio Solimeo, who collaborated in the book's conceptualization and editing. John W. Horvat II, TFP vice-president, contributed many timely observations. Veteran TFP member José Aloisio Schelini worked on translations from foreign languages into English. TFP director Robert E. Ritchie coordinated the creation of book's title and cover. TFP member Keith J. Douet assisted with research and library book loans and, along with several others, helped with the book's final editing.

My fellow TFP members encouraged me at this project's every step. To one and all, my sincere gratitude for their generous assistance.

Fr. Édouard-Marie Gallez was of invaluable assistance, answering questions, and authorizing the use of his research and writings.

LIST OF ABBREVIATIONS

II   Ibn Ishaq

JT   *Jami at-Tirmidhi*

MP   *The Meaning of the Glorious Quran*, translation by Mohammed Marmaduke Pickthall

MS   *The Holy Quran: Arabic Text With English Translation*, translation by Muhammad Sarwar

NA   New American Bible, Revised Edition.

QD   *The Holy Koran*, translation by Hasan Qaribullah and Ahmad Darwish

SAD   *Sunan Abi Dawud*

SB   *Sahih al-Bukhari*

SI   *The Qur'an: With Sura Introductions and Appendices*, translation by Saheeh International

SIM   *Sunan Ibn Majah*

SM   *Sahih Muslim*

The cowardly 9/11 attack on America and its 2,977 victims are an example of Islamist ideology and the Jihad directives found in the Koran in verses such as "Kill them wherever you find them." *Above*: Ground Zero, where the Twin Towers once stood.

Foreword

This book was written during the 100th anniversary of the apparitions of Our Lady of Fatima. It explains the incompatibility of Islam with Christianity and Western values. Peaceful coexistence with Islam is also a non-starter as it ignores the goal of all Sharia-adherent Muslims to impose Islam.

Therefore, many Christians today are confused over Pope Francis's "Outreach Program" to Islamists, while Christians continue to be slaughtered, and centuries-old churches destroyed or converted into mosques. It has been demonstrated repeatedly throughout time that interfaith dialogue is fundamentally flawed. Those who support it try to promote an angelic discourse on Islam that denies its inherent problem with violence. Furthermore, the pope's statement, "Don't proselytize, respect other beliefs," only adds to the confusion.

Luiz S. Solimeo clearly and concisely makes the case and provides the facts that support the belief that Islam is a totalitarian ideology bent on world domination, masquerading as a religion. There are 164 Jihad verses in the Koran that preach and incite violence against Christians and other "unbelievers." For example, in chapter 7, titled "Persecution of Christians"—"Kill them wherever you find them"—and never take one as a friend.

The fact of the matter is that Islam is an open declaration of war against all "unbelievers." The worst six words President George W. Bush ever uttered was, "Islam is a religion of peace." Nothing could be further from the truth, though it is also true that many Muslims are peaceful. With the Muslim Brotherhood (MB) penetration of all of our key national security and intelligence agencies, I am sure he was greatly influenced by their agents. That penetration by the MB, which should be designated as a terrorist organization, exists today.

This book clearly explains how Islamic fundamentalism is actually a continuation of the communist ideology of the twentieth century. It shows how the two combine efforts to destroy Western democracies. Islam, in effect, is the communism of our day.

The myth that Christians and Muslims worship the same God is nonsense. The Koran and the hadith not only deny the Blessed Trinity but see devotion to it as idolatry. Further, Islam's persecution of Christians is actually motivated by their hatred of the dogma of the Trinity.

Those who see and espouse the incompatibility of Islam with Western values are called Islamophobes, a term used by the MB to shut down any criticism of Islam. Acknowledged experts on Islam like Robert Spencer are often denied the opportunity to speak in order to expose the real threat of Islam. The same applies to those who try to confront the current Islamization of Europe under the banner of multi-culturalism.

The question is, will the West return to its Christian civilization roots inspired by the Gospel, or will it submit to Islamic totalitarianism? Belief in the message of Fatima provides the answer, as it implies a great conversion of Muslims and a complete victory of the Cross over the Crescent.

Admiral James A. Lyons, U.S. Navy (Ret.)

James A. Lyons, U.S. Navy retired admiral, was commander-in-chief of the U.S. Pacific Fleet and senior U.S. military representative to the United Nations.

Islam, a Danger Prowling About the World

Islam is the issue of the day. Through terrorism, mass immigration, and pressure groups in the West, Islamist expansionism begins to look like a quest for domination.

Over 70 years ago, when hardly anyone was attuned to the issue, the Brazilian Catholic scholar and founder of the Brazilian Society for the Defense of Tradition, Family, and Property—TFP, Prof. Plinio Corrêa de Oliveira, foresaw Islam's revival as a danger to the West.

Shortly after World War II, he wrote several articles in the Catholic weekly *Legionário* pointing out how Islamic forces were beginning to awaken and the danger this would represent in a few decades.

For example, a 1947 article, "Mohammed's Rebirth," described the impact that the First and Second World Wars had on the Islamic world, on the formation of new Islamic countries, and on the beginning of European decolonization. He commented:

> All this transformed the Islamic world and produced in all Mohammedan peoples, from India to Morocco, a shudder that means that the millennial slumber is over....
> The vital nerve of Islam revives in all these peoples, rekindling in them a sense of unity, a notion of common interests, concerns of solidarity, and a taste for victory....
> Does it take much talent, insight, and exceptional information to realize what this danger means?[1]

The dynamism of this expansionism and the support it receives from liberal leaders and media are reminiscent of communist expansionism during the Cold War.

Unfortunately, very few Catholic bishops raise the alarm, urging the faithful to defend the faith and remnants of Christian civilization. On the contrary, in the name of interreligious dialogue,

---

1. Plinio Corrêa de Oliveira, "Mohammed's Rebirth," Sept. 1, 2014, http://www.tfp.org /muhammad-s-rebirth/. First published as "Maomé renasce," *Legionário*, no. 775, Jun. 15, 1947, http://www.pliniocorreadeoliveira.info/leg_470615_maome_renasce.htm #.wpccaq6nhcs.

Catholic leaders usually support mass immigration, the building of mosques and Islamic cultural centers, the use of the hijab, with some even allowing it in Catholic schools, together with rooms set aside for Muslim prayer.[2]

Experts on Islamic terrorism have noted that the primary recruitment places, whether in the East or the West, are the madrasahs (Koranic schools) and mosques, most of them funded by Saudi Arabia.

The imams of these schools and mosques make use of the Koran (sometimes spelled *Qur'an* or *Quran*), and Islamic traditions (*hadith*) to transform young Muslims who were born in the West and enjoy its opulence into ferocious enemies. They fill them with hatred against that same West that gives them shelter and resources.

While it is true that not every Muslim, even devout ones, is a terrorist, we cannot deny that the Islamic religion has been the principal source of the new terrorism plaguing the world. It provides religious and moral justification for the use of brutal violence and killing, including the slaughter of moderate Muslims. Part One focuses on the resurgent threat.

Since the fundamental factor of Islamic expansionism is religious, then, to resist it seriously, we must have a general idea of Islam's beliefs, origins, doctrines, morals, and relationship to today's terrorism. We cover this in Part Two. In recent years, Islamicists have begun to study the role that the Ebionites (also called Judeo-Nazarenes) played in Islam's origins. The Ebionites were a religious sect that combined elements from Christianity and Judaism.[3] We shall present this hypothesis in this work as a historic contribution to better understand Islam, and, above all, the Koran's doctrine.

In this unpretentious work, we attempt to respond succinctly to

---

2.   "The construction of more official mosques will boost security in Western nations, said Archbishop of Bordeaux, Cardinal Jean-Pierre Ricard, Archbishop of Budapest, Cardinal Peter Erdo, and Archbishop Josip Bozani of Zagreb." "Vatican: Three Senior Clerics Back More European Mosques," *Adnkronos International*, Dec. 18, 2008, http://www1.adnkronos.com/AKI /English/Religion/?id=3.0.2829866770. "L'Islam et le voile dans les écoles catholiques?" *Le Peuple au Service de la Vérité*, May 6, 2016, http://lepeuple.be/lislam-et-le-voile-dans-les-ecoles -catholiques/65439; "Musulmans en école catholique," *Enseignement Catholique*, May 4, 2016, https://enseignement-catholique.fr/wp-content/uploads/2016/05/4-2-musulmansenecole -catholique.pdf.

3.   See Ray A. Pritz, *Nazarene Jewish Christianity: From the End of the New Testament Period Until Its Disappearance in the Fourth Century* (Leiden-Jerusalem: E.J. Brill and The Magnes Press at the Hebrew University, 1988); Patricia Crone, "Jewish Christianity and the Qur'an," *Journal of Near Eastern Studies* 74, no. 2 (October 2015): 225–53, https://www.journals.uchicago.edu /doi/abs/10.1086/ 682212; Édouard-Marie Gallez, *Le Messie et son prophète: Aux origines de l'Islam* (Versailles: Editions de Paris, 2005), 2 vols.

this need, based as much as possible on the Koran and Sunna, other old and current Islamic sources, and analyses by renowned Western specialists. Considering his Cambridge education and Indian Civil Service background, we draw mainly from Abdullah Yusuf Ali's English translation of the Koran, but other accepted translations were also used. We hope that the information presented here will help non-specialized readers to form a more accurate idea of Muhammad's religion and the West's imminent danger.

In writing this work, we are not moved by any personal animosity towards Muslims, not even terrorists. Our goal is only to present the truth and to provide facts and arguments for successful resistance to Islamic expansionism, in defense of what remains of the once glorious Christian civilization.

PART ONE

Islam's Renewed Onslaught

The open border mentality promoted by the far left and, regrettably, high ranking Catholic clergy, defies centuries-old established Catholic doctrine as well as common sense. *Above:* Syrian refugees in Budapest on their way to Germany.

Syrian refugees at the Turkish border.

Immigration or Invasion?

The right of immigration exists by natural law since the Earth as such belongs to all men.

Limits to the Natural Right of Immigration

Legitimately established states also have a natural right to regulate immigration into their territories to defend the common good of their citizens. This applies not only to economic and security matters but also cultural and spiritual goods, including national identity.

These two rights are not opposed but must be harmonized according to the Christian principles of justice and charity.

If there were no rules to regulate and serve as the norm for immigration, nations would plunge into chaos, and both natives and immigrants would suffer the consequences.

The individual good cannot dispense with or supersede the common good. Both goods have the same end and complete each other. Any exaggeration in one or the other causes a rupture in the proper legal order of a nation, harming individuals and society alike.

Those who immigrate must respect the laws and immigration rules of their host country. Every righteous law obliges both individuals and society since a just law manifests God's will, as known through human reason. Once welcomed into the host country, immigrants must integrate and assimilate into the local culture, instead of rejecting it, forming social cysts that disturb their new community.

Undoubtedly, it is legitimate for them to preserve their traditions and customs, but without opposing the characteristics of their country of adoption, seeking instead to harmonize with them in a spirit of true patriotism.

Immigration involves philosophical, moral, and even theological problems, which, to be correctly resolved depend on sound analyses of the facts and circumstances. We cannot be carried away by emotion, simplify problems, or treat them in a biased way wanting to see just one aspect of the issue.

In other words, it is useless to speak of morality and the principles of justice if, when the time comes to apply them to concrete situations, we do not assess the latter well, with objectivity.[4]

The Islamization of Europe

In a 2017 study, the Pew Research Center "assumed that only Muslim migrants who already have—or are expected to gain—legal status in Europe will remain for the long term, providing a baseline of 25.8 million Muslims as of 2016 (4.9% of Europe's population). However, this number could increase to 26.8 million "if *all* the approximately 1 million Muslims who are currently in legal limbo in Europe were to remain in Europe."[5]

The Russian Federation is the European country with the largest Muslim population, 15 million, some 11% of the population. "Muslims will represent between one third . . . and one half . . . of the Russian population by around 2050."[6] Most of Russia's Muslims do not stem from immigration, but from extending the Romanov Tsars' dominions to lands with followers of Muhammad.

Starting in 2011, the disruptions of the Arab Spring displaced ever larger numbers of people. Many made their way to Europe. In 2015 alone, a "record 1.3 million migrants applied for asylum in the 28 member states of the European Union, Norway and Switzerland."[7] The overwhelming majority came from Muslim countries.

Europe and North America have accepted millions of Muslim immigrants from around the world, but present instability in Northern Africa and the greater Middle East have catapulted the number of Muslims seeking admission.

Turkey is threatening to unleash its three million Syrian refugees into Europe. Should Jordan and Lebanon become destabilized, the millions of refugees they host, and many others, will seek shelter in the West as well. This new wave of Muslim refugees would effectively double Europe's already festering crisis.

This mass migration, combined with the brutal drop in the

---

4.   See Victor Cathrein, SJ, *Philosophia Moralis* (Fribourg: Herder, 1905).

5.   Pew Research Center, "Europe's Growing Muslim Population," Nov. 29, 2017, http://www
      .pewforum.org/2017/11/29/europes-growing-muslim-population/. (Emphasis in the original.)

6.   Marlene Laruelle, "How Islam Will Change Russia," *Jamestown.org*, Sept. 13, 2016,
      https://jamestown.org/program/marlene-laruelle-how-islam-will-change-russia/.

7.   Phillip Connor, "Number of Refugees to Europe Surges to Record 1.3 Million in 2015," *Pew
      Research Center*, Aug. 2, 2016, http://www.pewglobal.org/2016/08/02/number-of-refugees-to
      -europe-surges-to-record-1-3-million-in-2015/.

birthrate of European countries, makes for a very somber future of Christianity in Europe.

A Real Occupation Army

Looking at the sex and age of the new Muslim hordes arriving in Europe, they appear more like occupation troops than peaceful immigrants and refugees. According to the Pew Research Center, "Over half (53%) of asylum seekers to the European Union, Norway and Switzerland in 2015 were young adults—those ages 18 to 34. This was also generally the top age group among asylum seekers in Europe from the three leading origin countries. Roughly half of those from Syria (50%), Iraq (56%) and Afghanistan (45%) were young adults in 2015."[8]

Prof. Valerie Hudson, of Texas A&M University, shows the dangers of massive male immigration, not only regarding terrorism and sexual harassment, but also the balance between the sexes in Western countries. "According to official counts," she says, "a disproportionate number of these migrants are young, unmarried, unaccompanied males."[9]

She provides the following data:

- Over 66 percent of adult migrants registered through Italy and Greece in 2014 were male, according to the International Organization of Migration.

- According to Swedish government statistics, as of the end of November 2015, 71 percent of its asylum applicants in 2015 were male.

- Some 90% of minors traveling to Europe as *unaccompanied* minors are males.

- The Swedish government's figures report that 18,615 males aged 16 and 17 entered Sweden in 2015, compared with 2,555 females of the same age.

Many of these young people are behaving like conquerors in their European host countries. They believe they have a religious duty to impose Islam around the world. French Islamicist Marie-Thérèse

---

8. Ibid.
9. Valerie Hudson, "Europe's Man Problem: Migrants to Europe Skew Heavily Male—and That's Dangerous," *Politico Magazine*, Jan. 5, 2016, http://www.politico.com/magazine/story/2016/01/europe-refugees-migrant-crisis-men-213500.

Urvoy explains: "For Muslims, all humanity is born Muslim but loses the message either through personal forgetfulness or under the influence of the environment. . . . Thus, every Muslim has the role of bringing everyone back to his original and natural Islam."[10]

Burak Bekdil, a political analyst at the Middle East Forum, interviewed migrants on the island of Lesbos, Greece, one of the routes of Islamic immigration into Europe. He asked them why they left Turkey, a Muslim country that had welcomed them well, in exchange for a dangerous journey to reach Western Europe. One answered. "I want to go to Europe to increase the Muslim population there." Another commented, "'One day we good Muslims will conquer their infidel lands.'" "I asked," Bekdil writes, "why he was receiving 'infidel' money for a living. 'It's just halal,' he answered. 'They ['infidels'] are too easy to fool.'"[11]

Many of these migrants coming to Europe do not want to assimilate into the culture of their host countries, but to impose Islam. In Italy, a survey by IPR Marketing found that among Muslim immigrants, "31% (one-third of the total) do not want to integrate" into Italian society.[12]

Access Routes and the Role of NGOs

Muslim immigrants arriving in Western Europe come from the Middle East through Turkey, the Greek islands, and Eastern European countries. From Africa, they come by sea to Italy and Spain. They come from Libya, Morocco, and Tunisia, but also from countries in Sub-Saharan Africa.

In Italy, in 2015, there were 1,036,653 residents from Africa, of whom 59.4% were male. Most came from predominantly Muslim countries like Morocco, Egypt, Tunisia, and Senegal.[13]

Prof. Ana Bono, an expert on Africa at the University of Turin, points out that for the most part these immigrants cannot be qualified as refugees but rather as people seeking a better life (eco-

---

10. Élisabeth Caillemer, "Marie-Thérèse Urvoy: 'Le terrorisme islamique sent que l'Occident est fragile,'" *Famille Chrétienne*, Dec. 7, 2015, http://www.famillechretienne.fr/filinfo/marietherese -urvoy-le-terrorisme-islamique-sent-que-l-occident-est-fragile-183004.

11. Burak Bekdil, "What's on the Mind of a Muslim 'Refugee'?" *Middle East Forum*, Sept. 10, 2017, http://www.meforum.org/6917/what-on-a-muslim-refugee-mind.

12. Antonio Noto, "Musulmani in Italia, il sondaggio esclusivo di Ipr Marketing," *Quotidiano.net*, Sept. 19, 2017, http://www.quotidiano.net/politica/musulmani-in-italia-1.3406983.

13. See Comuni-Italiani, "Residenti in Italia dall'Africa," accessed Mar. 2, 2018, http://www.comuni -italiani.it/statistiche/stranieri/africa.html.

nomic migrants). Moreover, they are people with greater financial means, in contact through modern means of communication (especially the Internet), and who can afford the enormous expenses of the trip.[14]

If the NGOs (often funded by Western governments) worked to help migrants stay in their country, the tragedy of unsafe and overcrowded boats sinking in the Mediterranean could be avoided. Instead, their misdirected efforts effectively help the smugglers, who enrich themselves on human trafficking.

However, with the negligence or complicity of some governments and, sad to say, the misguided policy of the Holy See and many national episcopates, there is an orchestrated endeavor to bring as many Muslims to Europe as possible. Such mass migrations are only possible if someone promotes, finances, and organizes them.[15]

Muslim Immigration and Terrorism

Robert S. Leiken, of the Center for Immigration Studies, compares the terrorist attacks perpetrated in Europe in the seventies and eighties to those after 1990 when they acquired a predominantly Islamist note. He reports an alarming increase in both the number of attacks and the number of victims per attack:

> The sharp rise in casualties corresponds to the emergence of Islamist terrorism. During the 1970s and 1980's the predominant terrorist groups responsible for the most casualties were secular (largely nationalist, anarchist, or fascist). *In the 1990's those groups were supplanted by religious, typically Islamist, groups, and we witnessed a corresponding rise in both casualties per incident as well as lethality.* We calculated and compared the casualty rates for the two kinds of groups between 1968 and 2003. We found 3.27 casualties per incident for the secular nationalist groups and 27.05 casualties per incident for the religious groups.[16]

This rise in Islamist terrorism is not only due to the Muslim waves of recent years but also to the Islamization of the children of immi-

---

14. See Rodolfo Casadei, "Dall'Africa arrivano per lo più rifugiati economici, non profughi. I migranti separati dalle opinion," *Il Timone*, Jul. 5, 2017, http://www.iltimone.org/36269,News.html.

15. See Douglas Murray, "New NGO Racket: Smuggling, Inc.," *Gatestone Institute*, Sept. 2, 2017, https://www.gatestoneinstitute.org/10870/ngo-migrants-smuggling.

16. Robert Leiken, "Europe's Mujahideen: Where Mass Immigration Meets Global Terrorism," *Center for Immigration Studies*, Apr. 1, 2005, https://cis.org/Europes-Mujahideen.

grants from the fifties and sixties who were born in Europe and are recruited by Jihadists.

Leiken explains, "Jihad recruiters operate 'in makeshift prayer halls in Brussels, Islamic bookstores in 'Londonistan,' smoky coffee-houses in Amsterdam, prisons in Milan.' These candidates often subsist on the fringes of organized crime, frequently in gangs, regularly ending up in prisons where they are likely to encounter Islamist recruiters."[17]

According to the same author, the massive Islamic immigration in Western Europe favors the formation of a transnational terrorist network: "The Madrid bombers received illumination, advice, and assistance from imams and colleagues in Britain, Denmark, France, Germany, Italy and Norway as well as North Africa."[18]

Islamic Terrorism: A Stratagem of Revolutionary Psychological Warfare

Expounding on revolutionary psychological warfare, Prof. Plinio Corrêa de Oliveira wrote that it attempts, "To gradually and invisibly obtain th[at] victory in the interior of souls that it could not win through drastic and visible means, according to the classic methods, because of certain circumstances." Although only too few react to this psywar, "It is a . . . a true war of conquest—psychological, yes, but total—targeting the whole man and all men in all countries."

Plinio Corrêa de Oliveira, *Revolution and Counter-Revolution*, 3rd ed. (York, Penn.: The American Society for the Defense of Tradition, Family and Property, 1993, 141–2; 1st digital ed., Mar. 23, 2003, http://www.tfp.org/revolution-and-counter-revolution/.)

Lou Marinoff, a Philosophy professor at the City College of New York, sees Islamic terrorism from this psywar perspective. In an interview with Portugal's *Agência Lusa*, he stated that it "is just a tactic" for Westerners to "feel scared and inclined to appease Islam, giving it even more power."

Lusa, "Mundo muçulmano está a invadir Europa em 'câmara lenta,'" *RTP.pt*, May 30, 2017, https://www.rtp.pt/noticias/ mundo/mundo-muculmano-esta-a-invadir-europa-em-ca mara-lenta_n1005034.

---

17. Ibid.
18. Ibid.

Sexual Terrorism

In an article titled, "The New Terror Threat: Organized Rape," journalist Abigail R. Esman writes, "It was a different kind of terrorist attack: a carefully orchestrated, coordinated mass rape and sexual assault on hundreds of women across Cologne, Germany amongst the firework celebrations of New Year's Eve. Reports of the attacks describe women desperately fleeing as men pulled at them, groped between their legs, dragged them into alleyways, and witnesses who struggled to rescue them as men threw bottles and fireworks at the police."[19]

In fact, this new type of terrorism—rape jihad—has spread throughout Western Europe. The same journalist describes the phenomenon in the Netherlands, Belgium, and Austria.

According to Ingrid Carlqvist and Lars Hedegaard, when Sweden opened up to multiculturalism and immigration, it became the second country in the number of rapes, losing only to Lesotho: "Over the past 10–15 years, immigrants have mainly come from Muslim countries such as Iraq, Syria and Somalia. Might this mass influx explain Sweden's rape explosion," they ask? And they answer saying it is hard to know "because Swedish law forbids any registration based on people's ancestry or religion." But they recognize that "people from the Middle East have a vastly different view of women and sex than Scandinavians have."[20]

The refusal by authorities to objectively assess the cause of this rape explosion can only be described as dereliction of duty.

England's scandal of Muslim gangs that rape and traffic teenagers as young as thirteen is well-known. In his study, "British Girls Raped by Muslim Gangs on 'Industrial Scale,'" Soeren Kern, a specialist in European Islam, presents the following data:

> The report [Serious Case Review (SCR) published by the Government on March 3, 2015]—which reveals that there are "grounds for believing" that 373 girls have been sexually exploited by gangs in Oxfordshire since 2004—focuses on the accounts of six girls and their contact with the authorities. The girls were the victims in the "Operation Bullfinch" trial, in which seven Muslims were found

19. Abigail R. Esman, "The New Terror Threat: Organized Rape," *IPT News*, Jan. 15, 2016, https://www.investigativeproject.org/5130/the-new-terror-threat-organized-rape.
20. Ingrid Carlqvist and Lars Hedegaard, "Sweden: Rape Capital of the West," *Gatestone Institute*, Feb. 14, 2015, https://www.gatestoneinstitute.org/5195/sweden-rape.

guilty, in May 2013, of trafficking and raping the girls between 2004 and 2012.[21]

"Theology of Rape"

The New York Times investigative journalist Rukmini Callimachi covers al-Qaeda and ISIS. She published a 2015 report titled, "ISIS Enshrines a Theology of Rape."[22]

To write this story, she went to Iraq, where she interviewed 21 Yazidi women and girls imprisoned and enslaved by ISIS, but who managed to break free. They recounted their tragic experience as sex slaves, pointing out how Islamic State militants attached religious meaning to their continued sexual abuse. For example, a 12-year-old Yazidi girl said these militants would kneel and pray before raping her and do the same after the violence.

An already adult girl told about a younger one who suffered internal bleeding due to the sexual violence. Seeing the girl's condition, she said to the ISIS militant, "She's just a little girl," to which he answered, "No. She's not a little girl. She's a slave. And she knows exactly how to have sex. And having sex with her pleases God."[23]

Earlier in her story, the journalist discusses whether this ISIS view of slavery and sexual abuse runs counter to Islamic doctrine. Some scholars say that it does. However, she reports that "Cole Bunzel, a scholar of Islamic theology at Princeton University, disagrees, pointing to the numerous references to the phrase 'Those your right hand possesses' in the Quran, which for centuries has been interpreted to mean female slaves. He also points to the corpus of Islamic jurisprudence, which continues into the modern era and which he says includes detailed rules for the treatment of slaves."

The same scholar adds, "You can argue that it is no longer relevant and has fallen into abeyance. ISIS would argue that these institutions need to be revived, because that is what the Prophet and his companions did."[24]

---

21.   Soeren Kern, "British Girls Raped by Muslim Gangs on 'Industrial Scale,'" *Gatestone Institute*, Mar. 17, 2015, www.gatestoneinstitute.org/5386/british-girls-raped-oxford.

22.   Rukmini Callimachi, "ISIS Enshrines a Theology of Rape," *The New York Times*, Aug. 13, 2015, https://www.nytimes.com/2015/08/14/world/middleeast/isis-enshrines-a-theology-of-rape.html.

23.   Ibid.

24.   Ibid.

The Islamic site Islamweb.net would agree with him. On October 26, 2002, it posted a fatwa, a legal opinion or decree handed down by an Islamic mufti, a legal expert, and which believers should religiously follow. This "Fatwa No. 85061" explains the meaning of *Ma Malakat Aymaanukom*, the same Koranic term discussed by Cole Bunzel: "Those your right hand possesses."

The fatwa reads in part:

> Allah Says (interpretation of meaning): And those who guard their chastity (i.e. private parts, from illegal sexual acts) except from their wives or (the captives and slaves) that their right hands possess, for then, they are free from blame [23:5–6].
>
> This term includes the slave girls and slaves in general those who are under control of a free Muslim. . . .
>
> At last, a Muslim has the right to have sex with a slave girl since she is "in the possession of his right hand. Then, if she has a child, it becomes Haram to sell her, and when her master dies, she becomes free. Allah knows best."[25]

The Qatar-based *Islamweb.net* website is available in four languages—English, Spanish, German, and French. Despite Qatar's rank in the "very high human development" category by the United Nations Development Programme's *2016 Human Development Report*,[26] its wealth and status serve to scandalously and unashamedly uphold slavery and the sexual abuse of female slaves by their Muslim masters as an Islamic religious right.

In fact, the government of Qatar, through its Ministry of Endowments and Islamic Affairs, provides funding for this very website. Fahad Salman Al-Hajiri, *Islamweb*'s CEO, credits his site's success to its contributors "on top of whom is the Ministry of Endowments and Islamic Affairs (which is the sponsor and supervisor of the website), the Qatari Endowments Association (which is the main fi-

---

25. Islamweb.net, "Slaves Your Right Hands Possess: Fatwa No: 85061. Fatwa Date: 26-10-2002," accessed Feb. 28, 2018, http://www.islamweb.net/emainpage/index.php?page=showfatwa&Option=FatwaId&Id=85061. In Koranic citations, the first number is that of the *sura* or chapter, and the second that of the *ayah* or verse.

26. "Human Development Report 2016," United Nations Development Programme, Selim Jahan, Director, 22, http://hdr.undp.org/sites/default/files/HDR2016_EN_Overview_Web.pdf. See also: Lesley Walker "UN Ranks Qatar Highest Among Arab States for Human Development," *Doha News*, Dec. 15, 2015, https://dohanews.co/un-ranks-qatar-highest-among-arab-states-human-development/.

nancer of the website's projects),..."[27]

This continues seventy years after the December 10, 1948 United Nations adoption of the Universal Declaration of Human Rights. That Declaration's Article 4 unequivocally states, "No one shall be held in slavery or servitude; slavery and the slave trade shall be prohibited in all their forms."[28]

Unexpected Support

Given the above, we do not know how to explain Pope Francis's address to the national directors of pastoral care for migrants, participating in the meeting organized in Rome by the Council of European Episcopal Conferences, September 21–23, 2017:

> I cannot fail to express my concern about manifestations of intolerance, discrimination and xenophobia that have appeared in various parts of Europe. Often this reaction is motivated by mistrust and fear of the other, the foreigner, those who are different. I am even more worried about the disturbing fact that our Catholic communities in Europe are not exempt from these defensive and negative reactions, supposedly justified by a vague moral obligation to preserve an established religious and cultural identity.[29]

Is it not a moral obligation of Catholic communities to preserve the Christian religious identity of Europe—and is it not the pope's duty before God to do the same?

---

27. Islamweb.net, "Islamweb Wins World Summit Award 2007," accessed Aug. 2, 2018, http://www.islamweb.net/award/aw_e.htm.

28. "Universal Declaration of Human Rights," Dec. 10, 1948, http://www.un.org/en/universal-declaration-human-rights/

29. Francis, *Address of the Holy Father*, "Audience With the National Directors of the Pastoral Care of Migrants, Participating in the Meeting Organized by the Council of Episcopal Conferences of Europe (CCEE) (Rome, 21-23 September 2017)," *Bollettino Sala Stampa Della Santa Sede*, Sept. 22, 2017, https://press.vatican.va/content/salastampa/en/bollettino/pubblico/2017/09/22/170922d.html.

CHAPTER 2
Multiculturalism and Unfettered Immigration

Multiculturalism is the broad doctrinal justification that Western politicians and globalist opinion leaders in media and academia present to promote unbridled immigration, to the detriment of their nations' common good.

An Umbrella Term

According to the *Stanford Encyclopedia of Philosophy*,

> Multiculturalism has been used as an umbrella term to characterize the moral and political claims of a wide range of marginalized groups, including African Americans, women, LGBT people, and people with disabilities . . . . Contemporary theories of multiculturalism, which originated in the late 1980s and early 1990s, tend to focus their arguments on immigrants who are ethnic and religious minorities (e.g. Latinos in the U.S., Muslims in Western Europe), minority nations (e.g. Catalans, Basque, Welsh, Québécois), and indigenous peoples (e.g. Native peoples in North America, Australia, and New Zealand).[30]

An Old Communist Dream

On the sociological and cultural level, multiculturalism leads to the destruction of the wholesome characteristics of a people and the very existence of sovereign nations with their laws, history, culture, and ways of being.

This socio-political destruction turns an old dream of communist ideologues into reality. For example, we see this evil utopia expressed in *The Principles of Communism*, written by Frederick Engels in 1847: "What will be the attitude of Communism to existing nationalities? The nationalities . . . will be compelled to mingle with

---

30. Sarah Song, s.v. "Multiculturalism," in *The Stanford Encyclopedia of Philosophy*, ed. Edward N. Zalta (Spring, 2017 Edition), https://plato.stanford.edu/archives/spr2017/entries/multiculturalism.

each other . . . and thereby to dissolve themselves, just as the various estate and class distinctions must disappear through the abolition of their basis, private property."[31]

Later, the Italian Communist theoretician Antonio Gramsci (1891–1937) and the Freudian Marxists of the Frankfurt School laid the foundations for so-called Cultural Marxism. They expanded the concept of class struggle—proletariat versus bourgeoisie—to include the "oppressed" or "marginalized." Thus, for them, society unfairly oppresses and marginalizes the poor, prostitutes, homosexuals, and migrants. The subversive and revolutionary "liberation" of these "oppressed people" thus becomes a banner for class struggle.

More recently, the philosophers of postmodernism[32]—who deconstruct every concept by denying the existence of any objective truth—have taken subjectivism and relativism so far as to deny the very essence of things. If nothing has intrinsic worth, if everything is relative, then all cultures, institutions, and customs of peoples, civilized or savage, right or wrong, are equivalent. It is no longer possible, they argue, to make distinctions based on morality, the degree of cultural development, history, and so forth.

Hence, all peoples and all cultures—in the sense of usages and customs—must abandon their own identity, blend, and merge into a vast, undifferentiated mass, thereby fulfilling Engels's sinister forecast.

Anti-western and Anti-Christian

Historian Keith Windschuttle recounts that then–Italian Prime Minister Silvio Berlusconi, visiting Germany shortly after the 9/11 attacks, made the following statement: "We must be aware of the superiority of our civilization, a system that has guaranteed well-being, respect for human rights and—in contrast with Islamic countries—respect for religious and political rights."

When he said this, Windschuttle comments, "A bevy of European politicians rushed to denounce him. . . . Within days, Berlusconi was forced to withdraw."[33]

---

31. Frederick Engels, *The Principles of Communism*, in *Selected Works*, 1:81–97, accessed Mar. 6, 2018, https://www.marxists.org/archive/marx/works/1847/11/prin-com.htm.

32. See Gary Aylesworth, s.v. "Postmodernism," in *The Stanford Encyclopedia of Philosophy*, ed. Edward N. Zalta (Spring, 2015 Edition), https://plato.stanford.edu/archives/spr2015/entries/postmodernism/.

33. Keith Windschuttle, "The Cultural War on Western Civilization," *New Criterion*, Jan. 2002, http://www.discoverthenetworks.org/Articles/culturalwaronwesterncivilization.html.

Commenting on Berlusconi's cave-in, the same historian explains that "Though commonly known as multiculturalism, this position is defined by its supporters with a series of post prefixes: postmodernism, poststructuralism, postcolonialism. However, it is best understood as an anti phenomenon because it defines itself not by what it is for but by what it is against. It is entirely a negation of Western culture and values: whatever the West supports, this anti-West rejects."[34]

Feminism and Multiculturalism

Radical feminism is an example of this anti-Christian and anti-Western attitude. It combats Christian morality—which preaches respect for women's dignity. It defends abortion, homosexual practices, and the masculinization of women. It also advocates the greatest aberrations in the name of multiculturalism.

For example, radical feminist writer Germaine Greer, in her 1999 book, *The Whole Woman*, advocated female genital mutilation practiced in many Islamic countries in Africa and Asia.[35]

Reviewing her book for *The New York Times*, Michiko Kakutani writes,

> While Ms. Greer noisily assails the Western establishment for forcing women to conform to stereotyped standards of beauty, she denounces Western efforts to stamp out female genital mutilation in Africa as "an attack on cultural identity." Although she admits that genital mutilation "represents a significant health risk," she argues that "it must also be a procedure with considerable cultural value because it has survived 50 years of criminalization and concerted propaganda campaigns."[36]

Lord Carey of Clifton, former Archbishop of Canterbury, comments on the evils multiculturalism has brought women in the United Kingdom: "The fact is that for too long the doctrine of multiculturalism has led to immigrants establishing completely sepa-

---

34. Ibid.
35. See Thomas von der Osten-Sacken and Thomas Uwer, "Is Female Genital Mutilation an Islamic Problem?" *Middle East Quarterly*, Winter 2007, http://www.meforum.org/1629/is-female-genital-mutilation-an-islamic-problem.
36. Michiko Kakutani, "The Female Condition, Re-explored 30 Years Later," *The New York Times*, May 18, 1999, http://www.nytimes.com/1999/05/18/books/books-of-the-times-the-female-condition-re-explored-30-years-later.html.

rate communities in our cities. This has led to honor killings, female genital circumcision and the establishment of sharia law in inner-city pockets throughout the UK."[37]

One of the principal leaders of the radically feminist 2017 Women's March in Washington was Linda Sarsour, a Palestinian-American Muslim who wears the hijab, the Islamic symbol of feminine subjection.

On the March's official site we read that Linda Sarsour, "led the successful, progressive coalition to close New York public schools for the observance of two of Islam's most important holy days, Eid al-Fitr and Eid al-Adha. . . . Linda is the Executive Director of the Arab American Association of New York, co-founder of Muslims for Ferguson, and a member of Justice League NYC. She is most notably recognized for her focus on intersectional movement building."[38]

Journalist Giulio Meoti writes, "Under European multiculturalism, Muslim women *lost* many rights they should have had in Europe. They face 'honor crimes' for refusing to wear an Islamic veil; for dressing up in Western clothes; for meeting with Christian friends; for converting to another faith; for seeking a divorce; for resisting being beaten and for being too 'independent.'"[39]

---

37. Matthew Holehouse, "Multiculturalism Has Brought Us Honour Killings and Sharia Law, Says Archbishop," *The Telegraph*, Aug. 24, 2014, http://www.telegraph.co.uk/news/worldnews /middleeast/syria/11053646/Multiculturalism-has-brought-us-honour-killings-and-Sharia -law-says-Archbishop.html.

38. WomensMarch.com, "National Co-chairs—Linda Sarsour," accessed Mar. 6, 2018, https://www.womensmarch.com/march-committee.

39. Giulio Meotti, "Multiculturalism Is Splintering the West," *Gatestone Institute*, Oct. 9, 2017, https: //www.gatestoneinstitute.org/11118/multiculturalism-separation-secession. (Emphasis in the original.)

CHAPTER 3

Islamic Refusal to Assimilate

As seen in chapter 1, immigrants have a duty, by natural moral law, to assimilate into the culture of their host country. Not only is this an obligation in justice, as a form of gratitude. The virtue of piety, too, demands that they honor their adopted country. It is a duty under the Fourth Commandment of God's Law.[40]

Many analysts distinguish between integration and assimilation. In general, Muslims have fewer problems with the former. Many among them, however, resist the latter. In a 2004 article for the Middle East Policy Council, Mustafa Malik writes:

> In fact, assimilation into Western societies has never been an appealing idea to most Muslims. . . . Many contemporary Muslims, intellectuals and lay people, view the Muslim world's economic backwardness and military impotence as temporary, and the current Islamic resurgence as the precursor to the revival of Islamic civilization.
>
> Then there is the umma factor and the communications revolution, which also are helping shore up the Western Islamic space against assimilationist pressure.[41]

Erdoğan: "Assimilation Is a Crime Against Humanity"

On February 10, 2008, speaking in a Cologne stadium to a crowd of 20,000 Turks living in France, Belgium, the Netherlands, and Germany, then–Turkish Prime Minister, Recep Tayyip Erdoğan, told them to hold on to their Turkish culture and not assimilate: "Assimilation is 'a crime against humanity.'" "I can well understand that you are against assimilation."

Erdoğan's subversive statement drew a sharp rebuke from German Chancellor Angela Merkel, "'If you grow up in Germany in the third or fourth generation, if you have German citizenship, then I

---

40. See Marcellino Zalba, SJ, *Theologiae Moralis Summa* (Madrid: Biblioteca de Auctores Christianos, 1957), 2:5–7.

41. Mustafa Malik, "Muslims Pluralize the West, Resist Assimilation," *Middle East Policy Council*, vol. 11, no. 1 (Spring 2004), http://www.mepc.org/journal/muslims-pluralize-west-resist -assimilation.

am your chancellor.'"[42]

Two years, later, while speaking on February 28, 2010, to 10,000 Turks in Düsseldorf, Erdoğan returned to the theme:

> I am here to feel your yearning with you, I am here to enquire about your welfare. I am here to show that you're not alone! . . .
>
> They call you guest workers, foreigners, or German Turks. It doesn't matter what they all call you: You are my fellow citizens, you are my people, you are my friends, you are my brothers and sisters! . . .
>
> You are part of Germany, but you are also part [of] our great Turkey. . . . [43]
>
> Yes, integrate yourselves into German society but don't assimilate yourselves. No one has the right to deprive us of our culture and our identity.[44]

Turks in the crowd were heard to say: "Turkey is great!" "He is our savior."[45]

Germany has an estimated 5 to 5.6 million inhabitants of Turkish descent. Many are third- or fourth-generation Germans, but for Erdoğan, it is a "crime against humanity" for them to assimilate into German culture.

Europe's Muslim No-Go Zones

On Friday, November 13, 2015, ISIS terrorists killed 130 people and wounded hundreds of others in Paris, at the Stade de France stadium, in popular restaurants and cafes, and at the Bataclan concert hall.

France was stunned and President François Hollande called the attack "an act of war."

In the ensuing manhunt, two of the ISIS gunmen were arrested

42. Harry de Quetteville, "Turkish PM Speaks Out Against Assimilation," *The Telegraph*, Feb. 12, 2008, https://www.telegraph.co.uk/news/worldnews/1578451/Turkish-PM-speaks-out -against-assimilation.html.

43. Özlem Gezer and Anna Reimann, "'You Are Part of Germany, But Also Part of Our Great Turkey': Erdogan Urges Turks Not to Assimilate," *Spiegel Online*, Feb. 28, 2011, http://www.spiegel.de/international/europe/erdogan-urges-turks-not-to-assimilate-you-are -part-of-germany-but-also-part-of-our-great-turkey-a-748070.html.

44. Mike Gonzalez, "How to Know the Difference Between Multiculturalism and Assimilation," *The Federalist*, Oct. 6, 2015, http://thefederalist.com/2015/10/06/how-to-know-the-difference -between-multiculturalism-and-assimilation/.

45. Özlem Gezer and Anna Reimann, "'You Are Part of Germany, But Also Part of Our Great Turkey.'"

in the Brussels Molenbeek district. They were not the first terrorists to be connected to the neighborhood. Jihadists with Molenbeek ties arrested on other occasions include Moroccan Ayoub el-Khazzani, who fired on a passing train with a Kalashnikov assault rifle; Algerian Mehdi Nemmouche, who murdered four at a Brussels Jewish Museum; and two gunmen, killed in a police firefight in Verviers, Belgium.

Moroccans and Turks make Molenbeek a predominantly Muslim enclave. Brice De Ruyver, security adviser to Prime Minister Guy Verhofstadt for eight years, affirms: "We don't officially have no-go zones in Brussels, but in reality, there are, and they are in Molenbeek."[46]

Five days after the bloody attack, its main leader, second-generation Belgian-Moroccan Abdelhamid Abaaoud, who had spent time with ISIS in Syria, and two others died in a firefight with French security forces in Paris's Saint-Denis neighborhood.[47] Home to the medieval Saint-Denis Abbey-Basilica, the burial place of France's kings, Saint-Denis is another mostly Muslim enclave and no-go zone.

Writing after al-Qaeda's earlier terror attack on Charlie Hebdo's offices in Paris, Soeren Kern summarizes the findings of a 2,200-page study. He states:

> In October 2011, a landmark 2,200-page report . . . (Suburbs of the Republic) found that Seine-Saint-Denis and other Parisian suburbs are becoming "separate Islamic societies" cut off from the French state, and where Islamic Sharia law is rapidly displacing French civil law. The report said that Muslim immigrants are increasingly rejecting French values and instead are immersing themselves in radical Islam. . . .
>
> France—which now has 6.5 million Muslims . . . is on the brink of a major social explosion because of the failure of Muslims to integrate into French society.[48]

46. Leo Cendrowicz, "Paris Attacks: Visiting Molenbeek, the Police No-Go Zone That Was Home to Two of the Gunmen," *The Independent*, Nov. 15, 2015, https://www.independent.co.uk/news /world/europe/paris-terror-attacks-visiting -molenbeek-the-police-no-go-zone-that-was -home-to-two-of-the-gunmen-a6735551.html.

47. See *Wikipedia*, s.v. "November 2015 Paris Attacks," (San Francisco: Wikimedia Foundation), updated Jun. 22, 2018, 16:30, https://en.wikipedia.org/wiki/November_2015_Paris_attacks.

48. Soeren Kern, "European 'No-Go' Zones: Fact or Fiction? Part 1: France," *Gatestone Institute*, Jan. 20, 2015, https://www.gatestoneinstitute.org/5128/france-no-go-zones.

Failed Assimilation: A Muslim Conquest Strategy

Muslim social marginalization is deliberate and follows a strategy denounced by National Review columnist Andrew C. McCarthy:

> Highly influential Islamic leaders are embarked on a conquest strategy referred to as "voluntary apartheid": the establishment of sharia enclaves that would eventually merge into an Islamic state that dominates Europe and the United States.
>
> Sheikh Yusuf Qaradawi, regarded by many, including the Muslim Brotherhood, as the world's most respected sharia jurist, instructs Muslims that the "quest for an Islamic state" calls for integrating into Europe and then pressuring Western leaders to accept a Muslim "right to live according to our faith—ideologically, legislatively, and ethically."[49]

Linda Sarsour, a Muslim feminist leader and rising star in Democratic Party circles, seems to embrace this strategy of deliberate refusal to assimilate when she stated in her July 1, 2017, speech at the Islamic Society of North America annual meeting: "Our number one and top priority is to protect and defend our community. It is not to assimilate and please any other people and authority."[50]

As can be seen, Muslim slowness to assimilate into the culture of their host country dovetails well with the strategic objective of Muslim political and religious leaders.

---

49. Andrew C. McCarthy, "France's No-Go Zones: Assimilation-Resistant Muslims Are the Real Refugee Problem," *National Review*, Nov. 19, 2015, https://www.nationalreview.com/2015/11/frances-fifth-column-muslims-resist-assimilation/.

50. Jack Moore, "Women's March Organizer Linda Sarsour Says Standing Up to Trump Is a 'Jihad,'" *Newsweek.com*, Jul. 7, 2017, http://www.newsweek.com/womens-march-organizer-linda-sarsour-says-standing-trump-jihad-633118.

CHAPTER 4
Sharia, Islamic Law

Notwithstanding the September 11, 2001 attack on America and the many other terror attacks that have followed it, Muslim activism is growing and is increasingly assertive throughout the West. While we may see few "Sharia for America" signs in the U.S., it is no longer so in Europe. Protest images easily found on the Internet show excited Islamic protesters in England holding up signs saying, "Sharia for the UK," "Sharia the future for UK," and "Sharia will dominate the world."[51] Other searches show pictures of demonstrators in Holland with banners that read, "Sharia for the Netherlands."[52]

Sharia law is proof of Islamic rule, which is why Muslim activists demand its imposition in the Christian West.

What Is Sharia?

Baudouin Dupret, an expert on Islam, explains: "Sharia is first and foremost an Arabic word. It is not endowed with a proper, clear, manifest, universal meaning. Hence, only the uses made of it through time and space tell us what it is."[53]

Sharia means *way* or *path*, and, in Islamic understanding, it is the way to fulfill Allah's divine will. In this sense, it identifies with the law of God taken in its broadest sense.

The Koran uses the word just once: "Then We put thee on the (right) Way of Religion: so follow thou that (Way), and follow not the desires of those who know not" (45:18).[54]

In Islam, Sharia is the revealed law that regulates the conduct of

---

51. Google search – Images: "sharia united kingdom," accessed Mar. 6, 2018, https://www.google.com/search?q=sharia+united+kingdom&source=lnms&tbm=isch&sa=X&ved=0ahUKEwj_kpOlgJ7WAhXI34MKHf7-CGgQ_AUICygC&biw=1352&bih=612.

52. Google search – Images: "sharia Netherlands," accessed Mar. 6, 2018, https://www.google.com/search?q=sharia+NETHERLANDS&source=lnms&tbm=isch&sa=X&ved=0ahUKEwj2hI_ggZ7WAhUd3YMKHUgiBywQ_AUICygC&biw=1352&bih=612.

53. Baudouin Dupret, "La Charia en dix points. . . et quelques raccourcis," *Fondation Res Publica*, Jun. 5, 2013, https://www.fondation-res-publica.org/La-Charia-en-dix-points-et-quelques-raccourcis_a724.html.

54. Koranic citations without a letter prefix are always from Yusuf Ali's English Koran translation. Other Koran and Sunna translations are identified by one of the abbreviations in the List of Abbreviations.

a Muslim in all its aspects, including dietary rules, attire, financial transactions, family life, the number of wives, divorce, inheritance, criminal offenses, and judicial remedies.

Sharia is used as a synonym for Islam. It is that all-encompassing. See, for example, how it was used in the protest signs just mentioned. "Sharia"—in other words, Islam—"will dominate the world."

The problem is that Sharia is uncodified. It is loosely based on some eighty verses of the Koran and in the traditions of Muhammad, the canonical *hadith*, which number several thousand.

On the Way to Sharia

By opening the gates of the West to Islamic immigration, multiculturalism has also paved the way for its own increasing assimilation of Islamic customs and even laws. Why not, if all cultures, religions, and laws are equivalent?

We are thus witnessing, especially in Europe, a growing acceptance of Sharia and even of Islamic police that function in a parallel way to the legitimate law and law enforcement of the host country. Soeren Kern, in a 2011 article for the Gatestone Institute, presents unsettling information on the progress of Sharia in Europe.

- Denmark: A group that goes by the name "Call to Islam" works to implement autonomous "Sharia Law Zones" in cities of Denmark, including Copenhagen. It says that "it will dispatch 24-hour Islamic 'morals police' to enforce Sharia law in those enclaves."

- Great Britain: An organization that calls itself "Muslims Against the Crusades" wants to establish Islamic Emirates, autonomous areas in London and eleven other British cities where British law would be a dead letter and only Sharia law would be enforced. A Muslim group in East London, which goes by the name "Tower Hamlets Taliban," "issue death threats to women who refuse to wear Islamic veils," while apparently enjoying total impunity.

- Belgium: "Sharia4Belgium" set up its own Antwerp tribunal to adjudicate family matters using Sharia law. "Sharia4Belgium says the court . . . will eventually expand its remit and handle criminal cases as well."

- Germany: Joachim Wagner affirms in his book *Richter*

ohne Gesetz: Islamische Paralleljustiz gefährdet unseren Rechtsstaat, that "Sharia courts are now operating in all of Germany's big cities."

- France: "Islamic Sharia law is rapidly displacing French civil law in many parts of suburban Paris."

- Spain: "Salafi preachers in ... Catalonia have set up Sharia tribunals.... They also deploy Islamic 'religious police' ... to monitor and punish Muslims who do not comply."[55]

Sharia Police

According to media reports, a religious police force, the Sharia Police, runs through city districts of Europe's main countries harassing locals and tourists who are drinking alcohol, women who are unaccompanied or wearing short sleeves.

A few examples of these media reports include:

- "'Sharia Patrols' Harassing Citizens in London, Belgium, Sweden," is the title of an article by Barbara Boland on November 13, 2014, at the Media Research Center.[56]

- The BBC reported on December 10, 2015, "German court lets off 'Sharia police' patrol in Wuppertal."[57]

- On June 14, 2015, the program "60 Minutes Overtime" presented interviews by reporter Clarissa Ward in London with a Muslim preacher and one of his followers. Imam Anjem Choudary told her, "You know, the messenger Mohammad, he said, 'Fight them with your wealth, with your body, with your tongue.' So, I'm engaged here, if you like, in a verbal jihad." Regarding the religious police, Ward reports that, "Rumaysah and Choudary both live in east London, which is home to one of the largest Muslim populations in the U.K. In one part of town, Rumaysah and his associates have set up so-called 'Sharia patrols' to go out and discourage behavior that they deem un-Islamic."[58]

55. Soeren Kern, "Europe: 'You Are Entering a Sharia Controlled Zone': Hezbollah Pitches Tent in Denmark," *Gatestone Institute*, Oct. 24, 2011, https://www.gatestoneinstitute.org/2530/denmark-sharia-hezbollah.

56. Barbara Boland, "'Sharia Patrols' Harassing Citizens in London, Belgium, Sweden," *Media Research Center*, Nov. 13, 2014, https://www.mrctv.org/blog/sharia-patrols-harassing-citizens-london-belgium-sweden.

57. BBC, "German Court Sets off 'Sharia Police' Patrol in Wuppertal," *BBC News*, Dec. 10, 2015, http://www.bbc.com/news/world-europe-35059488.

58. Clarissa Ward, "Campaigning for ISIS in the West," *CBS News*, Nov. 2, 2014, https://www

Fiqh: The Application of Sharia

Fiqh jurisprudence exists to interpret Sharia and its concrete application. The Islamic site *Faith in Allah* gives this explanation on the relationship between Sharia and Fiqh: "The Sharia is the collection of values and principles derived from the Quran and Sunnah that form the moral, religious, and legal teachings of Islam. It is distinguished from *Fiqh* (jurisprudence) which is the practical application of those principles in real life. In other words, the Sharia may be called the spirit of the law, while Fiqh may be called the application of the law."[59]

No Equality Before the Law

One of the best-known Catholic Islamicists, the Egyptian Jesuit Fr. Samir Khalil Samir, explains: "*Al-sharia* is founded on a threefold inequality: the inequality between man and woman, the inequality between Muslim and non-Muslim, and the inequality between freeman and slave."[60]

Growing Trend to Traditional Islamic Law

In Islamic countries with more significant European influence, codes of civil law in the European mold exist alongside traditional Islamic law. However, the trend in Islam today is to return to traditional law.

Even in countries where Sharia plays a crucial role, there are differences in its application. Egypt, for example, applies Sharia more moderately than Saudi Arabia. The latter—which funds the construction and operation of thousands of mosques around the world, and millions of copies of the Koran and other Islamic literature[61]— is practically a Muslim theocracy, having even religious police to curb infractions of Islamic precept. In 2015, Rori Donaghy and Mary Atkinson published in the *Middle East Eye*—an online media outlet charged with "often writ[ing] sympathetically about the [Muslim]

.cbsnews.com/news/recruiting-for-isis-60-minutes/.

59. Abu Amina Elias, "Sharia, Fiqh, and Islamic Law Explained," *Faith in Allah*, Apr. 18, 2013, https://abuaminaelias.com/is-the-sharia-a-single-code-of-law-an-explanation-of-sharia-fiqh -and-islamic-law/.

60. Samir Khalil Samir, SJ, *111 Questions on Islam*, ed. trans. Wafik Nasry, SJ and Claudia Castellani (San Francisco: Ignatius Press, 2008), 91.

61   *Wikipedia*, s.v. "Petro-Islam," updated May 24, 2018, 08:24, https://en.wikipedia.org/wiki/Petro -Islam.

Brotherhood"[62]—a comparative study of the punishments and crimes considered grave by the Islamic State (ISIS) and Saudi Arabia. They are practically the same.[63]

Thus, multiculturalism, Muslim immigrants' refusal to assimilate into the local culture, and the application of Sharia are effecting Europe's Islamization. They are destroying the remnants of the once brilliant Christian civilization.

---

62. Gregg Carlstrom, "What's the Problem With Al Jazeera?" *The Atlantic*, Jun. 24, 2017, https://www.theatlantic.com/international/archive/2017/06/al-jazeera-qatar-saudi-arabia -muslim-brotherhood/531471/.
63. See Rori Donaghy and Mary Atkinson, "Crime and Punishment: Islamic State vs Saudi Arabia," *Middle East Eye*, Jan. 20, 2015, http://www.middleeasteye.net/news/crime-and-punishment -islamic-state-vs-saudi-arabia-1588245666.

The claim that Islam is a religion of peace is a lie that helps anesthetize the Christian West to the growing Muslim danger.

CHAPTER 5

Is Islam a Religion of Peace and Brotherly Love?

The media, academia, and the political and religious world of our decadent Western civilization see modern Islamic terrorism as an aberration, something at odds with true Islam, which, they claim, is a religion of peace. Their wishful thinking has no justification in the Koran, the *hadith*, or Islam's 1,400-year history.

Is Terrorism Incompatible With True Islam?

It is quite evident that not all believers of a religion follow every one of its precepts all the time. Therefore, as we analyze Islam's doctrine and history, it would be blatantly untrue for us to affirm that every Muslim is a jihadist and a terrorist. However, it is equally false to sustain that no Muslim is a jihadist and, moreover, that Islam as such, in its official writings and traditions, does not propose jihad.

The assertion that Islam is a religion of peace and brotherly love is not grounded in truth.

Jihad: Imposing Faith With the Sword

What is jihad?

The *Dictionary of Islam* defines it as follows: "JIHAD داهج *Lit.* 'An effort or a striving.' A religious war with those who are unbelievers in the mission of Muhammad. It is an incumbent religious duty, established in the Qur'an and in the Traditions as a divine institution, and enjoined specially for the purpose of advancing Islam and of repelling evil from Muslims."[64]

Father Samir explains that a distinction is made today between the *greater jihad* and the *lesser jihad*. While the latter would be a spiritual struggle against personal defects, the former would be armed struggle.

However, he explains, "In the Qur'an, the word *jihad* is always used to mean 'fight for God' according to the complete expression *jihad fi sabil Allah* (fight for the way of God); therefore [it] is trans-

---

64. *A Dictionary of Islam,* Thomas Patrick Hughes (London: William H. Allen, 1885), s.v. "Jihad."

lated into European languages by Muslims as 'holy war.'"[65]

He continues, "Therefore, on the sociohistorical level, from the Qur'an onward, the ordinary meaning of *jihad* is unequivocal. The term *jihad* indicates the Muslim war in the name of God to defend Islam. . . . *Jihad* is an obligation for all adult Muslims, in particular for males."[66]

In his biography, *Muhammad: Prophet and Statesman*, William Montgomery Watt emphasizes that, by giving religious meaning to the very common razzias (raids) among Arab tribes for pillaging or exacting revenge, Muhammad turned them into jihad:

> This transformation of the nomadic razzia has wider implications than are apparent from the English transla-tions used. The word translated 'strive' is *jahada*, and the corresponding verbal noun is *jihad* or 'striving' which came in the course of time to have the technical meaning of *holy war*. . . . It was this religious character of the *jihad* which channeled the energies of the Arabs in such a way that in less than a century they had created an empire which stretched from the Atlantic and the Pyrenees in the West to the Oxus and the Punjab in the East. It seems cer-tain that without the conception of the *jihad* that expan-sion would not have happened.[67]

The Myth of Islamophobia

Muslim leaders and Western liberals label as "Islamophobes" anyone who dares to criticize aspects of Islam or Islamic ter-rorism. While empty, this epithet psychologically hamstrings any valid criticism. In some countries, criticism is even crimi-nalized, shutting down any serious intellectual discussion. Fr. Édouard-Marie Gallez, CSJ, exposes this indecent sophism:

> In Islamic countries, it is forbidden to present this evidence [that the Koran calls for the employ-ment of all means to expand Islam] under pain of

---

65. Samir, *111 Questions*, 62.
66. Ibid.
67. William Montgomery Watt, *Muhammad: Prophet and Statesman* (London: Oxford University Press, 1961), 108–9.

State reprisals (which can mean death). Muslim leaders would like to see the same state terrorism gradually established in Europe, with the first step being to introduce the fallacious concept of "Islamophobia" in legislation as a punishable crime. Let us be clear: "Islamophobia" exists only in the minds of Islamic propagandists. . . .

Let us recall the origin of the "Islamophobia" concept: It was invented by Ayatollah Khomeini (during the years when he was royally hosted in France). It functions like the concept of "anticommunist," used by communists for fifty years to prevent any criticism of communism. . . . We can both love Muslims and take notice that Islam carries out something other than paradise on earth to the extent that it rigorously imposes itself somewhere. . . .

But how can we not say that a system that claims to be good and has always used every means, including the worst—starting with lies about its origins and terrorism—cannot be good per se, and cannot be righteous because of its "excesses"?

Édouard-Marie Gallez, "Un islam très normalement expansionniste," accessed Apr. 14, 2018, http://www.lemessieetsonprophete.com/annexes/Questions-debat.htm#expansionniste.

The Koran's 164 Jihad Verses

Under the title, "164 *Jihad* Verses in the Koran," Yoel Natan wrote a valuable research paper listing the Koran's jihad verses. It was published by the *Answering Islam* website, which is rich in data and refutations of Islam. He explains the method he adopted:

- Each of the 164 *Jihad* verses in this list was selected based on how clearly and directly it spoke about *Jihad*, at least when considered in its immediate context. Most of the listed passages mention a military expedition, fighting, or distributing war spoils. Verses NOT generally listed are those that speak about aspects of *Jihad* other than the raiding, fighting and looting, such as:

- Muhammad's poor opinion of those who did not go on *Jihad*, even though they were able-bodied and able financially (for instance, some verses in K 009:081–096),

- The heavenly rewards for *Jihadists,* and

- The many generic mentions of "victory" found in the *Koran.*[68]

The Koran Commands Jihad

In a June 10, 2017 interview with *National Catholic Register's* Edward Pentin, Egyptian Jesuit and Islamic expert Fr. Henri Boulad lists Koran verses that preach violence against Catholics and other "unbelievers":

- "Kill the unbelievers wherever you find them." – Koran 2:191.

- "Make war on the infidels living in your neighborhood." – Koran 9:123.

- "When opportunity arises, kill the infidels wherever you catch them." – Koran 9:5.

- "Any religion other than Islam is not acceptable." – Koran 3:85.

- "The Jews and the Christians are perverts; fight them. . . . " – Koran 9:30.

- "'Maim and crucify the infidels if they criticize Islam." – Koran 5:33.

- "Punish the unbelievers with garments of fire, hooked iron rods, boiling water; melt their skin and bellies." – Koran 22:19.

- "The unbelievers are stupid; urge the Muslims to fight them." – Koran 8:65.

- "Muslims must not take the infidels as friends." – Koran 3:28.

- "Terrorize and behead those who believe in scriptures other than the Qur'an." – Koran 8:12.

- "Muslims must muster all weapons to terrorize the infidels." – Koran 8:60.[69]

---

68. Yoel Natan, comp., "164 Jihad Verses in the Koran," *Answering Islam,* May, 2004, http://www.answering-islam.org/Quran/Themes/jihad_passages.html.

69. Edward Pentin, "Jesuit Scholar: Seeking to Defend Islam at All Costs Is Betraying the Truth," *National Catholic Register,* Jun. 15, 2017, http://www.ncregister.com/blog/edward-pentin/jesuit-scholar-seeking-to-defend-islam-at-all-costs-is-betraying-the-truth (Reprinted with permission.)

Muhammad, by his Words and Example, Also Commands Jihad

In addition to what is found in the Koran and the *hadith*, it is helpful to know how Muhammad acted, since Islam's sacred book presents him as a model for Muslims to emulate: "Ye have indeed in the Messenger of Allah a beautiful pattern (of conduct) for any one whose hope is in Allah and the Final Day" (33:21). In the same *National Catholic Register* interview, Fr. Henri Boulad explains how violent was the later part of Muhammad's life:

> [Here] are a few samples of Muhammad's teachings and life. . . . taken from Muslim sources:
>
> - "I have been commanded to fight against people till they testify that there is no god but Allah, and that Muhammad is the messenger of Allah" (Muslim 1:33).
>
> - "Fight everyone in the way of Allah and kill those who disbelieve in Allah." (Ibn Ishaq 992).
>
> - Muhammad's life was a succession of warfare, plundering and killings . . . and every Muslim is invited to imitate this supreme "model."
>
> - Muhammad owned and traded slaves (Sahih Muslim 3901), and ordered his followers to stone women for adultery. (Muslim 4206).
>
> - He himself beheaded 800 Jewish men and boys (Abu Dawud 4390) ordered the murder of women (Ibn Ishaq 819, 995) and killed those who insulted him. (Bukhari 56:369, 4:241).
>
> - According to him, Jihad in the way of Allah elevates one's position in Paradise by a hundred fold. (Muslim 4645).
>
> - In his last ten years, he ordered 65 military campaigns and raids. (Ibn Ishaq) and killed captives taken in battle. (Ibn Ishaq 451).
>
> - He encouraged his men to rape enslaved women (Abu Dawood 2150, Quran 4:24), he put apostates to death, plundered and lived off the wealth of oth-

ers, captured and enslaved non-Muslim people.[70]

Violence, a Constant in Islamic History

Father Boulad goes on to explain how Muhammad's violence informed Islam and its history:

- After Muhammad's death, his followers attacked and conquered the populations of 28 countries and declared holy war on the people of five major world religions. . . .

- In the first 240 years, 11 of the first 32 caliphs were murdered by fellow Muslims.

- Muslim clerics have always engaged in or condoned terrorism all along history and up until now.

- We witness daily religious violence against Hindus, Jews, Buddhists, Muslims, Christians. The converts to Christianity are beheaded.

- The victims of slave traffic done by the Arabs during almost ten centuries amount to tens of millions of people.

- Each year, thousands of Christian homes and churches are torched or bombed by Muslim mobs, and hundreds of Christians, priests, pastors, nuns and other church workers are murdered at the hands of Islamic extremists. The so-called justification varies, from charges of apostasy or evangelism, to purported "blasphemy" or "insulting" Islam. Innocent people have even been hacked to death by devout Muslims over cartoons. Islam is an open-ended declaration of war against non-Muslims.[71]

Jihad in the History of Islam

Jihad is at the very core of Islam's history. We can even say that the history of Islam is the history of jihad.

At the onset of Islamic expansion, the Middle East and North Africa were alternately dominated by the Sasanian (Persian) and Byzantine Empires. The former was Zoroastrian but with Christian minorities, while the latter was predominantly Christian. Both empires though contained heretical groups which rejected the Blessed

70. Ibid.
71. Ibid.

Trinity in one way or another, for example, the Arians, Nestorians, and Monophysites.

Besides waging wars continuously, both empires were decadent, and their troops were mostly mercenaries. The generals obtained their posts through courtly intrigue instead of military acumen. Both powers had been bled dry by the Byzantium-Sasanian War (602–628), and this weakened condition was a significant factor in assuring the success of expansionist Muslim jihad. The groups of anti-Trinitarian heretics frequently supported the Muslim invaders as they too were anti-Trinitarian.

After conquering the Mediterranean's southern rim, in 711 the Muslims invaded Spain, with help from Arians. From Spain, they invaded France where they were halted only by the military prowess of Charles Martel at the Battle of Tours-Poitiers, in 732. In the following century, the Muslims invaded Sicily (843) and later looted the city of Rome twice, in 843 and 846.[72]

In 1453, Mehmed II conquered Constantinople ending the Byzantine Empire. From there, Islam continued its advance into Eastern Europe. Its maritime impetus was broken only in 1571 in the naval battle of Lepanto when a European coalition fleet gathered by Pope Saint Pius V destroyed the Turkish one. On land, in the following century, the Turks were soundly defeated at the Battle of Vienna (1683). From then on, Muslim power began to wane.

But It All Started With Muhammad

From the Hijra (his migration to Medina in 622) on, when the Islamic era began, Muhammad's life was a succession of warfare, plundering, and slaughter. From 624 until his death in 632, Muhammad became a warlord and initiated the expansion of Islam through the sword. In his book *Muhammad: Islam's First Great General*, Richard A. Gabriel, a military historian and adjunct professor at the Royal Military College of Canada, writes:

> There is no biography written from the perspective of Muhammad's role as Islam's first great general and the leader of a successful insurgency....
>
> Had Muhammad not succeeded as a military commander Islam might have remained ... relegated to a ge-

---

72. See Rodney Stark, *God's Battalions: The Case for the Crusades* (New York: HarperOne, 2009), 11–23.

ographic backwater, and the conquest of the Byzantine and Persian empires by Arab armies might never have occurred. . . .

In the space of a single decade *he fought eight major battles, led eighteen raids, and planned thirty-eight other military operations* where others were in command but operating under his orders and strategic direction. . . .

Unlike conventional generals Muhammad's goal was not the defeat of a foreign enemy or invader but the replacement of the existing Arabian social order with a new one based on a radically different ideological view of the world.[73]

Is Jihadism un-Islamic?

Progressive ecclesiastics and Western scholars sympathetic to Islam insist that ISIS and other Muslim terrorist movements are not authentically Islamic. They stand by their claim despite terrorists' assertions that they are faithful Muslims, and intend to impose Islam on the world.

And when Fr. Samir Khalil Samir was asked "Are you of the view that Islamism is the true Islam?" he answered: "ISIS is the application of what is taught. It's not outside Islam, or something invented. No, they are applying Islam. When we hear it has nothing to do with Islam— that it means *salaam*; that it means peace—this is all false. It's not true. ISIS is not doing anything which is neither in the Quran nor in the Mohammedan tradition. Everything is taken after a decision taken by an imam. A mufti and imam will say this is or is not allowed."[74]

In statements to *The Atlantic* magazine, Prof. Bernard Haykel, a specialist on ISIS, agrees:

> According to Haykel, the ranks of the Islamic State are deeply infused with religious vigor. Koranic quotations are ubiquitous. "Even the foot soldiers spout this stuff constantly," Haykel said. "They mug for their cameras and repeat their basic doctrines in formulaic fashion, and they do it *all the time*." He regards the claim that the Islamic State has distorted the texts of Islam as prepos-

---

73. Richard A. Gabriel, *Muhammad: Islam's First Great General* (Norman, Okl.: University of Oklahoma Press, 2007), xviii–xx.

74. Edward Pentin, "Father Samir: Egypt's Palm Sunday Terror Reflects a Sickness Within Islam," *National Catholic Register*, Apr. 13, 2017, http://www.ncregister.com/daily-news/father-samir -egypts-palm-sunday-terror-reflects-a-sickness-within-islam.

terous, sustainable only through willful ignorance. "People want to absolve Islam," he said. "It's this 'Islam is a religion of peace' mantra. As if there is such a thing as 'Islam'! It's what Muslims do, and how they interpret their texts." Those texts are shared by all Sunni Muslims, not just the Islamic State. "And these guys have just as much legitimacy as anyone else."[75]

The fact that most Muslims likely reject the terrorist methods of these organizations does not prevent that majority from sharing the same religious principles and from accepting, in theory, punishments such as condemnation to death for apostasy from Islam, amputation of hands and feet for thieves, flogging or even death for adulterers, and crucifixion. After all, the Koran or the *hadith* mention these punishments (see 2:42; 5:33; 5:38; 5:33; SB 3018).[76]

Beyond all doubt, Muslim doctrine and history attest that Islam as a "religion of peace" is pure fantasy.

---

75. Graeme Wood, "What ISIS Really Wants," *The Atlantic*, Mar. 2015, https://www.theatlantic.com/magazine/archive/2015/03/what-isis-really-wants/384980/. (Emphasis in the original.)

76. See The Religion of Peace, "What Does Islam Teach About Torture?" *The Religion of Peace*, accessed Mar. 6, 2018, https://www.thereligionofpeace.com/pages/quran/torture.aspx.

Islam has greatly expanded its presence in Europe in the last thirty years.
Above: **a large banner held up during the Al Quds Day rally in London, 2018.**

Chapter 6
A Reenergized Islam

After World War II, the decline and slumber that had come to characterize Islam for 200 years ended and a reinvigorated Islam began to stir.

A Peaceful and Westernized Islam

Starting in the nineteenth century, and continuing with the dismemberment of the Ottoman Empire, almost all Islamic countries of the Middle East and North Africa became colonies or protectorates of France and England. In Asia, Indonesia, the most populous Muslim nation, was a Dutch colony from 1800 to 1945. India, with its large Muslim population (especially before the separation of Pakistan), was under British rule from 1858 to 1947.

With this political oversway, European culture, laws, and customs penetrated deeply into the Muslim elites. It was common for young people from important families to go to London, Paris, and other Western capitals, or to attend Christian schools that operated freely and safely in their own countries.

The Awakening of Islam

A casual observer assessing the Islamic world after the defeat of the Axis powers in World War II could easily believe that the irreducible opposition at the root of the millennial struggle between Muslims and Christians had been overcome, but keen analysts could see signs of change in the idyllic landscape. Thus, in 1947, Plinio Corrêa de Oliveira foresaw Islam's resurgence.[77]

Socialism and Islam

The winds of revolt that shook European colonies or protectorates in Asia and Africa in the fifties and sixties were largely instigated by international communism. Thus, in spite of legitimate aspirations, the struggle for decolonization took on a revolutionary character

---

77. See Introduction.

that was sharply anti-Western and anti-traditional.

In Egypt, nationalist-socialist officers deposed King Farouk, and then his son, Fuad II. In Iraq also, a military coup killed King Faisal II and most of his family. Similar movements spread throughout the Arab world.

The Arab coalition's defeats by Israel in 1967 and 1973 aroused deep fury in Arab public opinion against the nationalist-socialist military. There was a growing belief that the cause of the humiliating defeats had been secularism and Westernization, the abandonment of authentic Islam, the Koran, and Sharia.

Secret societies such as the Muslim Brotherhood, with its mixture of Islamism and socialism (as happened later in Latin America with so-called liberation theology, which interpreted Christianity in a Marxist way), expanded significantly.

The Muslim Brotherhood

The Brotherhood was founded in Egypt in 1928 by Hassan al-Banna, a Muslim imam and intellectual. It believes that the Koran and Sunna are the

> sole reference point for everything relating to the or-
> dering of the life of the Muslim family, individual, and
> community as well as the Muslim State[, in] all [of its]
> economic, social, political, cultural, educational, and also
> legislative and judiciary activities. . . .
> The call of the Muslim Brotherhood was based on two
> key pillars:
> 1-The introduction of the Islamic Shari'ah as the basis
> controlling the affairs of state and society.
> 2-Work to achieve unification among the Islamic
> countries and states, mainly among the Arab states, and
> liberating them from foreign imperialism.[78]

The Brotherhood was involved in the overthrow of the monarchies in Iran, Iraq, Libya, Yemen, and Egypt, and, more recently, in the so-called Arab Spring.

Through the writings of Sayyid Qutb (1906–1966), the Muslim Brotherhood's foremost theoretician, both al-Qaeda and the Islamic

---

78. "The Principles of the Muslim Brotherhood," Ikhwanweb.com, Feb. 1, 2010, http://www
.ikhwanweb.com/article.php?id=813.

State (ISIS) can be seen as Brotherhood offspring.[79]

The Brotherhood is fundamentally Sunni, but its revolutionary ideology transcends the great Muslim divide between Shia and Sunni, leading it to make common cause with revolutionary Shia. Writing for the *International Affairs Forum*, Mohammed Salama says that Ayatollah Khomeini translated two of Qutb's books and that, under Ayatollah Khamenei, Qutb's theories are taught in the schools of the Iran Revolutionary Guards Corps.[80]

Salafism

Salafis were among the Muslims rekindling their fervor at Islam's roots.

Graeme Wood states that Salafism is "a branch of Sunnism . . . after the Arabic *al salaf al salih*, the 'pious forefathers.' These forefathers are the Prophet himself and his earliest adherents, whom Salafis honor and emulate as the models for all behavior, including warfare, couture, family life, even dentistry."[81]

Thus, Salafis strive for a purer, more authentic Islam, the original Islam of Muhammad and his companions, as they understand it.

Saudi Arabia and Wahhabism

Wahhabism, a strict subset of Salafism, is dominant in Saudi Arabia. It takes its name from the reformer Muhammad ibn Abd al-Wahhab (1703–1792), born in Saudi Arabia.

According to Michael R. Dillon, "Wahhabism was founded in the eighteenth century as 'an Islamic puritanical doctrine of reform and renewal attributed to Muhammad Ibn Abd al-Wahhab, who allied himself with the House of Saud in 1744.' Wahhabism has since become the official ideology of the state or kingdom with the Qur'an serving as its constitution."[82]

---

79. See Fawaz A. Gerges, "The World According to ISIS," *Foreign Policy Journal*, Mar. 18, 2016, https://www.foreignpolicyjournal.com/2016/03/18/the-world-according-to-isis/.

80. See Mohammed Salama, "The Muslim Brotherhood and Their Relationship With Iran," *International Affairs Forum*, Jan. 30, 2015, http://www.iaforum.org/Content/View InternalDocument.cfm?ContentID=8287.

81. Wood, "What ISIS Really Wants."

82. Michael R. Dillon, *Wahhabism: Is It a Factor in the Spread of Global Terrorism?* (Monterey, Calif.: Naval Postgraduate School, 2009), 13, http://www.dtic.mil/dtic/tr/fulltext/u2/a509109.pdf.

The Jihad's Return

In their efforts to purify Islam, Salafi Sunnis re-energized jihadism. Prof. Bernard Haykel writes about the ideological basis of that Islamic terrorist movement: "The Islamic State is a Jihadi-Salafi movement, which means that its members adhere to a strict literalist interpretation of the texts of the Quran and the sayings of the Prophet Muhammad. They also privilege armed struggle (jihad) as a means for implementing their austere, intolerant, and muscular vision of Islam. Salafis—not all of whom preach armed violence; only the Jihadi-Salafists do—have been a minority group, albeit an influential one, throughout the history of Islam."[83]

In his abovementioned analysis, Dillon shows the role played by Wahhabism and Saudi Arabia in today's Islamic terrorism:

> The Saudis can be held accountable for creating a permissive environment through their campaign of spreading Wahhabism that provided, whether intentional or not, groups like Al-Qaeda the opportunities to spread. The Saudi campaign of financing charities, mosques, *madrasas* and Islamic centers throughout the world with no government regulation of the funds being contributed nor the manner in which they were distributed provided Al-Qaeda with a means of raising, laundering and distributing funds worldwide to support attacks against U.S., Saudi and other Western targets. . . .
>
> Al-Qaeda's ideology is a mixture of neo-Wahhabi/neo-Salafi and radical Islamist ideologies influenced by the politics, economics and jihadi movements of the late 1970s and onward.[84]

OPEC's Use of the Oil Weapon

A first oil embargo was launched against the U.S. and the United Kingdom on the second day of the 1967 Six Day War. Its impact was minimal compared to the 1973 oil embargo imposed on the U.S. and other countries during the Yom Kippur War. U.S. oil prices

---

83. Bernard Haykel, "ISIS: A Primer–A Leading Scholar Explains the Beliefs and Goals of the Islamic State," *Princeton Alumni Weekly* 115, no. 14 (Jun. 3, 2015): 22, https://paw.princeton.edu/article /isis-primer.
84. Dillon, *Wahhabism*, 73–4.

quadrupled, gas rationing was implemented, and a 55-m.p.h. speed limit imposed nationwide.

U.S. oil prices doubled again during the 1979 oil crisis caused by the Iranian Revolution. Given oil's vital role in industrialized economies, its higher cost triggered a rise in inflation. The extra trillions flowing from the U.S. and oil-importing nations into OPEC coffers over the following decades helped fund the Islamic resurgence in those countries and around the world.

The Iranian 1979 Revolution

Under a growing swell of protests, Iran's 2,500-year-old monarchy collapsed in January 1979, and Shah Mohammad Reza Pahlavi went into exile. On February 1, 1979, Ayatollah Ruhollah Khomeini, who had been living in exile himself, in France, returned to Iran in triumph, and by year's end was the country's Supreme Leader. His regime was revolutionary Islamic, anti-American, and anti-Western. Iran quickly became a radiating hub for further Islamic agitation, helping to found Lebanon's Hezbollah movement in 1985. On January 19, 1984, the U.S. State Department designated Iran as a state sponsor of terrorism. Through Iraq's Shia majority, Iran has considerable influence in that country's current government.

Turkey Under Erdoğan's Justice and Development Party

Though only founded in 2001, Turkey's Justice and Development Party (JDP) has been in power most of the time since 2002. Its current leader, Recep Tayyip Erdoğan, was prime minister from 2003 to 2014 and has been president since 2014. While calling itself a conservative democratic party, JDP follows pan-Islamist and neo-Ottomanist policies and is implementing an Islamic cultural revolution in the country.

Under Erdoğan, Turkey is becoming less reliable as a NATO ally and is increasingly aligned with Russia's Vladimir Putin and Iran's ayatollahs.

Erdoğan wants the Ottoman borders back: "Those who think we have forgotten the lands from which we withdrew in tears a hundred years ago, are mistaken. Every time the occasion arises we say that Syria, Iraq and other places on the geographic map of our hearts, are no different from our homeland. We will be fighting until there is no foreign flag waving in any place where an '*adhan*' [the Islamic call to prayer in mosques] is recited. What we have done until now, is nothing compared to the even greater attacks we are planning for the coming days, *inshallah* (if Allah wills)."[85]

Turkey is also the power behind the "common political will" of the Turkic Council—The Cooperation Council of the Turkic Speaking States.[86] The member states of this intergovernmental organization are Turkey, Azerbaijan, Kazakhstan, and Kyrgyzstan (Uzbekistan and Turkmenistan are potential members), with a combined population of some 113 million.

Pakistan

With its predominantly Muslim population, Pakistan is currently the only Islamic country with declared nuclear weapons. Muhammad Ali Jinnah, the nation's founder and independence leader, was a pan-Islamist who wanted a politically united Islam from Morocco to Indonesia.[87] Under the rule of General Muhammad Zia ul-Haq (1977–1988), Pakistan's Islamization intensified with the establishment of Sharia courts and blasphemy laws.

Egypt

During the Barack Obama Administration–supported turmoil of the Arab Spring, Hosni Mubarak resigned from Egypt's presidency on February 11, 2011. That fall, the Muslim Brotherhood's Freedom and Justice Party won the most seats in Parliament. Its candidate,

---

85. Roberto de Mattei, "Europe Will Be Muslim If It Is the Will of Allah," trans. Francesca Romana, *Rorate-Caeli*, Mar. 28, 2018, https://rorate-caeli.blogspot.com/2018/03/de-mattei-europe-will -be-muslim-if-it.html.

86. See Information Note, Turkic Council, accessed Apr. 14, 2018, http://www.turkkon.org/Assets /dokuman/Information_Note.pdf.

87. "Maulana Shabbir Ahmad Usmani (founder of the *Jamiatul Ulama-i-Islam* and later acclaimed as Pakistan's *Shaikhul Islam*) declared that Pakistan would recreate the Islamic utopia first fashioned by the Prophet in Medina, inaugurating an equal brotherhood of Islam by breaking down barriers of race, class, sect, language and region among Muslims and establishing an example worthy of emulation by the global *ummah*. . . ." "Usmani asked Pakistanis to remember the *Qaid*'s [Muhammad Ali Jinnah] ceaseless message of Unity, Faith and Discipline and work to fulfill his dream 'to create a solid bloc of all Muslim states from Karachi to Ankara, from Pakistan to Morocco. He [Jinnah] wanted to see the Muslims of the world united under the banner of Islam as an effective check against the aggressive designs of their enemies. This is the hour of trial for Muslims. Those who face it with courage and determination will reign supreme.'" Venkat Dhulipala, *Creating a New Medina: State Power, Islam, and the Quest for Pakistan in Late Colonial North India* (Cambridge: Cambridge University Press, 2015), 5, 489.

Mohamed Morsi, won the following year's spring presidential elections and he was sworn in as president on June 30, 2012. Protests followed his attempts to replace Egypt's constitution with an Islamist one, and on July 3, 2013, he was ousted by a military coup. Egypt's military has governed the country for decades but, like the public at large, its officer corps is not immune to the influence of the Muslim Brotherhood and the other clashing forces in the secularist-religious-revolutionary struggle at Islam's core.

Growing Numbers of Muslims Worldwide

The number of Muslims around the world is rising. In Western countries, their numbers are increasing due to migration, conversions, and a birth rate that is substantially higher than that of demographics infected with the Sexual Revolution's mindset of contraception and abortion. Already in 2007, Muhammad was the most popular name for baby boys in Brussels.[88] In 2008, it became London's top name for newborn boys.[89] By 2014, it had "been the favorite name for baby boys in Oslo for the past four years."[90]

The Muslim World League

The Muslim World League was founded in Mecca, in 1962, at a conference of 22 prominent Islamic religious leaders, under the auspices of Crown Prince Faisal Bin Abdul-Aziz.[91] Its primary funding comes from the Saudi government. Its Charter of Commitment states:

> We the members of the Muslim World League, representing it religiously, hereby undertake before God, Almighty to: Discharge our obligation towards God, by conveying and proclaiming His Message all over the world. We also reaffirm our belief that there shall be no

88. See "Mohammed Tops Baby Name List in Brussels," *Sydney Morning Herald*, Sept. 17, 2008, https://www.smh.com.au/world/mohamed-tops-baby-name-list-in-brussels-20080917 -4ikl.html.

89. See Rebecca Lefort and Ben Leapman, "Mohammed Is Most Popular Name for Baby Boys in London," *The Telegraph*, Sept. 15, 2009, https://www.telegraph.co.uk/news/religion/6194354/Mohammed-is-most-popular-name-for -baby-boys-in-London.html.

90. Camilla Skarra, Henriette Mordt, & Grethe Kielland Jenssen, "Nå er Mohammed det vanligste navnet i Oslo," *NRK.no*, Aug. 27, 2014, https://www.nrk.no/ostlandssendingen/mohammed -vanligste-navn-i-oslo-1.11898780.

91. "History," Muslim World League, accessed Apr. 15, 2018, http://en.themwl.org/mwl-history.

peace in the world without the application of the principles of Islam. . . . Hence, in order to further these goals,
we intend to: Unite the ranks of the Muslims, and remove
all divisive forces from the midst of the Muslim communities around the world. Remove obstacles in the way of
establishing the Muslim world union."[92]

Although, as seen, the Koran and the *hadith* command jihad, the
League's website states that "The League, which employs all means
that are not at variance with the Sharia (Islamic law) to further its
aims, is well known for rejecting all acts of violence and promoting
dialogue[93] with the people of other cultures."[94]

The Organization of Islamic Cooperation

Founded in 1969, the Organization of Islamic Cooperation "is the
collective voice of the Muslim world."[95] Its original name was the
Organization of the Islamic Conference, as referenced above.

While the Muslim World League acts as a religious body, the
O.I.C. acts socio-politically. It is an intergovernmental organization
with 57 member states and a combined population of over 1.6 billion. Its Permanent Secretariat is located in Jeddah, Saudi Arabia.

Its member-nations' heads of state meet every three years for the
Islamic Summit. Its Conference of Foreign Ministers meets annually.[96]

Islam's Sunni-Shia Divide

Contrary to the widespread impression favored by the media, Islam
is not a cohesive and hierarchical religious and political bloc with
a central authority. On the contrary, it has neither cohesion nor
hierarchy. It is divided into numerous sects, factions, currents, and
many varying degrees of Islamic fervor. The result is a spectrum of
different interpretations of Koranic doctrine and practice, with the
more radical ones fomenting jihad and Islamic terrorism.

When Muhammad imposed Islam on the Arabian Peninsula, he

---

92. "Charter of Commitment," Muslim World League, accessed Apr. 15, 2018, http://en.themwl
    .org/node/38.
93. For a full discussion on the talismanic word "dialogue," see chapter 12.
94. "About MWL," Muslim World League, accessed Apr. 15, 2018, http://en.themwl.org/about-mwl.
95. "History," Organization of Islamic Cooperation: The Collective Voice of the Muslim World,
    accessed Apr. 14, 2018, https://www.oic-oci.org/page/?p_id=52&p_ref=26&lan=en.
96. See OIC Charter, ch. 5, art. 10, Mar. 14, 2008, https://www.oic-oci.org/page/?p_id=53&p
    _ref=27&lan=en.

became a spiritual and political leader, as well as the supreme legislator of the Muslim community. He died in 632, without leaving a male heir to succeed him, or instructions in a will. His closest relative was Ali ibn Ali Talib, his cousin and son-in-law. Ali was married to Fatima, Muhammad's daughter by his first wife, Khadija. A serious succession problem arose. It was unclear how to effect the transition and what powers a successor should have. Muhammad's spiritual power came from being considered God's Messenger. Since he was deemed the last of the prophets, that spiritual leadership could not be claimed by any successor. Thus, a successor could only inherit Muhammad's political leadership.

As his closest relative, Ali thought that he should succeed his cousin and father-in-law. Instead, one of Islam's first converts, Abu Bakr (father of Aisha, Muhammad's favorite wife), was chosen. He received the title of caliph (meaning "deputy," "successor," or "steward"). After him came Umar ibn al-Khattab who was assassinated in 644. Umar was succeeded by Uthman ibn 'Affan, who was assassinated in 656.

Ali was then elected caliph. His election was not accepted peacefully though, and opposition arose, led by Aisha. After numerous disputes, Ali was assassinated in 661 by some of his most radical supporters (who gave rise to Islam's *khâridjite* current).

Ali was succeeded by his son Hasan ibn 'Ali, who abdicated after six months of government to prevent a civil war. His stepping down resulted from an agreement with Al-Hasan Muawiyah, who became the new caliph. Muawiyah reneged on the deal and designated his eldest son, Yazid ibn Muawiya, as successor, making the caliphate hereditary. Yazid succeeded his father in 680.

Husayn, Ali's second son, and his followers did not accept Yazid as the new caliph. Their faction became known as the Shia—literally "*Shiat Ali*" (Ali's Party). Shias claimed that Ali and his heirs were Muhammad's rightful successors. A feud ensued, and on October 10, 680, Yazid's troops killed Husayn in the Battle of Karbala, Iraq. The Shias considered Husayn a martyr, and their break with the Sunnis became irreversible and historic.

Further Doctrinal Divisions

Divisions between Sunnis and Shias began over a problem of

succession, but as Islamicist Sabrina Mervin points out, it later led to contentions "not only about the caliphate but also about theological problems and questions concerning the sources of Islamic law and its application."[97] Both groups were further fragmented into dissenting currents, factions, and sects.

Other Fracture Lines

Over time, Islam underwent further splintering resulting from historical, ethnic, and tribal disputes and rivalries. Varying degrees of religious fervor separated radicals from moderates. Even the attraction of many to the Western lifestyle acted as a dividing wedge.

The Muslim Brotherhood and other forces have been diligently laboring to smooth over these multiple fracture lines for generations. Their goal is to make Islam work together as a united political bloc. Others openly toil to restore the caliphate and its unifying effect. All of them appreciate the wisdom in the ancient adage attributed to Aesop, "United we stand, divided we fall." Our Lord's teaching is no different: "Every kingdom divided against itself shall be made desolate: and every city or house divided against itself shall not stand" (Matt. 12:25).

This practical wisdom should also unite the West in collective self-defense. Furthermore, it should bind Western religious and political leaders in an effort to obstruct and foil the Muslim Brotherhood's revolutionary efforts to weld together Islam's many fractious blocs.

---

97.   Sabrina Mervin, *Histoire de l'islam: Fondements et doctrines* (Paris: Flammarion, 2000), 99.

CHAPTER 7
Persecution of Christians

The flourishing Christian communities in the Middle East and North Africa produced countless saints and several Church Fathers and Doctors. Islam's armed expansion in the seventh and eighth centuries, however, almost annihilated them. Its invasion of Visigothic Spain led to an Islamic domination that took some eight centuries to overturn. Islam has attacked and persecuted the Church in many other European, African, and Asian countries.

"Kill the Polytheists [Christians] Wherever You Find Them"

The Koran's well-known verse 9:5 is variously translated as "kill the polytheists," "slay the idolaters," or "slay the Pagans."[98] The *Quranic Arabic Corpus* presents the Arabic words of this verse's command: *fa-uq'tulū* (meaning, "then kill") *l-mush'rikīna* (meaning, "the polytheists").

The Saheeh International translation prepared by three American women who became Muslim, and which ISIS favors in its English-language propaganda,[99] renders 9:5 as follows: "And when the sacred months have passed, then kill the polytheists [Christians] wherever you find them and capture them and besiege them and sit in wait for them at every place of ambush. But if they should repent, establish prayer, and give zakah, let them [go] on their way. Indeed, God is Forgiving and Merciful" (SI 9:5).

Twenty-four verses later, the Koran insists that even Jews and Christians ("the People of the Book") must be fought: "Fight those who believe not in Allah nor the Last Day, nor hold that forbidden which hath been forbidden by Allah and His Messenger, nor acknowledge the religion of Truth, (even if they are) of the People of the Book, until they pay the Jizyah with willing submission, and feel themselves subdued" (9:29).

---

98. "Verse (9:5)," *Quranic Arabic Corpus*, accessed Mar. 8, 2018, http://corpus.quran.com/translation.jsp?chapter=9&verse=5.

99. See Katie Zavadski, "How Three American Women Translated One of the World's Most Popular Qurans, *TheDailyBeast.com*, Mar. 26, 2017, https://www.thedailybeast.com/how-three-american-women-translated-one-of-the-worlds-most-popular-qurans.

According to the Koran, Christians, whom it calls "associators" (*Mushrikun*), must everywhere be imprisoned, forced to pay a protection tax,[100] and killed. Such is the mercy of this misrepresented religion of peace.

A 1,400-Year Trail of Blood

Islam's 1,400-year history is a trail of blood not just for the millions killed in its unjust wars, but for the countless Christians it has martyred.

On December 20, 2012, Pope Benedict XVI canonized Otranto's 813 martyrs. In 1480, an Ottoman fleet conquered this Italian city by storm. After the Turkish victory, these 813 men were taken to a nearby hill and killed for refusing to apostatize and become Muslim. Theirs has been the fate of countless other Christians in Islam's path.

Untold others were captured in raids and dragged away from their Christian homelands into Muslim territories where they were made slaves. Deprived of the help of the sacraments and the ministry of the clergy, these Christians were at high risk of losing the Faith. Two religious orders were founded in medieval Christendom to minister to these enslaved Christians and ransom them. In 1198, Saint John of Matha founded the Order of the Most Holy Trinity and of the Captives. In 1218, Saint Peter Nolasco founded the Order of the Blessed Virgin Mary of Mercy, known as the Mercedarians. Saint Peter Armengol stands out among the later order's heroes.[101]

For centuries, the Ottomans imposed the *devshirme* or blood tax on Christian families, taking boys from their parents, forcing them to convert to Islam, and then turning them into soldiers and civil servants of the State. The Janissaries, Turkey's elite and respected warriors, were drawn from their ranks.[102]

---

100. The *jizyah* is a tax paid by the *dhimmi*, the non-Muslim subjects of a Muslim state, to receive protection and be able to practice their religion. See Bat Ye'or, *The Dhimmi: Jews and Christians Under Islam*, trans. David Maisel, Paul Fenton, and David Littman (London, Ont.: Associated University Press, 1985), 53.

101. Having traveled to Bejaia, Algeria, to ransom 119 captives, he was about to return to Aragon when he heard that 18 Christian children were still prisoners and in danger of apostatizing. He negotiated their ransom and took their place until the ransom money arrived. When the deadline came and the funds had not yet arrived the Muslims hanged him on charges of blasphemy. Our Lady kept him alive miraculously on the gallows. The ransom funds arrived six days later, and he was released from the gallows, and returned to Barcelona. See Felipe Barandiarán, "Saint Peter Armengol," *TFP.org*, Apr. 27, 2011, http://www.tfp.org/saint-peter-armengol/.

102. *Wikipedia*, s.v. "Devshirme," updated Jun. 20, 2018, 04:21, https://en.wikipedia.org/wiki

Persecution Today

Islam's persecution of Christians today is no different from what we have seen in the historical record. Raymond Ibrahim's well-documented, *Crucified Again: Exposing Islam's New War on Christians* presents an in-depth report of this abomination.[103] Here we will describe just a few highlights of this persecution.

Syria-Iraq

On October 31, 2010, the world was shocked by al-Qaeda's slaughter of 58 Catholics in the church of Our Lady of the Deliverance in Baghdad. Three-year-old Adam Udai shouted, "Enough! Enough! Enough!" but the Muslim terrorists mercilessly killed him.[104]

When ISIS captured Mosul, it gave its Christian population five and a half weeks to leave, convert to Islam, pay the *jizyah* tax, or be killed.[105]

Nicole Russell wrote in a 2017 article: "Before the U.S. invaded in 2003, about 1.4 million Christians lived in Iraq. After being killed or driven out, there are now only about 250,000."[106]

In the civil war that has devastated Syria since its 2011 Arab Spring, Christians living in regions controlled by ISIS were given the same desperate choice.[107]

Nigeria

On January 1, 2012, ISIS-aligned Boko Haram, whose name means "Western education is forbidden," gave Christians an ultimatum: They had three days to leave northern Nigeria.[108]

"'Boko Haram wants to destroy Christianity in the northeast, in

---

/Devshirme.

103. See Raymond Ibrahim, *Crucified Again: Exposing Islam's New War on Christians* (Washington, D.C.: Regnery Publishing, Inc., 2013).

104. Michael Terheyden, "Anniversary of Massacre in Iraq and the Future of Christianity," *Catholic.org*, Nov. 13, 2011, https://www.catholic.org/news/international/middle_east/story.php?id=43627.

105. "Convert, Pay Tax, or Die, Islamic State Warns Christians," *Reuters*, Jul. 18, 2014, https://uk.reuters.com/article/uk-iraq-security-christians/convert-pay-tax-or-die-islamic-state-warns-christians-idUKKBN0FN29N20140718.

106. Nicole Russell, "Persecuted Christians in Iraq Are Being Forgotten," *Washington Examiner*, Aug. 22, 2017, https://www.washingtonexaminer.com/persecuted-christians-in-iraq-are-being-forgotten.

107. See "Syria's Beleaguered Christians," *BBC News*, Feb. 25, 2015, http://www.bbc.com/news/world-middle-east-22270455.

108. See Tim Lister, "Islamist Militants Warn Christians to Leave North Within Three Days," *CNN*, Jan. 2, 2012, https://www.cnn.com/2012/01/02/world/africa/nigeria-sectarian-divisions/index.html.

Nigeria and beyond, even the whole world,' said Bishop [Oliver] Doeme," of the Catholic Diocese of Maiduguri, Borno State, in an interview with the *National Catholic Register*.[109] His diocese was devastated, 350 churches and rectories were burned down, and many of his clergy, religious, and faithful fled to safer areas.

Pakistan

On March 2, 2011, Shahbaz Bhatti, a Roman Catholic and Pakistani Federal Minister for Minorities Affairs, was shot dead in Islamabad while driving to work. His assassins were Islamist terrorists from Tehrik-i-Taliban Pakistan. They said they killed him for blaspheming Muhammad.[110]

In an earlier interview with Al Jazeera, Minister Bhatti was asked who was threatening his life. He replied that it was the Taliban and al-Qaeda. He then declared: "I believe in Jesus Christ who has given His own life for us. I know what is the meaning of [the] Cross, and I'm following [Him to] the Cross. . . . I prefer to die for my principles and for the justice of my community rather than compromise on these threats."[111]

As a minister, Bhatti opposed Pakistan's blasphemy laws. He protested the death of six Christians burned alive in their Gorja home during Muslim riots over an alleged Koran desecration. He also protested the death sentence given to Asia Bibi.

Asia Bibi (Aasiya Noreen), a Pakistani Catholic married woman, was arrested in 2009 and sentenced to death on spurious blasphemy accusations. Although she has not yet been executed thanks to international pressure, as of this writing, she is still locked up in a windowless jail cell.

During Holy Week 2016, she composed a beautiful prayer that was published in the West:

> Resurrected Lord, allow your daughter Asia to rise
> again with you. Break my chains, make my heart free and
> go beyond these bars, and accompany my soul so that it

---

109. Daniel Blackman, "Nigerian Bishop Doeme Combats Boko Haram With 'Rosary Battle Plan,'" *National Catholic Register,* Oct. 12, 2016, http://www.ncregister.com/daily-news/nigerian-bishop-doeme-combats-boko-haram-with-rosary-battle-plan.
110. See *Wikipedia*, s.v. "Shahbaz Bhatti," Jun. 20, 2018, 13:21, https://en.wikipedia.org/wiki/Shahbaz_Bhatti.
111. Shahbaz Bhatti Interview With *Al Jazeera,* accessed Apr. 15, 2018, https://www.youtube.com/watch?v=oBTBqUJomRE.

is close to those who are dear to me, and that it remains always near you. Do not abandon me in the day of trouble, do not deprive me of your presence. You who have suffered torture and the cross, alleviate my suffering. Hold me near you, Lord Jesus.[112]

She continues:

On the day of your resurrection, Jesus, I want to pray for my enemies, for all those who hurt me. I pray to you for them and beg you to forgive them for the evil they have done. I ask you, Lord, to remove every obstacle so that I can obtain the good gift of freedom. I ask you to protect my family and me.[113]

Asia's prayer, composed amidst suffering and tribulation, shows the strength of faith and the help of God's grace, which never abandons those who remain faithful. What an example for us to ever confide in Divine Providence, even in the most extreme situations.

These snapshots are just a quick overview of Islam's persecution of Christians today. Wherever it could, Islam has persecuted Christians, inflicting much injustice and many deaths. Erdoğan is wrong. The true "crime against humanity" is this centuries-old cruel persecution.[114]

112. Isabelle Cousturie, "Asia Bibi has spent more than 3,000 days in prison for blasphemy," *Aleteia*, Sept. 18, 2017, https://aleteia.org/2017/09/18/asia-bibi-has-spent-more-than-3000-days-in -prison-for-blasphemy/.

113. Paolo Affatato, "Asia Bibi: 'Signore, spezza le mie catene,'" *La Stampa/Vatican Insider*, Apr. 15, 2017, http://www.lastampa.it/2017/04/15/vaticaninsider/ita/nel-mondo/asia-bibi-signore -spezza-le mie-catene-ceogCdpydp6bVzhvWrkToI/pagina.html.

114. "On May 24, 1915, the Allied Powers, England, France, and Russia, jointly issued a statement explicitly charging for the first time ever another government of committing 'a crime against humanity.'" "HRes.316-Affirmation of the United States Record on the Armenian Genocide Resolution," 109th Congress (2005-2006), 1st session, introduced Jun. 14, 2005, https://www .congress.gov/bill/109th-congress/house-resolution/316/text.

In the famous July, 1212 battle of Las Navas de Tolosa, four Catholic Kings defeated the Caliph al-Nasir. It was one of many battles between Christian and Muslim forces during Spain's eight centuries-long Reconquista.

The Myth of Peaceful Coexistence Between Catholicism and Islam in Medieval Spain

Earlier, we discussed the multiculturalist utopia that provides intellectual cover for the unfettered Muslim immigration into the West.[115] Here we shall focus on the historical myth that helps support this utopia regarding Islam. It is the myth of harmonious coexistence and peaceful collaboration between Catholicism and Islam in Crescent-dominated Spain.

The Conquest of Spain

In 711, Islam took advantage of internal strife in Visigothic Spain to invade it. The Iberian country had just gone through a civil war over the succession of King Witiza.[116] Having defeated and exiled Witiza's three sons, Count Rodrigo was proclaimed king in 710. The three princes requested the support of North Africa's Muslim governor, Moussa Ibn Noçaïr, and agreed that their partisans would join any troops Moussa sent across the straits.

In the decisive Battle of Guadalete, on July 31, 711, the Christian troops commanded by King Rodrigo were superior in number to the invaders. However, supporters of Witiza's sons joined the enemy or, according to one version, deserted the battlefield. Their defection resulted in the defeat and death of the Visigoth King.

By 718, the Muslims dominated most of the Iberian Peninsula. Only in the north did the resistance continue, headed by a Visigoth noble, Don Pelayo (685–737). In the famous Battle of Covadonga in 722, he defeated the Moors and founded the Christian kingdom of Asturias. It was the beginning of the *Reconquista*, which ended only with the fall of the Moorish kingdom of Granada in 1492.

---

115. See Chapter 2.
116. The history of King Witiza, his death, succession, ensuing revolution, and the Islamic conquest of Spain is very confusing, with varying versions depending on the sources. See Francisco Javier Simonet, *Historia de los Mozárabes en España* (Madrid: Real Academia de la Historia, n.d.), 31–47.

Imposing Islam by Force

The conquest of Spain followed the strategy Muslims have used since the beginning: First, take advantage of internal divisions in the target nation; second, make alliances; and third, impose submission on both the defeated and allies after the victory.

To imagine that peaceful coexistence with Islam is possible is to ignore the goal of all Muslim conquest: the imposition of Muhammad's religion.

Historian Ibn Khaldun (1332–1406), whose ancestors had moved to Tunisia after Seville's recapture by King Saint Ferdinand in 1248, states this clearly: "In the Muslim community, the holy war is a religious duty, because of the universalism of the (Muslim) mission and (the obligation to) convert everybody to Islam either by persuasion or by force."[117]

The Koran itself imposes the state of submission on Christians and Jews: "Fight those who believe not in Allah nor the Last Day, nor hold that forbidden which hath been forbidden by Allah and His Messenger, nor acknowledge the religion of Truth, (even if they are) of the People of the Book, until they pay the jizya with willing submission, and feel themselves subdued" (9:29).

As in earlier conquests, Muslims allowed the vanquished Visigoths to retain their religion and customs and to be governed to some extent by their own authorities. That freedom was only relative, however. It existed in a state of submission.

The Moors applied to Spain the norms of the Koran and the Sunna as they did everywhere else. The condition of peoples conquered by Islam is one of *dhimmitude*, from the term *dhimmi*, which means *protected people*. This so-called protection, which requires paying taxes such as the jizya and others, allows Christians to keep their lives and have a modicum of freedom, as long as they "feel . . . subdued."[118]

A Certain Splendor, Concealing a Dark Reality

Whoever contemplates the architectural splendor of the Alhambra

---

117. Abd ar Rahman bin Muhammed ibn Khaldun, *The Muqaddimah*, trans. Franz Rosenthal, no. 31, 405, accessed Mar. 24, 2018, https://archive.org/stream/ibn_khaldun-al_muqaddimah_201611/ibn_khaldun-al_muqaddimah_djvu.txt.
118. See Bat Ye'or, *The Dhimmi*.

or the ancient Mosque of Córdoba, today a Catholic cathedral, may have the impression that Andalusia—Islam-dominated Spain—was a real paradise.

It was precisely to undo this false impression and to destroy the myth created around it that Northwestern University professor Darío Fernández-Morera wrote the book, *The Myth of the Andalusian Paradise: Muslims, Christians and Jews under Islamic Rule in Medieval Spain*.[119] He shows how Muslim protection (*dhimma*) was applied to Christians:

- Processions and other public manifestations of Catholic worship were forbidden;
- Christians could rarely build new churches or repair old ones, and to do so they needed a special license;
- Churches could not have towers higher than the mosques;
- It was forbidden to ring church bells;
- Christians could not wear a cross or place one atop churches;
- Christians had to stand up for Muslims;
- Christians could not bear arms or ride a horse, a noble animal, but only donkeys;
- Christians had to use the Arabic language in all commercial transactions, petitions, and dealings with authorities, thus slowly causing the loss of their cultural identity;
- The country's name, Hispania, was changed to Andalusia;
- The church of Saint Vincent in Córdoba was demolished and its materials used for the construction of the famous "Córdoba mosque."[120]

Ultimately, the Church in Spain under Islam's so-called protectorate was a frozen Church that could survive only at the cost of renouncing its normal development and fidelity to Our Lord's great commission: "Going therefore, teach ye all nations; baptizing them

---

119. Darío Fernández-Morera, *The Myth of the Andalusian Paradise: Muslims, Christians and Jews Under Islamic Rule in Medieval Spain* (Wilmington, Del.: ISI, 2017).

120. See Ibid., 209–16.

in the name of the Father, and of the Son, and of the Holy Ghost"
(Matt. 28:19).

Humiliation, to Coerce Apostasy

In her book *The Dhimmi: Jews and Christians Under Islam,* Bat Ye'or
cites this Arab document teaching how Christians should pay the
jizya to their Muslim tax collectors:

> On an appointed day the *Dhimmi*—Christian or Jew—
> must present himself in person . . . before the emir respon-
> sible for the collection of the *jizya.* The latter must be
> seated on a chair raised in the form of a throne; the
> *dhimmi* will come forward bearing the *jizya* held in the
> middle of the palm of his hand, whence the emir will take
> it in such a way that his hand is above and the *dhimmi's*
> hand underneath. Following this, the emir will strike the
> *dhimmi* on the neck with his fist; a man will stand near
> the emir to chase away the *dhimmi* in haste; then a sec-
> ond [*dhimmi*] and a third will come forward to suffer the
> same treatment as well as all those to follow. All [Mus-
> lims] will be admitted to enjoy this spectacle.[121]

Francisco Javier Simonet comments that the protection law was
"all set to favor Muslim subjects and humiliate Christians with the
undisguised end of making them apostatize from their faith."[122] The
weight of taxes, humiliations, and persecution caused many Christians to abandon the Faith.

In his lecture, "Cristianos en Al-Andaluz (Siglos VIII–XII)," José E.
Lopez de Coca Castañer says that, according to Richard Bulliet,
"10% of the population of Andalusia was integrated [Islamized] by
around 750; one hundred years later, that figure was 20% and in 950,
50%. At the turn of the millennium the Muslims are said to have an
overwhelming majority of around 75 or 80%."[123]

Figures are difficult to ascertain because, as Christian kingdoms
gradually formed in Spain, Mozarabic Christians fled the Crescent-
dominated lands *en masse* for those under the Cross. As a result, it
is not known to what extent the decline in the number of Christians

---

121. Bat Ye'or, *The Dhimmi,* 201.
122. Simonet, *Mozárabes en España,* 73.
123. José E. Lopez de Coca Castañer, "Cristianos en Al-Andaluz (Siglos VIII– XII)," XVIII Semana de
    Estudios Medievales, Najera, Jul. 31–Aug. 3, 2007, Biblioteca Gonzalo de Berceo,
    Vallenajerilla.com, http://www.vallenajerilla.com/berceo/lopezcoca/cristianosenal-aldalus.htm.

is due to apostasies to Islam or mass exodus. However, there is no doubt that there was a considerable number of defections from the Faith over time.

Intellectual and Artistic Collaboration

According to the current liberal narrative, it was through Spain that the Arabs transmitted to the West their superior culture, enabling Western progress.

The myth of a culturally refined Arab world in the face of a supposedly barbaric and uncultivated Christian Europe at the time of the Crusades is demonstrated by Rodney Stark to be an Enlightenment fabrication. Its proponents claimed that medieval times in the West were a Dark Age in contrast with Islam. Based on expert studies, Stark shows not only that European technical knowledge was superior, but that the learning Arabs displayed was not developed by them, as they were nomads, but by the dominated peoples of the Byzantine and Persian Empires.[124]

In his book, *The Closing of the Muslim Mind*, Robert R. Reilly, carefully describes the internal struggle between the two currents of medieval Islam, a rationalist one (the Mu'tazilites) and a voluntaristic one (the Ash'arites). He explains: "For the Mu'tazilites, God must be who He is and no other. . . . He is *bound* to be who He is. He cannot act against or deny His own nature. For instance, God does not have reason: He is reason. Therefore, He cannot do anything unreasonable. This is not a constraint; it is freedom. The ability to negate who and what you are is not freedom; it is nihilism."

The other current, the Ash'arites, held an opposing view:

> For the Ash'arites, however, God, as pure will, is not *bound* by anything, including Himself. His freedom of will is absolute. He has no "nature" to deny. He has reason, but is not reason. Therefore, by removing God's attributes from His essence, the Ash'arites made these attributes products of His will. In other words, God was not mercy, but merciful when He wished to be. Likewise, there was no impediment to His acting unreasonably when He wished to do so.[125]

---

124. See Stark, *God's Battalions*, 56–67; also Fernández-Morera, *Myth of the Andalusian Paradise*, 236.

125. Robert R. Reilly, *The Closing of The Muslim Mind: How Intellectual Suicide Created the Modern Islamist Crisis* (Wilmington, Del.: ISI, 2010), 31–2. (Emphases in the original.)

Reilly explains that the struggle between these two currents was finally won by the Ash'arites in the eleventh century. This victory closed off the Islamic mind to philosophy and scientific thinking by denying the principle of causality and secondary causes. Supposedly, everything depends on the arbitrary will of Allah.[126]

When in the following century, basing himself on Aristotle, Averroes (Ibn Rushd, 1126–1198), sought to refute al-Ghazali (1058–1111), the great theorist of anti-intellectualists, his book was burned in 1195 in Córdoba's public square, and the teaching of philosophy was forbidden. The result was that Averroes became better known in the West than in the Islamic world.[127]

The Martyrs of Córdoba

The penal laws burdening Christians in Andalusia made it difficult for them to show their zeal for the Faith, thus favoring the emergence of heresies and apostasies. Between 850 and 859, the most fervent Christians, aware of this danger, decided to proclaim their Faith publicly, knowing they would be martyred.

Between 850 and 859, forty-eight Christians suffered martyrdom. The authorities exposed their mutilated bodies in public places as a warning to others. The effect was the opposite. Seeing the martyrs' relics, other Christians were encouraged to follow their example. Emir Abd al-Rahman II then pressed the Catholic bishops to dissuade Christians from imitating their martyred brethren, which Seville archbishop, Don Recafredo, a Muslim collaborator, did.[128]

Saint Eulogius (d. 859) stands out among the martyrs of Córdoba. He was a highly cultured priest and monk. While in prison, he wrote a *Memorial of the Saints* on the lives of the martyrs and a *Documentum Martyriale* in which he sought to encourage two Christian women awaiting martyrdom. Also, he opposed Archbishop Recafredo.

---

126. See Ibid., 91–127.

127. See Ibid., 120–1. The consequences of this closing to scientific thinking is felt until today: "Pakistani physicist Pervez Hoodbhoy is particularly trenchant. In the August 2007 issue of *Physics Today*, he notes that after the major scientific contributions of Islam's Golden Age in the ninth to thirteenth centuries, 'science in the Islamic world essentially collapsed. No major invention or discovery has emerged from the Muslim world for well over seven centuries now.'" Ibid., 161.

128. See Fernández-Morera, *Myth of the Andalusian Paradise*, 232; San Eulogio de Córdoba, *Memorial de los Santos,* in *Obras Completas de San Eulogio de Córdoba,* ed. Pedro Herrera Roldán (Madrid: Ediciones Akal, 2005).

Saint Eulogius was made the bishop of Toledo but never installed because of Archbishop Recafredo's opposition. He was finally arrested for giving shelter to Leocrícia, a Muslim woman who converted to Catholicism. Both were condemned to death and martyred.[129]

A Shattered Myth

The myth of cordial understanding and collaboration between Muslims, Jews, and Christians in the Andalusian "paradise" is nothing but ideological fantasy. It has no basis in historical fact and is inconsistent with Islamic doctrine.

---

129. See Roldán, *Introducción,* in *Obras Completas de San Eulogio,* 24–7.

The Islamic and Communist world views overlap to some extent. Both deny man's God-given and natural freedom and basic human rights. *Above*: Turkish President Recep Tayyip Erdoğan, with Russian President Vladimir Putin in September, 2017.

CHAPTER 9
Islam's Affinity with Communism and Nazism

In her apparitions in Fatima, Portugal, in 1917, Our Lady warned that the "errors of Russia," that is Communism, would spread everywhere. As we will see, the errors of Russia and those of Islam have much in common, although this is not clear at first sight.

Both Are Totalitarian . . .

In the name of atheism, Communism creates a totalitarian regime in which the *god-state* is the almighty lord that owns and controls all things.

In the name of an Almighty God, lord of all things, or rather, in strict Islamic interpretation, a tyrannical and oppressive God, Islam subjects all creatures to its despotic power and creates a totalitarian theocracy like that seen in the Taliban's Afghanistan or ISIS' caliphate.[130]

. . . And Deny Man's God-Given Freedom

With its materialistic determinism, Communism reduces man to a mere cog in the wheel in the evolution of matter and economic factors.

With its fatalist historical determinism, Islam turns man into the plaything of a capricious God.

In both systems, man is no longer considered a free and rational being endowed with free will, capable of guiding himself, and responsible for his actions.

Both Communism (and other totalitarian ideologies) and Islam eventually lead to a destructive nihilism.

---

130. Worldatlas.com presents these countries as theocracies: Afghanistan, Iran, Mauritania, Saudi Arabia, Sudan, and Yemen. Oishimaya Sen Nag, "Countries With Theocratic Governments Today," Worldatlas.com, updated Apr. 19, 2018, http://www.worldatlas.com/articles/countries -with-theocratic-governments-today.html.

Totalitarian Conception of Divine Omnipotence

For example, Sayyid Qutb takes the Muslim conception of Allah as a god who is pure omnipotence, bereft of wisdom or love, to its ultimate consequences. Based on the premise that everything belongs to Allah, Qutb rejects all human law or government, as well as the legitimacy of private property.

In his book *Milestones*, he states:

> This religion [Islam] is really a universal declaration of the freedom of man from servitude to other men and from servitude to his own desires, which is also a form of human servitude; it is a declaration that sovereignty belongs to Allah alone and that He is the Lord of all the worlds. It means a challenge to all kinds and forms of systems which are based on the concept of the sovereignty of man; in other words, where man has usurped the Divine attribute.

Later on, he continues, "This declaration means that the usurped authority of Allah be returned to Him and the usurpers be thrown out—those who by themselves devise laws for others to follow, thus elevating themselves to the status of lords and reducing others to the status of slaves."

He ends by proclaiming a universal totalitarian theocracy, with the elimination of all nations: "In short, to proclaim the authority and sovereignty of Allah means to eliminate all human kingships and to announce the rule of the Sustainer of the universe over the entire earth."[131]

Elimination of Private Property

Concerning private property, in his book *Social Justice in Islam*, Sayyid Qutb rejects private land ownership, accepting only its private *use*.

For him, "[What man] can possess [of the land] is its irrigation and its crops, which means that the matter is one of the profitable use of a possession rather than one of actual ownership."[132]

---

131. Sayyid Qutb, *Milestones: Ma'alim fi'l-tareeq*, ed. A.B. al-Mehri (Birmingham, U.K.: Maktabah, 2006), 67, PDF edition, https://ia800708.us.archive.org/34/items/SayyidQutb/Milestones%20Special%20Edition.pdf.
132. Sayyid Qutb, *Social Justice in Islam*, trans. John B. Hardie, rev. Hamid Algar (Kuala Lumpur: Islamic Book Trust, 2000), 134.

The abolition of private property is the objective of Communism. Private property enables man to hold on to and increase his possessions, thereby improving his condition. Marx contemptuously called it "bourgeois property." As Marx and Engels proclaimed in the 1848 Manifesto of the Communist Party: "The theory of the Communists may be summed up in the single sentence: Abolition of private property."[133]

"Islam May Be Considered as Co-extensive With Communism"

Muhammad Hamidullah (1908–2002) was an influential Muslim scholar. He was born in Hyderabad into a scholarly family and studied both in India and in Europe. A polyglot, he was the first Muslim scholar to translate the Koran into French. He was a specialist in Islamic law and economics and the author of a two-volume biography of Muhammad, besides many other books on Islamic subjects.

In 1950, at the height of the Soviet Union's power, he wrote a study titled *Islam and Communism: A Study in Comparative Thought.* He writes, "Although Islam and Communism are not the same thing, it is possible that they do not differ in each and every thing. The object of this short study is to find out how far Islam may tolerate the teachings of Communism."[134]

After mentioning different types of Communism, he analyzes its political aspect and affirms that communists are committed to the creation of a single World State. "Taking this question alone, without any reference to dogmas or economic set-up, I think Islam can accommodate this arrangement, which simply means a World State, a single central Government for the whole of the human race . . . . Thus Islam may be considered as co-extensive with Communism."[135]

In support of this conclusion, Hamidullah's study contains a picture of a Tajik Muslim girl performing a national dance at a festival, with the following commentary praising communist ideology:

---

133. Karl Marx and Frederick Engels, *Manifesto of the Communist Party*, 22, accessed Mar. 1, 2018, https://www.marxists.org/archive/marx/works/download/pdf/Manifesto.pdf.

134. Muhammad Hamidullah, *Islam and Communism: A Study in Comparative Thought*, 3, accessed May 7, 2018, http://ebooks.rahnuma.org/religion/Dr.Hamidullah/Dr.HamidUllah-Islam-and -Communism.pdf .

135. Ibid., 8.

These young men and women are the inhabitants of Tajikistan, Soviet Russia, whose destinies are controlled by Communist ideology, whose one positive value, it must be admitted, lies in the fact that it has been a corrective of one-sided spiritualistic conceptions of life that have been dominant in the world of Islam and made Islam misunderstood by friend and foe.[136]

Continuing, he addresses the question of the center of this World State: "There remains the question of subordination to Moscow.... As I am examining different aspects of Communism individually, and in a theoretical manner, I should say that with the idea of a World State there ought to be a political center."[137]

He sees no problem with Moscow being that center: "As a center of purely political field of the proposed World State, Moscow or New York are as good as Mecca or Medina. Was not Medina preferred by the Prophet himself to be his political metropolis instead of the Meccan religious center? Was not Kufa preferred to Medina by the Caliph 'Ali, Damascus by the Umaiyyads, Baghdad by the Abbasids, Istanbul by the Osmani Caliphs?"[138]

Summing up, Hamidullah says, "In short, in the political doctrine of Communism, there is essentially no difficulty for Islam."[139]

He does not advocate a violent revolution, however, preferring Fabian-type socialism which promotes egalitarianism through taxes. He states: "If other freedoms are conceded, why not also the freedom to possess? Tax the rich to any extent necessary for providing the poor with the minimum required by them. That is the Islamic principle of general law."

Similarly, he explains that "Accumulation of very large wealth in limited hands is further remedied by Islam by its laws of testaments and inheritance . . . its prohibition of interest and other things to which I shall revert again. Large fiefs and landed properties cannot exist in Islam for more than one generation; the law of inheritance divides and subdivides in the course of time."[140]

For him, the decadence of capitalism is a consequence, not of pri-

---

136. Ibid., 9.
137. Ibid., 12.
138. Ibid.
139. Ibid.
140. Ibid., 19–20.

vate property, but of its attachment to materialism. Similarly, for Communism, the problem is not collective property, but the danger of an alliance with materialism.

> Capitalism has degenerated not because private and individual ownership of capital and means of production was the order of the day, but, I maintain, because its worst advocates professed and practised materialism, that is, rejection of all moral values and striving for nothing except material gain, even at the expense of all that is dear to human morality. Communism, that is collective ownership of the means of production, may as such not lead to anything unbearable; what I fear for it is its alliance, or rather conspiracy, with materialism.[141]

Islam Replaces Communism

André Glucksmann (1937–2015) was a French philosopher of the extreme left and one of the intellectual leaders of the 1968 anarchist Sorbonne student uprising, but who later abandoned the Red creed. For him, Islam replaces Communism: "Islamism replaces the final secular struggle of Communism with a theological apocalypse, its mechanisms work in the same way in all societies it seizes. It is a vehicle of terror. In the name of a radiant future, all is allowed."[142]

Contemporary Islamic Nihilism

As Glucksmann explains, the nihilist philosophy underpinning Islamic fundamentalism is the continuation of the Fascist and Communist ideologies of the twentieth century:

> The nihilist, Islamic fundamentalist, Bolshevik, or Fascist does not recoil in face of anything. . . .
> . . . The fantasy of a great anti-liberal, anti-Western, and anti-capitalist global revolution has fed the fanaticism of the Nazis, Communists, and Islamists. This is their secret nihilistic convergence. Hence the taste for redemptive violence that they share.[143]

In another place, Glucksmann states, "My question is: what do

---

141. Ibid., 20.
142. André Glucksmann, "Les trois délires, rouge, vert et brun," *Le Figaro Magazine*, Sept. 6, 2003 (no. 18376), 44.
143. Ibid., 44–5.

extremist ideologies like the Communism or Nazism of yesteryear and the Islamism of today have in common? After all, they support ostensibly very different ideals—the superior race, mankind united in socialism, the community of Muslim believers (the *Umma*). . . . But the common characteristic is nihilism."[144]

Italian Islamicist Stefano Allievi also highlights this nihilistic aspect of contemporary Islamic ideology: "Even if ISIS were defeated in its own terrain in Iraq and Syria, its supporting ideology, this disturbing form of contemporary Islamic nihilism which is at the same time the incubator and the product, will not end."[145]

It is this nihilism that leads to suicide attacks, in which the individual destroys himself while destroying countless lives in cruel atrocities and mass attacks. It causes the vandalizing of monuments and works of art. It reduces churches, monasteries, and historical sites such as Palmyra, Syria, to rubble, to give just one example.

Communists Adhere to Islam

It is not surprising, therefore, that communists express sympathy for, ally themselves with, or even convert to Islam without ceasing to be communists.

■ Roger Garaudy

A typical example is Roger Garaudy (1913–2012), a theoretician of the French Communist Party and member of its political bureau. He became a Muslim in 1982.

In 1983, he published a statement on his conversion. He affirms that he joined Islam without abandoning Marxism: "I joined [Islam] without denying anything that brought Jesus into my life, as in the Koran he is a prophet of Islam, nor what Marxism had taught me to analyze in our societies and how to act effectively in them since the Muslim faith does not exclude any science or technology, but on the contrary integrates them and places them in the way of God."[146]

144. André Glucksmann, "Bin Laden, Dostoevsky and the Reality Principle: An Interview With André Glucksmann," *OpenDemocracy*, May 2, 2011, https://www.opendemocracy.net/faith -iraqwarphiloshophy/article_1111.jsp.

145. Stefano Allievi, "Dopo Barcellona: Il nichilismo islamico contemporaneo e i suoi obiettivi," Aug. 19, 2017, http://www.stefanoallievi.it/2017/08/dopo-barcellona-il-nichilismo-islamico -contemporaneo-e-i-suoi-obiettivi/.

146. Roger Garaudy, "Pourquoi je suis musulman," *Revue Proche-orient et Tiers-Monde*, 7 (Jun. 1983): 57–65, republished as "Marx, Jésus et Mohammed," Jun. 25, 2016, http://rogergaraudy

■ Carlos "The Jackal"

Even more meaningful is the statement by the notorious Marxist-Leninist terrorist Carlos, the Jackal. His name is Ilich Ramírez Sánchez, and he was born in Venezuela, on October 12, 1949. In 1970, he became a member of the Marxist-Leninist terrorist organization *Popular Front for the Liberation of Palestine* (PFLP).[147] The Jackal became known worldwide with the 1975 raid on OPEC's Vienna headquarters in which three people were killed and more than 60 people taken hostage. He participated in many other terrorist acts until his 1994 arrest and subsequent sentencing to life imprisonment.

In 1975, Illich converted to Islam. In 2004, he published from prison a book-manifesto titled, *L'Islam révolutionnaire* [Revolutionary Islam], in which he states:

> I converted to Islam on the eve of my twenty-sixth birthday, at the beginning of October 1975.
>
> I've not changed one iota, revolutionary and communist I was, such am I, and I will stay.
>
> I am a *professional revolutionary*, a soldier, a combatant, in the purest Leninist tradition.
>
> My communist ideal remained totally unchanged through the tribulations of life. It obviously did not contradict my faith in the one God. . . . Islam has reinforced my revolutionary convictions. . . .
>
> Islam is from the beginning a revolution. Islam is essentially revolutionary. I would define "revolutionary Islam" as the return to the origins of the Islamic *Fatah*, the time when Koranic revelation was the source of all political sovereignty.[148]

Support From the Leftist Establishment

The above data, although necessarily condensed, help to understand

---

.blogspot.com/2016/06/marx-jesus-et-mohammed.html.

147. "[T]he Popular Front adopts Marxist-Leninist theory as a basic strategic line for the building of the revolutionary party." Popular Front for the Liberation of Palestine. *Strategy for the Liberation of Palestine*. Chap. 13—"No Revolutionary Party Without Revolutionary Theory," accessed Mar. 1, 2018, http://pflp.ps/english/strategy-for-the-liberation-of-palestine-no-revolutionary-party-without-revolutionary-theory/.

148. Ilich Ramírez Sánchez (Carlos), *L'Islam révolutionnaire: Texte et propos recueillis, rassemblés, et presentés par Jean-Michel Vernochet* (Monaco: Rocher, 2003), 23, 31, 37, 38, 89. (Emphasis in the original.)

why the leftist establishment—media, entertainment industry, academia, politicians, feminists, homosexual, and transgender movements—look sympathetically at Islam despite everything that seems to separate them.

This totalitarian common denominator of Communism and Islam, as well as their shared nihilism, is what leads the left (and those nostalgic for Nazi-Fascism)[149] to find in Islam an ally for the destruction of what remains of Christian civilization.

Upending the observation attributed to sociologist Max Weber that Communism "is the Islam of modern times,"[150] we can say that Islam is the Communism of our days.

Hitler: Nazism Is More Compatible With Islam Than Christianity

Adolph Hitler admired Islam. He would not have minded a Muslim victory over the Franks at the Battle of Tours/Poitiers since he considered Islam more compatible with Nazism than Christianity. He expressed these views several times, as his confidant Albert Speer (1905–1981), Nazi Germany's World War II Minister of Armaments and War Production, recorded in his memoirs. Léon Degrelle (1906–1994), a Belgian collaborator, also attests to them.

Hitler's Admiration for "a Religion That Believed in Spreading the Faith by the Sword and Subjugating All Nations"

Hitler had been much impressed by a scrap of history he had learned from a delegation of distin-

---

149. See Glucksmann, "Les trois délires, rouge, vert et brun."
150. Hichem Djait, *Europe and Islam*, trans. Peter Heinegg (Berkeley: University of California Press, 1985), 132.

guished Arabs. When the Mohammedans attempted to penetrate beyond France into Central Europe during the eighth century, his visitors had told him, they had been driven back at the Battle of Tours. Had the Arabs won this battle, the world would be Mohammedan today. For theirs was a religion that believed in spreading the faith by the sword and subjugating all nations to that faith. The Germanic peoples would have become heirs to that religion. Such a creed was perfectly suited to the Germanic temperament. Hitler said that the conquering Arabs, because of their racial inferiority, would in the long run have been unable to contend with the harsher climate and conditions of the country. They could not have kept down the more vigorous natives, so that ultimately not Arabs but Islamized Germans could have stood at the head of this Mohammedan Empire.

Hitler usually concluded this historical speculation by remarking: "You see, it's been our misfortune to have the wrong religion.... The Mohammedan religion too would have been much more compatible to us than Christianity. Why did it have to be Christianity with its meekness and flabbiness?"

Albert Speer, *Inside The Third Reich: Memoirs*, trans. Richard and Clara Winston [New York: The Macmillan Company, 1970], 96.

Hitler Would Not Have Minded a Muslim Victory at the 732 Battle of Poitiers (Tours)

According to Léon Degrelle, "Hitler certainly had a soft spot for Islam. Originally a Catholic, he was highly interested in Islam and its civilization. He almost regretted that its armies failed to triumph over Charles Martel at Poitiers."

Léon Degrelle, "Hitler et l'Islam," *Rebelle*, no. 2, (Fall 1984), republished in *Revue d'Histoire non conformiste*, 107–13, accessed Mar. 6, 2018, https://web.archive.org/web/201709120606 26/https://radioislam.org/degrelle/islam.htm.

In an Open Letter to America after the 9/11 attacks, Osama Bin Laden stated, "The first thing we are calling you to is Islam." The letter ends with threats of destruction should America refuse to submit to Islam. *Above*: Osama Bin Laden with his lieutenant, the Egyptian doctor Ayman al-Zawahiri, in November 2001.

Chapter 10

Islamist Universalism

Islam divides the world in two: those who are Muslim and those who are not. It engages the latter, through *dawah* (missionary efforts), and, as we have seen, jihad, and Sharia.

Muslims of the World, Unite!

In 1848, Karl Marx and Friedrich Engels launched the rallying cry, "Workers of the world, unite!" in their *Communist Manifesto*. It could be said that pan-Islamism's slogan is, "Muslims of the world, unite."[151]

The *Oxford Dictionary of Islam* defines *pan-Islamism* as an "ideology calling for sociopolitical solidarity among all Muslims. [It h]as existed as a religious concept since the early days of Islam."[152]

While some Muslim activists struggle for this Islamic world government through non-violent means, others do so through jihad.

Bin Laden's "Letter to America"

On 9/11, war was declared on America by a dishonorable enemy. In an open "Letter to America" published around the world in 2002, Osama bin Laden tried to explain why America was attacked. He also stipulated what Islam wanted from America. For him, Islam transcends sovereign nations and borders:

> What are we calling you to, and what do we want from you?
> The first thing that we are calling you to is Islam.
> The religion of the Unification of God; of freedom from associating partners with Him, and rejection of this; . . .
> It is to this religion that we call you; . . . It is the religion of Jihad in the way of Allah so that Allah's Word and religion reign Supreme. . . .
> It is saddening to tell you that you are the worst civi-

---

151. Ervand Abrahamian, "The Making of the Modern Iranian State," in *Introduction to Politics of the Developing World*, ed. William A. Joseph, Mark Kesselman, and Joel Krieger, 5th ed. (Boston: Wadsworth Cengage Learning, 2010), 324.

152. *The Oxford Dictionary of Islam*, John L. Esposito, ed., (New York: Oxford University Press, 2003), s.v. "Pan-Islamism." See also, *Oxford Islamic Studies Online*, http://www.oxfordislamicstudies.com/article/opr/t125/e1819.

lization witnessed by the history of mankind. . . .

(7) We also call you. . . .

If you fail to respond to all these conditions, then pre-pare for fight with the Islamic Nation. The Nation of Monotheism, . . .

The Nation of honor and respect. . . .

The Nation of Martyrdom. . . .

The Nation of victory and success. . . .

The Islamic Nation that was able to dismiss and de-stroy the previous evil Empires like yourself; the Nation that rejects your attacks, wishes to remove your evils, and is prepared to fight you. . . .

If the Americans refuse to listen to our advice and the goodness, guidance and righteousness that we call them to, then be aware that you will lose this Crusade Bush began, just like the other previous Crusades in which you were humiliated by the hands of the Mujahideen fleeing to your home in great silence and disgrace. . . .

This is our message to the Americans.[153]

The Islamic State's Caliphate

In June 2014, Mosul fell to ISIS (or ISIL), and its spokesman, Abu Mohammed Al Adnani, by audio file distributed over the Internet, proclaimed the caliphate, and al-Baghdadi as the new caliph. He also declared the terrorist organization's statehood, changing its name to Islamic State. The declaration called on Muslims worldwide to pledge allegiance to the caliph and help the jihad. It declared null and void the political independence of all states, upon the arrival of the Islamic State's soldiers to their territories: "The legality of all emirates, groups, states, and organizations, becomes null by the expansion of the caliph's authority and arrival of its troops to their areas."[154]

In 2017, the caliphate lost much of the territory it controlled in Iraq and Syria. Nevertheless, like an aerosol, its venomous spray reached other continents, with terrorists far and wide pledging allegiance to it. It became a symbol for Islamist unity, making it evident to the West and jihadis alike that a worldwide caliphate can be restored.

---

153. "Full text: bin Laden's 'Letter to America,'" *The Guardian*, Nov. 24, 2002, https://www.theguardian .com/world/2002/nov/24/theobserver.

154. Matt Bradley, "ISIS Declares New Islamist Caliphate," *Wall Street Journal*, Jun. 29, 2014, https://www.wsj.com/articles/isis-declares-new-islamist-caliphate-1404065263.

CHAPTER 11

Christian Civilization vs. Islamic Totalitarianism

In his memorable encyclical *Immortale Dei*, of November 1, 1885, Pope Leo XIII (1878–1903) refers to a philosophy of the Gospel that shaped Christian civilization: "There was a time when the philosophy of the Gospel . . . permeated the laws, institutions, and customs of the peoples, all categories and all relations of civil society."[155] In this sense, that philosophy governed the states.

The Philosophy of the Gospel Governed the States

Having the philosophy of the Gospel as the foundation of civilization is appropriate because it highlights the role of the human intellect and the assistance the mind receives from divine grace. This philosophy of the Gospel helps us take the sublime teachings of the Savior and draw doctrinal principles from them. These principles impart a Christian undertone to the laws, arts, social customs, and civil governance of a people.

Among the many doctrinal principles contained in the philosophy of the Gospel is the distinction Our Lord Jesus Christ introduced between religious and civil authority: "Render therefore to Caesar the things that are Caesar's; and to God, the things that are God's" (Matt. 22:21). Consequently, there was no fusion, let alone confusion, between the two powers. Instead, the pope says, "Church and State were happily united in concord and a friendly interchange of good offices."[156]

As a whole, the Catholic nations of Europe formed Christendom, which saw the pope as the natural arbitrator to resolve their disputes. This ascendancy of the pope did not come from his power of the keys—that is, his apostolic power—but from the consensus of Christian nations. Therefore, the pope's decision in those disputes

---

155. Leo XIII, Encyclical *Immortale Dei* (On the Christian Constitution of States), Nov. 1, 1885, no. 9, http://w2.vatican.va/content/leo-xiii/la/encyclicals/documents/hf_lxiii_enc_01111885 _immortale-dei.html. (Our translation from the Latin original.)

156. Ibid.

did not have a properly religious character. It could freely be rejected, as it was a specifically temporal matter.[157]

Islamic Theocracy

In opposition to the concept of Christendom, Islam presents the *ummah*, the community of believers and followers of Muhammad.

However, the two concepts are entirely different. In Christendom, the laws, customs, and institutions are informed by the Christian Faith but cannot be confused with it. On the contrary, the *ummah* is not only inspired by religion but is also its expression: Laws, customs, and institutions are said to have been established by Allah directly, through the Koran and the Sunna.

In fact, Fr. Antoine Moussali writes, "Islam puts the community before the individual. The notion of the *ummah* overrides any other consideration. *Ummah* comes from umm, mother. *Ummah* means 'the gathering of believers into the fold of faith.'"

Earlier, the Lebanese Islamicist states, "The Islamic system, as it was born in Medina, has naturally taken the form of a theocratic system." [158]

According to the Koran, Islam considers itself the chosen people. "You are the best nation that ever existed among humanity" (MS 3:110).[159] Having taken the privileged Old Testament place of the Jewish people—a theocratic people ruled directly by God, Yahweh—Muslims believe they must dominate the world.[160]

Commenting on this same verse, Maududi explains, "This is the same declaration that has been made in Al-Baqarah [2:143]. The followers of the Holy Prophet are being reminded that they have been appointed to the leadership of the world from which the children

---

157. See Charles Journet, *L'Église du Verbe Incarné*, 3rd edition enlarged (Bruges-Paris: Desclée de Brouwer, 1963), 1:343.

158. Antoine Moussali, C.M., "Ce qu'un Chrétien doit savoir sur l'Islam," Jun. 12, 2015, https://questionsislam.wordpress.com/2015/06/12/ce-quun-chretien-doit-savoir-de-lislam -pere-antoine-moussali/. Fr. Antoine Moussali, C.M. (1921–2003) knew the Koran by heart and could recite it like a muezzin. He was thus able to perceive later additions to the Koran, as they broke the rhythm of the psalmody.

159. Father Moussali's translation from the Arab. Yusuf Ali renders it as: "Ye are the best of peoples, evolved for mankind" (3:110).

160. On the theocratic character of the Jewish people and its limits when they adopted the monarchic government, see James F. Driscoll, s.v. "Theocracy," in *The Catholic Encyclopedia*, vol. 14 (New York: Robert Appleton, 1912), New Advent online edition, http://www.newadvent.org /cathen/14568a.htm.

of Israel had been deposed on account of their incompetence."[161]

The same Muslim commentator presented a similar idea earlier regarding 2:142,[162] which changed the direction in which Muslims pray, from Jerusalem to Mecca:

> This is the declaration of the leadership of the Muslim Community [umma]. . . . It was the change of the *qiblah* [direction of the prayer] from the Temple to the *Ka'bah* that was an indication that the Israelites had been deposed from the leadership and the Muslims had been appointed to it. Therefore the change of the *qiblah* from the Temple to the *Ka'bah* was not merely a change of direction as the foolish people took it to be, but it was really the formal declaration of the change of leadership from the Israelites to the followers of Muhammad.[163]

Therefore, Islam believes in a universal Islamic community whose mission is to dominate the world and impose not only the religion of Muhammad but also Sharia and all its consequences.

This is what the French Islamicist Marie-Thérèse Urvoy explains:

> The *ummah* is the people of Muhammad. . . . This brotherhood has a specific bond of unity which is the Book, uncreated and eternal according to orthodox doctrine. . . . It contains the law that God wants for humanity. First come the rights of God, such as the obligation of combat by stigmatizing those who remain "seated" (*al-qâ'idûn*), the Koran encourages "effort" (*jihad*) to promote these "rights of God" all over the world by a political-religious organization.[164]

Likewise, Egyptian Islamicist Father Samir comments, "Islam from its beginning presented itself as a global project that includes all the aspects of life . . . religion, society, and state . . . the religious law determines the civil law and organizes the private and commu-

---

161. Maududi, *Meaning of the Qur'an* (3:110 – note 88), accessed Mar. 6, 2018, http://www.englishtafsir.com/quran/3/index.html#sdfootnote89sym.
162. "Thus have We made you a Community of the 'Golden Mean' so that you may be witnesses in regard to mankind and the Messenger may be a witness in regard to you." Ibid. (2:142), accessed Mar. 6, 2018, http://www.englishtafsir.com/quran/2/index.html#sdfootnote144anc.
163. Ibid., note 144, accessed Mar. 6, 2018, http://www.englishtafsir.com/quran/2/index.html#sdfootnote144sym.
164. Dominique et Marie-Thérèse Urvoy, "Oumma, Communauté (*Ummah*)," Jan. 13, 2009, http://Jesusmarie.free.fr/islam_urvoy_oumma.html.

nal life of all those who live in a Muslim society or environment."[165]

Consequently, the Islamic community or *ummah* is a "political-religious organization" to impose the beliefs and law of Muhammad.

Unfortunately, starting in the fourteenth century, the West increasingly abandoned the philosophy of the Gospel and the concept of Christendom and sank into a process of moral decadence.[166] Today, seven centuries later, it is confronted with Islamic totalitarianism from within and without.

Will the West follow the example of the Prodigal Son and choose to return to the Father's House, to a Christian civilization inspired by the "philosophy of the Gospel," or will it submit to an Islamic totalitarianism that highly resembles communist ideology?

---

165. Samir, *111 Questions*, 100–1.
166. See Corrêa de Oliveira, *Revolution and Counter Revolution*.

Chapter 12

Dialogue, a Talismanic Word Used to Create a Mindset

Toward the end of 1965, as the Second Vatican Council was coming to a close amidst euphoria and optimism, Plinio Corrêa de Oliveira wrote a still timely essay: "Unperceived Ideological Transshipment and Dialogue."

Optimism and Relativism

The eminent Catholic thinker analyzes the then-reigning optimism and how the Church's dialogue with non-Catholics was replacing militancy in defense of Truth and the struggle against evil and error.

In the post-Conciliar Church, relations with non-Catholics were no longer directed toward converting them to the Faith, by logical persuasion, using philosophical, historical, and theological arguments, but merely to establish friendship between religions that were doctrinally incompatible.

Dialogue thus assumed the character of a magic word. It later became something of a talisman or charm capable of resolving all disputes with non-Catholics, even communists. The word acquired a peculiar, artificial glow that spoke more to feelings than to reason and caused its users to eschew reality and allow themselves to be carried away by wishful thinking.

The TFP founder called dialogue and other words that underwent the same transformation, "*talismanic words*," and explained that,

> [The talismanic word] is a word whose legitimate meaning is congenial and, at times, even noble; but it is also a word that has some elasticity. When it is used tendentiously, it begins to shine with a new radiance, fascinating the patient and taking him much farther than he could have imagined.
>
> Twisted out of shape and distorted, wholesome and even dignified words have been used to label a number of mistakes, errors and blunders. . . . Some words with a dignified connotation that have been transformed into

deceitful talismans and placed at the service of error are: social justice, ecumenism, dialogue, peace, irenicism, and coexistence. . . .

Passing to the religious field as such, we have irenic dialogue favoring interconfessionalism and weakening all religions, throwing them into a state of absolute confusion.[167]

"Talismanic Word" and Interreligious Dialogue With Islam

Interreligious dialogue with Islam has taken on this talismanic character since it willfully ignores the irreconcilable doctrines of Catholicism and Islam. It further disregards Islam's history, worldwide expansionism today, cruel persecution of Christians, and use of terrorism.

A Wrongheaded Dialogue From the Beginning

Dialogue with Muslims was flawed from the outset because it was based on extremely ambiguous statements in Second Vatican Council documents. Such statements were influenced by the theories of Louis Massignon.[168] Massignon was such an Islamophile that when Pope Pius XI received him in audience in 1934, he jokingly called him a Muslim-Catholic.[169]

The Constitution on the Church, *Lumen Gentium* reads, "The plan of salvation also includes those who acknowledge the Creator. In the first place amongst these there are the Muslims, who, professing to hold the faith of Abraham, along with us adore the one and merciful God (*nobiscum Deum adorant unicum, misericordem*)."[170]

The Declaration *Nostra Ætate* states:

The Church regards with esteem also the Moslems.

---

167. Plinio Corrêa de Oliveira, "Unperceived Ideological Transshipment and Dialogue," *Crusade for a Christian Civilization*, vol. 12, no. 4 (Oct.–Dec. 1982), ch. 3, 2. C.; Concl., 1; pp. 20, 38; digital ed., http://www.tfp.org/unperceived-ideological-transshipment-and-dialogue.

168. See Christian S. Krokus, "Louis Massignon's Influence on the Teaching of Vatican II on Muslims and Islam," *Islam and Christian–Muslim Relations* vol. 23, issue 3 (2012): 329–45, http://www.tandfonline.com/doi/abs/10.1080/09596410.2012.686264; Neal Robinson, "Massignon, Vatican II and Islam as an Abrahamic religion," *Islam and Christian–Muslim Relations* vol. 2, issue 2 (1991): 182–205, http://www.tandfonline.com/doi/abs/10.1080/09596419108720957?src=recsys.

169. See Lorenzo Perrone, "'Abraham, père de tous les croyants' Louis Massignon et l'apostolat de la prière," *Proche-Orient Chrétien* no. 60 (2010): 106, http://www.academia.edu/1287868.

170. Second Vatican Council, *Lumen Gentium* (Dogmatic Constitution on the Church), Nov. 21, 1964, no. 16, http://www.vatican.va/archive/hist_councils/ii_vatican_council/documents/vat-ii_const_19641121_lumen-gentium_en.html.

> They adore the one God, (Muslimos respicit qui unicum
> Deum adorant) . . . merciful and all-powerful the Cre-
> ator of heaven and earth, who has spoken to men; they
> take pains to submit wholeheartedly to even His in-
> scrutable decrees, just as Abraham, with whom the
> faith of Islam takes pleasure in linking itself, submitted
> to God. Though they do not acknowledge Jesus as God,
> they revere Him as a prophet. They also honor Mary,
> His virgin Mother; at times they even call on her with
> devotion.[171]

Strictly speaking, the statements that Muslims "along with us
adore the one and merciful God," and that they "adore the one God"
and subject themselves to Him "just as Abraham . . . submitted" suggest that Christians and Muslims worship the same God, and thus
both have the same God.

This is tantamount to saying that the Trinitarian God of Scripture
and the Koran's non-Trinitarian deity are one and the same. This is
further reinforced by the mention of Abraham's faith and by showing esteem for the fact that Muslims see Jesus as a prophet, a
prophet who Islam says came to announce the future advent of
Muhammad!

However, in the Scriptures, God unfailingly revealed that He is
One and Triune, and Jesus Christ made this clear in the Gospels.
Therefore, we cannot deny the Trinity without rejecting the true
God, since God's Trinity of Persons is not accidental but derives
from His very essence.[172]

In turn, to transform the Word Incarnate, Our Lord Jesus Christ,
into a mere man is to deny the principal mysteries of our Faith: the
Incarnation, Passion, and Death of Our Lord Jesus Christ.

The Koran and the *hadith* not only deny the Blessed Trinity but
see devotion to it as idolatrous, polytheist, and punishable by death.

Nothing in the conciliar texts quoted above suggests they refer
only to those Muslims who find themselves in a state of invincible
ignorance regarding the true Faith. Such Muslims are unaware of

---

171. Second Vatican Council, *Nostra Ætate* (Declaration on the Relation of the Church to Non-
  Christian Religions), Oct. 28, 1965, no. 3,
  http://www.vatican.va/archive/hist_councils/ii_vatican_council/documents/vat-ii_decl
  _19651028_nostra-aetate_en.html.
172. See George Joyce, s.v. "The Blessed Trinity," in *The Catholic Encyclopedia*, vol. 15 (New York: Robert
  Appleton, 1912), New Advent online edition, http://www.newadvent.org/cathen/15047a.htm.

the dogma of the Trinity, and consequently have never knowingly adhered to Islam's rejection of it. Helped by grace, such people— whom Saint Thomas Aquinas calls unbelievers "merely because [they have] not the faith," "by way of pure negation"[173]—earnestly desire to worship a God who rewards and punishes according to merits and demerits. This subjective state, "implicitly, by way of desire *fides in voto*), includes belief in Christ and the Trinity."[174]

Instead, the quoted Conciliar texts deal with Muslims in general, as "they," thereby including those who adhere to Muhammad's erroneous doctrines and reject the dogma of the Trinity. This is all the more so since these documents speak of Muslims who accept Our Lord Jesus Christ as a prophet while denying His Divinity.

The Popes and Islam: From Belligerence to Friendship

ISIS online magazine *Dabiq* sees a change of attitude toward Islam in today's popes:

> While previous popes spoke against Islam due to the actual reality they faced, based on mutual enmity between the pagan Christians and monotheistic Muslims, recent popes—and especially Pope Francis—have attempted to paint a picture of heartwarming friendship, seeking to steer Muslim masses away from the obligation of waging jihad against disbelief.

Dabiq [online ISIS magazine], "In the words of the enemy," *Dabiq* (1437 Shawwal) 15, 76, accessed Feb. 28, 2018, https://clarionproject.org/factsheets-files/islamic-state-magazine-dabiq-fifteen-breaking-the-cross.pdf.

Ominous Consequences

Since these conciliar texts are the foundation for dialogue with Islam, that dialogue can only increase the confusion among Catholics while favoring Muslims.

---

173. St. Thomas Aquinas, *Summa Theologiae*, II–II, q. 10, a. 1, trans. Fathers of the English Dominican Province, 2nd rev. ed., 1920, rev. and ed. Kevin Knight for New Advent, http://newadvent.org/summa/.

174. Msgr. Joseph Pohle, *Grace, Actual and Habitual: A Dogmatic Treatise*, ad. and ed. Arthur Preuss, 3rd, rev. ed. (Toronto: W. E. Blake & Son, 1919), part 2, ch. 1, sec. 1, http://biblehub.com/library/pohle/grace_actual_and_habitual/title_page.htm.

Several Catholic priests who participated in this dialogue attest to this fact. For example, Father Moussali describes the dialogue fever and its consequences: "Encounters, sessions, seminars, speeches, and colloquia followed one another at a brisk pace for two decades, as one got carried away by an immense, irrepressible optimism. . . . Forced, compelled by impatience for dialogue, one had changed imperceptibly from an attitude of goodwill to one of complacency, and from a search for the truth to a search for compromise."[175]

In a 2016 *Le Figaro* interview with Eléonore de Vulpillières, Fr. François Jourdan, an author of books on Islam, also shows how incoherent that dialogue is:

> We are fooled by constantly deceptive similarities with Islam, which is a syncretism of pagan elements (jinn, Ka'ba), Manichaean (Gnostic prophetism reshaped out of real history with Mani, the 'seal of prophets'), Jews (Noah, Abraham, Moses, David, Jesus . . . who become Muslims before Muhammad and do not function alike: Solomon is a prophet and speaks with ants. . .), and Christians (Jesus has another name, 'Îsâ'; he is neither dead nor resurrected but speaks in the cradle and gives life to birds of clay. . .). The phonetics make it seem as if both names refer to the same thing. Not to speak of the deep axes of the Koranic vision of God and the world: A heavy God who overhangs and manages everything without leaving real and autonomous room to what is not Him (a fundamental problem of lack of otherness due to divine transcendence without the biblical covenant). Now if we have 'the same God,' everyone sees it in his own way and, to be reassured, believes that the other sees it likewise. . . . This is total misunderstanding and permanent political exploitation in mutual relations (naturally without saying it: someone had to dare figure it out).[176]

---

175. Antoine Moussali, C.M., *La Croix et le croissant: Le Christianisme face à l'Islam* (Versailles: Editions de Paris, 1998), 13.

176. Eléonore de Vulpillières, "Islam et christianisme: les impasses du dialogue interreligieux–L'islamologue François Jourdan revient sur les différences spécifiques qui distinguent l'islam du christianisme," *Le Figaro*, Jan. 22, 2016, http://www.lefigaro.fr/vox /religion/2016/01/22/31004-20160122ARTFIG00344-islam-et-christianisme-les-impasses-du -dialogue-interreligieux.php. (Reprinted with permission.)

What Is the Purpose of This Dialogue?

A dialogue between people who think differently only makes sense when you either want to convince the other of your position or need his cooperation to solve a practical problem, such as preventing a catastrophe or hammering out a peace agreement.

Interreligious dialogue, and ecumenism in general, though, do not aim to convert anyone to the Catholic Faith. The Pontifical Council for Interreligious Dialogue's document called *Dialogue in Truth and Charity: Pastoral Orientations for Interreligious Dialogue*, states: "Interreligious dialogue, in itself, does not aim at conversion." As a concession, it adds, "Nevertheless, it does not exclude that it might be an occasion of conversion."[177]

Not excluding conversion is very different from seeking conversion. The whole philosophy of post-Vatican II religious dialogue runs counter to conversion, as can be seen from these statements by Pope Francis: "Don't proselytize; respect others' beliefs."[178] "Proselytism is the strongest venom against the path of ecumenism."[179]

In addition, this Catholic-Muslim dialogue has not served to alleviate any persecution of Christians and their forced diaspora from their homelands in the Middle East.

Dialogue has become an end in itself, the vapid occupation of some professionals. It ignores the fact that Islam has no hierarchical authority to impose doctrinal conclusions and decisions, and, therefore, interfaith summit meetings will never have practical consequences for other Muslims.

It does have consequence, however, for Catholics. A mindset of Catholic-Muslim dialogue has spread among bishops and clerics and is shaping their attitude towards Islam. For example, in February 2013, Bishop Robert J. McManus of Worcester, Mass., forbade Islamicist Robert Spencer to speak at the annual Worcester

---

177. Pontifical Council for Interreligious Dialogue, *Dialogue in Truth and Charity: Pastoral Orientations for Interreligious Dialogue* (Vatican City: Libreria Editrice Vaticana, 2014), 4–5, http://www.pcinterreligious.org/uploads/pdfs/DIALOGUE_IN_TRUTH_AND_CHARITY _website-1.pdf.

178. Carol Glatz, "In Latest Interview, Pope Francis Reveals Top 10 Secrets to Happiness," *Catholic News Service*, Jul. 29, 2014, http://www.catholicnews.com/services/englishnews/2014/in -latest-interview-pope-francis-reveals-top-10-secrets-to-happiness.cfm.

179. *ANSA*, "Proselytism Venom Against Ecumenism—Pope: Francis Addresses Lutheran Pilgrims," *ANSA*, Oct. 13, 2016, http://www.ansa.it/english/news/vatican/2016/10/13/proselytism-venom- against-ecumenism-pope_f39b848d-c170-46ba-b2ae-a58366ec391e.html; Claire Chretien, "Pope: It's a 'Very Grave Sin' for Catholics to Try to Convert Orthodox," *LifeSiteNews*, Oct. 4, 2016, https:// www.lifesitenews.com/news/pope-very-grave-sin-for-catholics-to-try-to-convert-orthodox.

Catholic Men's Conference. The prelate sought to justify his action by citing the text of *Lumen Gentium* on Islam and interreligious dialogue.[180] Thus, he denied a group of Catholics the benefit of a talk by an acknowledged expert on Islam to avoid harming an interreligious dialogue that only benefits Muslims.

Even more incredible was the case of Mark Smythe, a teacher at Blessed Trinity Catholic School in Ocala, Florida. He was rebuked by diocesan officials and threatened with dismissal for having distributed a text of Saint John Bosco on Islam!

According to the *Catholic World Report* of May 8, 2017:

> A Catholic teacher in Florida remains under fire in his diocese, three weeks after the *Huffington Post* reported that he assigned "anti-Muslim" material to sixth-grade students. Mark Smythe . . . faces termination unless he signs a letter of reprimand. Theresa Simon, Human Resources Director for the Diocese of Orlando, in consultation with Henry Fortier, Superintendent of Schools, informed the school's principal that Mr. Smythe "must" be reprimanded because he caused an incident that distressed Muslim community members and furthermore it was an "embarrassment for BT (Blessed Trinity) School, the Office of Schools, and the Bishop's Office."[181]

In statements to the leftist *Huffington Post*, Jacquelyn Flanigan, an associate superintendent at the Diocese of Orlando's Catholic school system, said that "the information provided in the sixth-grade class is not consistent with the teachings of the Catholic Church." She mentioned the document of Vatican II, *Nostra Ætate*.[182]

Because of a conciliar document and dialogue's disarming mindset, Islam's historical reality, which Saint John Bosco accurately described, is silenced and declared non-Catholic. However, except for dogmatic facts, and Islam's 1,400-year war on Christendom is not

---

180. See *Catholic Free Press*, "Catholic Men's Conference Opens Ticket Sales," Feb. 8, 2013, http://www.catholicfreepress.org/local/2013/02/08/catholic-mens-conference-opens-ticket-sales/.

181. Mary Jo Anderson, "Catholic Teacher in Ocala, Florida Faces Termination Over Presentation about Islam," *The Catholic World Report*, May 8, 2017, http://www.catholicworldreport.com/2017/05/08/catholic-teacher-in-ocala-florida-faces-termination-over-presentation-about-islam/.

182. Christopher Mathias, "Teacher Gave 6th-Grade Students Reading That Called Islam 'Immoral And Corrupting,'" *Huffingtonpost.com*, Apr. 19, 2017, https://www.huffingtonpost.com/entry/teacher-anti-muslim-assignment-ocala-florida-blessed-trinity_us_58f65e67e4b0da2ff863d21b?23w.

among them, history belongs to the realm of science, not theology.[183]

Sympathy for the Muslim Advance in Europe

Another practical consequence of this spirit of interreligious dialogue is that most European bishops do not utter a single word against the slow invasion of their continent by Muslim "immigrants" and "refugees," often young and violent propagators of Islam, including its "rape jihad."[184]

In his book, *Église et immigration: le grand malaise*, French Catholic writer Laurent Dandrieu addresses the Church authorities' new approach to Islam. He says that contrary to great popes like Saint Pius V, who formed the Holy League that won the decisive victory of Lepanto against the Turks in 1571, recent popes seem to have abandoned the "fierce resistance they have led for centuries against any hint of Islamization of Europe."[185]

In an interview, Dandrieu also points out that, "Since the 1960s, the Church has entered an active phase of interreligious dialogue which, with regard to Islam, seems to me fundamentally flawed because it is not done in a spirit of truth: Under the pretext of preserving the 'fruits of this dialogue'—which are in fact nonexistent—they have come to make *an angelic discourse on Islam that denies its problem with violence and ignores its incompatibility with Western values*."[186]

In the same article Dandrieu denounces the naiveté of Church authorities who see the influx of millions of Muslims into Europe as nothing more than "migratory phenomena." They seem completely blind to any possible ulterior motive. Moreover, though shepherds, they seem unconcerned with the expansion of the Islamic faith in Europe. They see it as the inevitable "manifestation of religious freedom."[187]

---

183. "By a *dogmatic fact*, in wider sense, is meant any fact connected with a dogma and on which the application of the dogma to a particular case depends." Daniel Coghlan, s.v. "Dogmatic Facts," in *The Catholic Encyclopedia*, vol. 5 (New York: Robert Appleton, 1909), New Advent online edition, http://www.newadvent.org/cathen/05092a.htm.

184. See David French, "Have Afghan Refugees in Europe Launched a 'Rape Jihad?'" *National Review*, Jul. 14, 2017, http://www.nationalreview.com/article/449526/afghan-refugees-rape-jihad-europe.

185. Laurent Dandrieu, *Église et immigration: le grand malaise* (Paris: Renaissance, 2017), 23.

186. Laurent Dandrieu, "Sur les migrants, l'Eglise se tire une balle dans le pied," *Atlantico*, Jan. 15, 2017, http://www.atlantico.fr/decryptage/pour-laurent-dandrieu-migrants-eglise-se-tire-balle-dans-pied-2935709.htmlDuAiksouZzLwkXfX.99. (Emphasis in the original.)

187. Ibid.

Bitter Fruits of Dialogue:
Churches Turned Into Mosques

While the Vatican and bishops engage in dialogue with Islam, Catholic churches are emptying out. Then, for lack of parishioners, churches are being sold to Muslims and turned into mosques!

Europe, which sent missionaries who built churches in the most remote corners of the earth, now sees its own churches being demolished or transformed into places of worship for the enemies of the Cross of Christ! Here are some examples of this sad reality in France:

- In Graulhet, in 2015, the church was turned into a mosque. It is now called Al-Mohammadi mosque and still belongs to the town hall.

- In 2015, at Quai Malakoff, in Nantes, Saint-Christophe chapel suffered the same fate. It was topped by a 55-foot high minaret and is now called El-Forqane mosque.

- Saint Joseph's, at Clermont-Ferrand, was lent for 33 years to the city's Muslim community, which covered the Christian symbols with new decorations. Having become too small, the Muslims returned its keys in 2011 and built a large mosque nearby.

- In Lille, the Chapel of the Dominican Sisters also became a mosque after being lent free of charge in 1973 by the bishop of the time.[188]

188. *InfoCatho*, "Ces églises qui deviennent des mosques," Oct 19, 2017, https://www.infocatho .fr/eglises-deviennent-mosquees/; *Dreuz.com*, "Les Français se réveilleront lorsque Notre Dame deviendra une mosque . . . et encore," May 29, 2016, http://fr.igihe.com/religion /les-francais-se-reveilleront-lorsque-notre-dame.html.

"The One God Who Attacks the Trinity Cannot Be Confused With the One God Who Is Triune"

Roger Arnaldez (1911–2006), a renowned French Islamicist and consultant to the Vatican Secretariat for Non-Christians, was quoted by Pope Benedict XVI in his famous 2006 Regensburg speech.[189] In this book chapter, he explains how it is a logical impossibility for the Koran's God to be the same as Christianity's Triune God:

> The fundamental rule of formal logic is that one of two contradictory propositions is true and the other false. . . .
>
> Obviously, if God is one and not triune it is wrong to affirm the Trinity; conversely, if God is one and triune, it is wrong to affirm that He is one and not triune. It is therefore logically inadmissible that the one and triune God be identical to the one and not triune God. Now the Koran, the Word of God [for Muslims], attacks the Trinity. The one God who attacks the Trinity cannot be confused with the one God who is triune."

Roger Arnaldez, "Réflexion sur le Dieu du Coran du point de vue de la logique formelle," *Vivre avec l'Islam: Réflexions chrétiennes sur la religion de Mahomet*, ed.
Annie Laurent (Versailles: Éditions Saint-Paul, 1996), 131–2.

---

189. See Chapter 15, The Koran, An Anti-Trinitarian Book.

CHAPTER 13
Jihad and Crusade: Nothing in Common

Islamic apologists and secularist intellectuals try to compare jihad—the Muslim holy war—with the Crusades. However, they have nothing in common. Jihad is a military offensive aimed to impose the Islamic religion and dominion throughout the world. Those who die for Allah in such wars are seen as martyrs who go straight to the Muslim Paradise, each with his harem of 72 virgins.

Different in Origin, Nature, and Purpose

The Crusades are entirely different in their origin, nature, and purpose. They were never intended to impose the Catholic Faith by the sword. Instead, they arose from the need to deal with a Muslim enemy which had conquered many Christian lands and made continual incursions into others. They were a defensive response to Islam's pillaging and massacring of populations throughout the Mediterranean basin and to its threat to overwhelm the Byzantine Empire.

According to Baylor University professor Rodney Stark, "The Crusades were precipitated by Islamic provocations: by centuries of bloody attempts to colonize the West and by sudden new attacks on Christian pilgrims and holy places. Although the Crusades were initiated by a plea from the pope, this had nothing to do with hopes of converting Islam."[190]

Paul Fregosi adds that "When, in 1096, the Crusades were launched, the Jihad had already been in action against Christendom for nearly five hundred years. It was the Jihad's recent successes in Spain that inspired, so to speak, the pope to create [convoke] the Crusades and to order the Crusaders to march to the Holy Land."[191]

Thus, the Crusades were not wars of aggression or conquest but rather of self-defense. They countered and blocked Islam's centuries-old offensive. Although religiously motivated, they were just wars in defense of a threatened Christendom. They sought to free

---

190. Stark, *God's Battalions,* 8.
191. Paul Fregosi, *Jihad in the West: Muslim Conquests From the 7ᵗʰ to the 21ˢᵗ Centuries* (Amherst, NY: Prometheus, 1998), 17.

the Holy Sepulcher from the hands of Muslims, who were preventing pilgrimages by the Catholic faithful.

In addition to this general motivation, individuals made the Crusader vow to do penance for their sins and obtain the plenary indulgence granted by the pope. The indulgence represented the remission of temporal punishment due either in this life or Purgatory for sins already absolved sacramentally.

In one of its decrees, the 1095 Council of Clermont, France, in which Pope Urban II convoked the first Crusade, makes clear this penitential aspect: "Whoever for devotion alone, not to obtain honor or money, shall set out to free the church of God at Jerusalem, that shall be counted to him for all penance (*pro omni penitentia*)."[192]

No One Should Be Forced to Convert

The Crusades are also entirely different from the jihad because their scope was never to force the conversion of Muslims. Catholic doctrine is explicit on this. Conversion is an interior act of the intellect and the will, moved by grace; hence, the prohibition of coerced conversions.

After giving the above-mentioned reason why we cannot force anyone to convert, Saint Thomas Aquinas adds: "It is for this reason that Christ's faithful often wage war with unbelievers, not indeed for the purpose of forcing them to believe, because even if they were to conquer them, and take them prisoners, they should still leave them free to believe, if they will, but in order to prevent them from hindering the faith of Christ."[193]

The Crusaders Are Not Considered Martyrs

Another fundamental difference between the Crusades and the jihad is that Islam considers as martyrs those who "slay and are slain" (9:111; see SM 1899) for Allah. The Church has never recognized the worthy soldier who dies in combat, even in the most legitimate of wars, as a martyr.

Commenting on a text in which Saint Thomas Aquinas explains that the Church does not venerate as martyrs those who die fight-

---

192. Lambert, "From Liber Lamberti" (p. 74), 2, in "Decrees of Pope Urban II at the Council of Clermont, 1095," accessed Mar. 11, 2018, http://falcon.arts.cornell.edu/prh3/259/texts/clermont.html.
193. *Summa Theologiae*, II–II, q.10, a.8.

ing, the great Spanish canonist Francisco de Vitoria, OP (1483–1546) illustrates this notion with the example of the Crusaders. The father of international law states that although they die fighting in defense of the Faith and are, therefore, worthy of admiration, they are not martyrs.[194] A martyr is one who voluntarily accepts death inflicted out of hatred for the Catholic Faith or some virtue (such as purity, for example).

As stated, the Crusades were just wars in defense of Christendom. The just war theory developed by the great Doctors of the Church helps us understand better the difference between them and Muslim jihad.

Saint Augustine Lays the Foundations on Just War Doctrine

The great Saint Augustine (354–430) provided the basis of Catholic doctrine on just war. Considering whether war is always wrong or if there are circumstances when it can be just, he wrote:

> John, when the soldiers who came to be baptized asked, what shall we do? Would have replied, Throw away your arms; give up the service; never strike, or wound, or disable any one. But knowing that such actions in battle were not murderous but authorized by law, and that the soldiers did not thus avenge themselves, but defend the public safety, he replied, "Do violence to no man, accuse no man falsely, and be content with your wages." (Luke 3:14)[195]

Therefore if military life is legitimate, then so also is an army's purpose: To wage war. Nevertheless, the saint argues, there are Gospel precepts like "resist no evil" or "turn the other cheek" that seem to condemn the use of force and thus contradict the legitimacy of military life and, therefore, of war.

He replies to these objections by showing how these precepts apply to the interior life and how we must be meek even when punishing another. Based on this, Moses condemned the Jewish idolaters to death, not out of personal hatred, but out of charity, thus

194. See Charles Journet, *The Church of the Word Incarnate* (New York: Sheed and Ward, 1955), 1:320, note 5.
195. St. Augustine, *Contra Faustum*, bk. 22, no. 74.

preventing them from remaining in sin.

In this way, Saint Augustine teaches that what is forbidden is to take advantage of the military life to do evil. Therefore, what is bad is not the military life per se but its abuses, and that abuse is forbidden. The Church does not prohibit the military, but only malice.[196]

According to the saintly bishop of Hippo, just war must seek to obtain peace or to restore it, and in this sense, it is an instrument of peace. By peace, he understands "the tranquility of order."[197] By order, he means, the right disposition of things according to their proper end.[198]

Saint Augustine also defines just war as a means to re-establish and vindicate violated justice, and thus obtain peace. Therefore we can wage war to punish a nation for the violation of just order. Nevertheless, in the Augustinian concept of justice, this applies not only to the natural law of individuals and peoples but also to justice due to God as Sovereign and Lord. Thus both the systematic violation of natural law and the denial of the right worship of God can be motives for just war.

Likewise, just war was ordered by God in many episodes narrated in the Old Testament. On the other hand, just war can also be waged against a country that refuses to punish adequately its citizens who acted unjustly against an offended nation.

In other words, according to Saint Augustine, just war can be waged when recovering goods or legitimate situations or when restoring order and justice violated by a people.[199]

Saint Bernard of Clairvaux (1090–1153)

Saint Bernard, the great troubadour of Our Lady, the meek and mellifluous Church Father and Doctor, was also a great orator and preacher of the Crusades. He was the official preacher of the Second Crusade.

In his famous *Opusculum, De laude novæ militæ* ("In Praise of the New Knighthood"), Saint Bernard addressed the Knights Templars—using Saint Augustine's arguments on the famous reply of

---

196. "Non enim benefacere prohibet a militia, sed a malitia." St. Augustine, *Sermo 302*, no. 15.
197. St. Augustine, *The City of God*, bk. 19, ch. 13.
198. See Ibid.
199. See *Contra Faustum*, bk. 22, nos. 74–76.

Saint John the Baptist to the soldiers. He wrote: "What then? If it is never permissible for a Christian to strike with the sword, why did the Savior's precursor bid soldiers be content with their pay, and not rather ban military service to them?"

Acclaimed as the Church's central figure in the twelfth-century, Saint Bernard states in the preceding paragraph: "This is not to say that the pagans are to be slaughtered when there is any other way of preventing them from harassing and persecuting the faithful; but only that now it seems better to destroy them than to allow the rod of sinners to continue to be raised over the lot of the righteous, lest perchance the righteous set their hand to iniquity."[200]

Saint Thomas Aquinas Summarizes the Church's Just War Teaching

Saint Thomas Aquinas (1225–1274) built upon and further developed the teachings of the Church concerning just war. This greatest of all Church Doctors completed the doctrine of just war in several aspects.

Quoting Saint Augustine, Saint Thomas returned to Saint John the Baptist's argument favoring the legitimacy of military life and, therefore, of war, and added many other points. He introduced the concept of the common good as an essential element for the legitimacy of war.

The military profession must have as its goal the defense of the public good, the poor, the oppressed, the Church, and the worship due to God. Soldiers are therefore instruments of legitimate authority, which prevents or punishes, even with death, the misdeeds of evildoers.

Quoting the sermons of Saint Gregory the Great, he justified capital punishment as a means to avenge outraged justice, to correct and instill fear in evil, and thus re-establish and to guarantee both the peace of society and the Church, and a nation's stability and prosperity. Such actions are virtuous when motivated by the love of justice and charity.

For soldiers to fight in just wars, the saint explained, what is

---

200. St. Bernard of Clairvaux, *In Praise of the New Knighthood, A Treatise on the Knights Templar and the Holy Places of Jerusalem*, trans. M. Conrad Greenia, OCSO (Trappist, Ky.: Cistercian Publications, 1977), 40.

needed is supernatural or divine help, in other words, the virtues. The first such virtue is fortitude, a supernatural help that makes man more courageous and persevering in the fight.

Bellicose action, he added, can only be performed with wisdom and ability, when executed with prudence, which directs man's actions in life with uprightness.

Therefore, according to Saint Thomas Aquinas, there are three conditions for just war:

1. It must be *declared by legitimate authority*. Developing the teaching of Saint Augustine, Saint Thomas states,

   > It is not the business of a private individual to declare war. . . . And as the care of the common weal is committed to those who are in authority, it is their business to watch over the common weal of the city, kingdom or province subject to them. And just as it is lawful for them to have recourse to the sword in defending that common weal against internal disturbances, when they punish evil-doers . . . so too, it is their business to have recourse to the sword of war in defending the common weal against external enemies. . . . For this reason Augustine says (Contra Faust. xxii, 75): "The natural order conducive to peace among mortals demands that the power to declare and counsel war should be in the hands of those who hold the supreme authority."

2. *The cause must be just*. Again, he quotes Saint Augustine: "A just war is wont to be described as one that avenges wrongs, when a nation or state has to be punished, for refusing to make amends for the wrongs inflicted by its subjects, or to restore what it has seized unjustly."

3. *It must be waged with good intention*. For it may happen that the war is declared by the legitimate authority, and for a just cause, and yet be rendered unlawful through a wicked intention. Hence Augustine says (*Contra Faust.* xxii, 74): "The passion for inflicting harm, the cruel thirst for vengeance, an unpacific and relentless spirit, the fever of revolt, the lust of power, and such like things, all these are rightly condemned in war."[201]

---

201. *Summa Theologiae*, II–II, q. 40, a.1.

Crusades and Just War

Summarizing the above explanations and applying them to the Crusades:

- The Crusades were born as a response to Islam's prolonged violent aggression;
- The Crusades were acts of self-defense for a threatened Christendom;
- The Crusades were also in defense of pilgrims and Christians living in the territories occupied by Islam who were the victims of severe persecution.

Thus, the Crusades fulfilled all the requirements set by natural law and Catholic doctrine for a war to be considered just. On the contrary, jihad fulfills none.

PART TWO

Islam's Anti-Christian Doctrines and Origins

Shutterstock

The Koran is a confusing book filled with contradictions and repetitions. The story of Moses and the Pharaoh is repeated some 30 times. *Above*: Young Thai students reading the Koran in school.

The Koran, an Unconventional Book

The Koran, Islam's sacred book, is a collection of apologetic sheets arbitrarily assembled in 114 chapters called *suras* and numbered by verses called *ayah* (plural: *ayat*).

A Confusing Book

Unlike the Bible, whose books and chapters are arranged in a well-established order according to their literary genre and divided into the Old and New Testaments, the Koran is utterly confusing. *Suras* are arranged by size, from longest to shortest. Thus, the second *sura*, its longest, has 286 verses, while the last thirteen *suras* have fewer than ten *ayat* each, with *suras* 103, 108, and 110 having just three apiece.

Such a structuring of the Islamic book, coupled with continuous repetition of ideas, stories, and narratives, makes both reading and understanding difficult. Even Muslim scholars recognize this.

"It Is Unlike Conventional Books"

Thus, in his introduction to Abdullah Yusuf Ali's English translation of the Koran, Islamic scholar Sayyid Abula A'la Maududi states:

> It [the Koran] is unlike conventional books in that it does not contain information, ideas, and arguments about specific themes arranged in a particular literary order. A stranger to the Qur'an is baffled in the beginning because he does not find the enunciation of its themes, its division into chapters and sections, a separate treatment of varied topics, or separate instructions for different aspects of life arranged in serial order. Conversely, there is an obscurity because it does not conform to the conception of "a book".... Subjects are repeated in different ways, and one topic follows another without any apparent connection. Intermittently, a new topic emerges in the middle of another following no obvious structure. The speaker, the receiver, and the direction of the address may change without any prior notice. There are no signs of chapters or divisions, and historical events are pre-

sented unlike those in ordinary history books.[202]

A Book to Confirm What Had Already Been Revealed

The Koran itself states that it confirms the divine revelation men received from Moses and Jesus:

> He has sent down upon you, [O Muhammad], the Book in truth, confirming what was before it. And He revealed the Torah and the Gospel (SI 3:3).
>
> Before, as guidance for the people. And He revealed the Criterion [i.e., the Qur'ān] (SI 3:4).
>
> And do not argue with the People of the Scripture except in a way that is best, except for those who commit injustice among them, and say, "We believe in that which has been revealed to us and revealed to you. And our God and your God is one; and we are Muslims [in submission] to Him" (SI 29:46).
>
> And thus We have sent down to you the Book [i.e., the Qur'ān]. And those to whom We [previously] gave the Scripture believe in it. And among these [people of Makkah] are those who believe in it. And none reject Our verses except the disbelievers (SI 29:47).

"For Each Period Is a Book (Revealed)."

However, the same Koran sustains that there are successive revelations from God for each new period, and each new revelation presupposes a new book. "For each period is a Book (revealed) (3:38). Allah doth blot out or confirm what He pleaseth: with Him is the Mother of the Book" (13:39).

The Koran also states that both the Pentateuch and the Gospels were corrupted, justifying God's new revelation in the Koran; it would complete and correct the previous ones. Without explanation, we are told the Koran was God's final revelation, and Muhammad, His last prophet. However, if there is a new revelation for every historical period, why would the Koran be the last one?

Nevertheless, such is Islamic belief, and we see it reaffirmed by the Islamic Educational Services of Mt. Holly, New Jersey: "The

---

202. Sayyid Abul A'la Maududi, "An Introduction to The Qur'an," introduction to *Translation of the Qur'aan: Old Testament for Jews, New Testament for Christian, Final Testament for Humanity,* trans. Abdullah Yusuf Ali, 3rd US ed. (Mt. Holly N.J.: Islamic Educational Service, 1998), 5–6.

Qur'aan is a complete and original compilation of the Final Revelation from God to mankind through the last Prophet, Muhammad."[203]

A Book Shorter Than the New Testament

According to Islam, the Koran was dictated by the Archangel Saint Gabriel (*Jibreel* in the Koran) to Muhammad over the course of 22 years, from 610 to 632.

Compared to the Bible, the Koran is a small book. While Sacred Scripture has about 800,000 words, the Koran has only 86,000.[204] It is shorter than the New Testament, which has 138,020 words.[205]

Moses is the person mentioned most in the Koran. His story with the Pharaoh is recounted some 30 times, more or less entirely. He is named 136 times, followed by Abraham, 69 times, Noah, 43, and Jesus, (as 'Îsâ), 25, and many other times as the "son of Mary." Muhammad is only mentioned four times, by name, and once as Ahmad. Many of the references are drawn from the Pentateuch.[206] Thus, much of the Koran can be traced back to the Bible, with added stories about Jesus and Mary being taken from the apocryphal gospels.[207]

The Use of Apocryphal Gospels

French Islamicist Fr. Jacques Jomier, OP, in his book *The Bible and the Qur'an*, says that the Koran has:

1. *Accounts that occur in the Bible with some variants.* It should be noted that in the Qur'an there are no narratives in the exact wording of the Bible. What we find are summaries, varying accounts on the same themes that preserve the essential thought.

2. *Accounts known only from rabbinic literature or apocryphal literature* [mainly Gnostic Gospels].

203. Yusuf Ali, *Translation of the Qur'aan*, back cover.

204. See "How Many Words Are There in the Bible?" *Word Counter*, Dec. 8, 2015, https://wordcounter.net/blog/2015/12/08/10975_how-many-words-bible.html; "Statistics of Al Quran," accessed Mar. 2, 2018, http://myonlinequran.com/quran-facts.php.

205. See Felix Just, SJ, comp. "New Testament Statistics," accessed Mar. 2, 2018, http://catholic -resources.org/Bible/NT-Statistics-Greek.htm.

206. See Kamil Mufti, "Prophets of the Kuran: An Introduction (Part 1 of 2), *The Religion of Islam*, Apr. 22, 2013, https://www.islamreligion.com/articles/10228/viewall/prophets-of-quran/.

207. *Apocryphal Gospels* are Christian era religious writings that the Church ruled were not inspired by the Holy Spirit, and, therefore, did not incorporate them into the New Testament. In contrast, the four divinely inspired and accepted Gospels are called *canonical*.

3. *Other narratives.*[208]

For example, the Koran tells us that Mary Most Holy was raised in the Temple by Zechariah (3:37). It affirms that the Child Jesus spoke in the cradle to defend the purity of His Mother (19:29–33). It says that the Infant Jesus made sparrows of clay and gave them life (3:48–50 and 5:110).

These stories are mentioned in the several apocryphal gospels about Jesus' childhood, for example, *The Protoevangelium of James*, *The Infancy Gospel of Thomas*, and the *Arabic Gospel of the Infancy of the Savior.*

Paganism in the Koran: *Jinn* or Genies–The *Ifrit*

The sacred book of Islam is not only indebted to Holy Scripture, the apocryphal gospels, and the rabbinical commentaries of the Talmud. It also contains pagan conceptions.

■ *Jinn* or Genies

The Koran retained the pagan belief in genies (jinn) common in early Arabia. It describes them as rational creatures that enjoy free will but are neither men nor angels. It refers to them in 16 different *suras*, with one of them, *sura* 72, being titled, *The Jinn.*

Muhammad preached that Allah created the jinn before man (15:26–27). While the latter was made of clay, the jinn were made from fire. They were created to worship God (51:56), but they can choose between good and evil and go to heaven or hell. The same book affirms that the *Iblis*, the devil, "was one of the Jinns" (18:50), but if he was also an angel is disputed.[209] According to the Koran, God commanded the angels to venerate Adam, but Iblis, the devil, refused (7:11–18). Some among the jinn supposedly heeded the message of the Koran (46:29; 72:1), and others helped Solomon (27:17; 27:39).

■ The *Ifrit*

According to Islamic mythology, the *ifrit* are a class of malevolent supernatural beings. They are among the most powerful and high-ranking of the jinn. Folktales depict an *ifrit* as "an enormous winged creature of smoke, either male or female, who lives underground

---

208. Jacques Jomier, OP, *The Bible and the Qur'an* (San Francisco: Ignatius Press, 2002), 46–7.
209. See Esposito, "Satan," *Oxford Dictionary of Islam*, 279.

and frequents ruins."[210]

Curiously, although they are creatures of smoke, they lead a life similar to that of men. "*Ifrits* live in a society structured along ancient Arab tribal lines, complete with kings, tribes, and clans. They generally marry one another, but they can also marry humans."[211]

These powerful creatures can only be overcome by magic, which men use to kill or enslave them. "As with the jinn, an *ifrit* may be either a believer or an unbeliever, good or evil, but is most often depicted as a wicked and ruthless being."[212]

Though mentioned only once in the Koran (27:39), where it seems to designate a rebellious member of the jinn, *ifrit* appear abundantly in the *hadith* and Islamic literature.

In spite of being a perverse spirit, an *ifrit* comes to the aid of Solomon, whom the Koran presents as a prophet:

> He [Solomon] said (to his own men): "Ye chiefs! which of you can bring me her throne [of the Queen of Sheba] before they come to me in submission?"
>
> Said an 'Ifrit, of the Jinns: "I will bring it to thee before thou rise from thy council: indeed I have full strength for the purpose, and may be trusted."
>
> Said one who had knowledge of the Book: "I will bring it to thee within the twinkling of an eye!" Then when (Solomon) saw it placed firmly before him, he said: "This is by the Grace of my Lord! - to test me whether I am grateful or ungrateful!" (27:38–40).

Solomon Talks to Birds and Ants

The Koran is full of fantasies. Some of the stories told therein look more like children's fairy tales than divine revelation. For example, concerning Solomon, the third king of Israel, the book states that he knew the language of the birds and talked with them as if they were human. According to the Islamic book, he also understood the language of the ants.

Sura 27 (titled *An-Naml*–The Ants), after saying that Solomon

---

210. *Encyclopedia Britannica*, s.v. "Ifrit," https://www.britannica.com/topic/ifrit.

211. Ibid.

212. Ibid.

had "been taught the speech of birds" (27:16), tells the story of an expedition the king undertook in the company of "his hosts, of Jinns and men and birds, and they were all kept in order and ranks" (27:17). On the walk, the Jewish monarch heard an ant say to the others: "'Ye ants, get into your habitations, lest Solomon and his hosts crush you (under foot) without knowing it'" (27:18). Solomon smiled and waited for them to hide, and then proceeded (27:19).

On the same expedition, Solomon realized that one of the birds, a hoopoe, had disappeared. He asked the other birds where he was. The hoopoe then came back saying that he had been at the Court of the Queen of Sheba and he informed Solomon, "'I found her and her people worshipping the sun besides Allah: Satan has made their deeds seem pleasing in their eyes, and has kept them away from the Path, so they receive no guidance'" (27:24). The king gave the bird a letter to take to the Queen, and await her answer (27:28).

The Ant Prays for Rain

During the time of the Prophet Sulaiman (King Solomon), there was a widespread famine in Palestine. The king went to an open place in the desert with his people to pray for rain. Suddenly, he saw an ant standing on two legs, raising its hands up towards the sky and saying, "Oh Allah! We are but very small among all Thy creatures. We cannot survive without Thy grace. Please bestow upon us Thy sustenance and do not punish us because of the sins of human beings. Please send down the rains so that trees can grow, farms become green and grains become available and we have our food to eat."

Prophet Sulaiman knew the language of all animals. He told his people, "Let us go home. The prayer of this ant is enough." It then rained heavily and all the land became green and productive.

"The Ant Prays for Rain," Al-Islamic.org, accessed Apr. 27, 2018, https://www.al-islam.org/islamic-stories/ant-prays-rain.

Who Dictated the Koran to Muhammad?

The Koran recounts the discussions Muhammad had with his listeners and the mistrust he aroused in them. He was accused of falsifying doctrine with someone's help: "But the misbelievers say: 'Naught is this but a lie which he has forged, and others have helped him at it'" (25:4).

They said that his preaching was nothing but a repetition of what had been already taught before, which he received from someone daily: "And they say: 'Tales of the ancients, which he has caused to be written: and they are dictated before him morning and evening'" (25:5). "'It is a man that teaches him'" (16:103). "'No messenger art thou'" (13:43).

They accused him of saying what they already knew: "'We have heard this (before): if we wished, we could say (words) like these: these are nothing but tales of the ancients'" (8:31).

Burning the First Korans

According to Islamic traditions (*hadith*), Muhammad was illiterate and dictated his revelations to various people, who wrote them down on date palm leaves, tree bark, bones, and other materials. All these writings were placed in a bag. Some companions of Muhammad also wrote down what they heard, and consigned other things to memory by reciting them continuously.[213]

Unfortunately, none of these contemporary written texts have come down to us. Arab traditions vary on how the Koran as we know it came into recorded form, but it is known that Uthman, the third caliph to succeed Muhammad, who reigned from 644 to 656, decided to make a standard text and eliminate all prior versions. Among others, he commissioned Zayd ibn Thabit, Muhammad's secretary, to compile the definitive book. Muhammad al-Bukhari (810–870) states: "They did so, and when they had written many copies, . . . Uthman sent to every Muslim province one copy of what they had copied, and ordered that all the other Qur'anic materials, whether written in fragmentary manuscripts or whole copies, be burnt" (SB 4987).

---

213. Maududi, "Introduction to the Qur'an," 14.

The *Sunna* Explains the Koran

Although the Koran is regarded as divine revelation, it does not resolve doubts raised by its reading. During his lifetime, Muhammad was the supreme authority on its interpretation, but who would do this after his death? His followers resolved to use his sayings and deeds as the criterion for solving future doubts and for imparting teaching on religious practices that are not explicitly mentioned in the Koran.

These acts and words of Muhammad—known as the *hadith*—were transmitted orally from one generation to another. In the ninth century, some scholars compiled and wrote them down.

The Al-sīra (commonly referred to as *Sira*) are traditional Muslim biographies of Muhammad. They are mainly based on the *hadith*.

Together, Muhammad's *hadith* and the Sira constitute the *Sunna* or custom. Its importance is almost equivalent to that of the Koran. Islamicist Fr. Henri Lammens, SJ (1862–1937), explains: "The doctrinal sources of Islam are contained in the collection called the Qoran and in the Corpus of the *Sunna*. The Qoran is the written revelation; the *Sunna* represents oral revelation transmitted through the channel of tradition."[214]

Moreover, since the *Sunna* would be as it were a continuation of Muhammad's authoritative interpretation, it would explain the Koran. Sheikh Yûsuf al-Qaradâwî explains this in his work, "Introduction to Islam": "[The Koran] contains all the foundations and bases on which the edifice of religion is built in terms of Creed and legislation. Among its foundations: the Messenger expresses and elucidates what is revealed to him. In other words, the Sunna explains the Koran: 'We have sent down unto thee (also) the Message; that thou mayest explain clearly to men what is sent for them, and that they may give thought (16:44).'"[215]

Difficulties in Proving the Veracity of the *Hadith*

One of the problems in proving the truthfulness of the *hadith* is that by the time they were compiled two hundred years had elapsed and their numbers had reached astronomical proportions. Bukhari

---

214. Henri Lammens, SJ, *Islam Beliefs and Institutions*, trans. Sir E. Denison Ross, 2nd ed. (New Delhi: Oriental Books Reprint Corporation, 1979), 37.

215. Yûsuf Al-Qaradâwî, "Introduction à l'Islam: Section: Les sources primaires de l'islam—La sunna prophétique," *Islamophile.org*, Jul. 17, 2001, http://www.islamophile.org/spip/La-sunna -prophetique.html.

alone collected some three hundred thousand *hadith*, which, after years of painstaking sorting, he reduced to about 7,400.

Even that rigorous process would prove insufficient, because the sole criterion adopted was a rudimentary external critique, namely, trying to establish source authenticity by showing a chain of narrators. Did the *hadith* indeed go all the way back to Muhammad or to someone who had heard the report directly from the prophet of Islam, like his wives or early companions? Proving such a chain could only establish who passed on the story. It could never prove that the first version of the report matched what Bukhari wrote down two centuries later. Accordingly, if Bukhari had subjected the *hadith* to an internal critique, examining their meaning, for example, many more would have been eliminated as contradictory or improbable.[216]

Father Gallez summarizes Father Lammens' views on Islam's vicious circle—the *Sunna* explains the Koran, but the Koran is the basis for the *Sunna*:

1. On the one hand, the tradition (*Sunna*) and its collections of *hadith* attributed to the Prophet or his relatives, show how the Koranic text is to be understood;

2. On the other hand, the Koranic text provides much of the content of these oral traditions.[217]

In his book *Le problème de Mahomet*, Régis Blachère comes to the same conclusion: "The vicious circle was now closed. The allusions contained in the Koran were to serve as a support for the biographical tradition—without which these allusions remained a dead letter."[218]

---

216. See Lammens, *Islam Beliefs*, 69–71.

217. Gallez, *Le Messie et son prophète*, 2:54; see Henri Lammens, SJ, "Qoran et tradition, comment fut composée la vie de Mahomet," *Recherches de Science Religieuse,* 1910, 1:27–51.

218. Régis Blachere, *Le problème de Mahomet* (Paris: Presses Universitaires de France, 1952), 7.

CHAPTER 15

The Koran, an Anti-Trinitarian Book

While the Koran may be confusing, its anti-Trinitarian stance is clear. It continually insists that Allah is one. It denies the divinity of Jesus, the Word Incarnate, and the Holy Spirit as the third person of the Blessed Trinity.

Moreover, because of their misrepresentation of the doctrine of the Blessed Trinity, Muslims call those who believe in one God in three Persons *polytheists* and *associators,* accusing them of associating other gods to Allah. They equate fidelity to this Christian dogma with unbelief (*kufr*) and idolatry. In fact, according to the Koran, polytheism or idolatry (*shirk*) is the gravest sin possible; for it, there is no forgiveness.

Islam's millennial persecution of Christians is motivated mostly by this hatred of the dogma of the Trinity.

The Myth of a Polytheistic Arabia

According to Islamic legend, the Arabia of Muhammad's time, especially the region around Mecca where he began his preaching, was pagan and polytheistic. He is said to have put an end to that polytheism.

Since the Trinity is strictly a Christian dogma, if Muhammad were preaching to pagans, there would be no point in attacking a tenet of a faith they knew nothing about. Since Muhammad did rail against the Blessed Trinity, however, then the obvious conclusion is that his jabs must have been aimed at Christians and spoken to those familiar with Christian doctrine.

Before quoting the Koran in this regard, let us see the opinion of a specialist, Father Gallez, the author of a remarkable work on Islam's origins:

> It is necessary to radically question the conventional discourse presenting seventh century Arabs (of Hejaz [the Mecca region] or elsewhere) as "polytheists" hitherto ignorant of any biblical or Judeo-Christian tradition. Besides, can one teach or believe that caravan traders, after six centuries

of close contact with Jews and Christians because of their commerce, were ignorant of Judeo-Christian revelation?

In the Koran, the term believed to designate the polytheist Arabs is *mušrikûn*, which, according to its etymology and all the authors of the eighth and ninth centuries, means *associators*, which is the reproach continuously addressed to Christians (to whom other verses or passages of the Koran are also explicitly addressed). The supposed "Arab polytheism," in the middle of which Islamic doctrine brings forth the new Revelation and Proto-Islam, is unconvincing regarding the Koranic text itself: Many verses expressly attest to the *monotheistic* faith of those supposedly polytheistic *mušrikûn*. . . .

"Associators" who claim to believe in one God

First, they believe in the existence of the Creator and that this Creator is called Allah: "If indeed thou ask them who has created the heavens and the earth. . . . they will certainly reply, '(Allah).'" (29:61, 63; 31:25; 39:38).

Allah was the name used by Christian Arabs long before Islam and corresponded to El or Elohim in Hebrew. Moreover, this time, mušrikûn is not only monotheistic but Trinitarian, as the anti-Trinitarian polemic in another verse (6:23) indicates: "They will say: 'By God our Lord! We are not people who associate [gods with Allah]!'"

Who are those whom the author [of the Koran] accuses of being associators and who deny being so? Are polytheists saying they are not polytheists? In this verse, the author wishes to forestall, in the spirit of his disciple, the protest that Christians will make in defense of their faith by saying that they adore one only God. The answer comes in the following verse: It consists in calling these Christians liars (6:24): "Behold! how they lie against their own souls!"[219]

---

219. Édouard-Marie Gallez, "Aperçus relatifs au supposé polythéisme arabe," accessed Mar. 28, 2018, http://www.lemessieetsonprophete.com/annexes/onze.htm. On his website, Father Gallez reproduces parts of his book, as well as updates to it. Therefore, we sometimes quote from the printed text, indicating the pages, sometimes from the website. Here we quote from his website. In a footnote on this website update Father Gallez adds: "The first name '*Abd-Allah* (meaning *servant of God*) is an Arab Christian first name known before Islam. Even if this is banal, it is well to recall, along with François Nau, that "*Allah*" is 'the Christian name of the Divinity, by which millions of Arab Christians invoked God morning and evening, before Muhammad.'" (François Nau, *Les Arabes chrétiens* [Paris, n.p. 1933], 126). Gallez, "Aperçus," no. 1; "Such anti-Trinitarian polemic is very present in the Koran; see also 6,41.136; 10,12.22; 16,38.54; 23,86–89 || 31,32 || 43,87 and the remarks by Sfar Mondher, *Le Coran, la Bible et l'Orient ancien* (Paris: Diffusion Cerf, 1998), 108–9." Ibid., no. 2.

Saint John Damascene "They Call Us *Associators*"

Saint John Damascene (676–749), a Father of the Church who lived in an Islamic environment and knew Koranic doctrine well, wrote of Muslims: "they call us *Hetaeriasts*, or *Associators*, because, they say, we introduce an associate with God by declaring Christ to be the Son of God and God."

St. John Damascene, *On Heresies*, 155

Günter Lüling

Günter Lüling (1928–2014), was a German Protestant theologian and philological scholar. In his book based on Islamic sources, *A Challenge to Islam for Reformation*, Lüling writes:

> That the Meccan (and central Arabians) adversaries of the Prophet, the so-called musrikūn ("associators," that is associators of a child to God), were trinitarian Christians… [T]he Prophet in reality and in principle did not fight against heathendom but almost exclusively against "associators," that is, against trinitarian Christianity.

Günter Lüling, *A Challenge to Islam for Reformation: The Rediscovery and Reliable Reconstruction of a Comprehensive pre-Islamic Christian Hymnal Hidden in the Koran Under Earliest Islamic Reinterpretations*, 1ˢᵗ English Edition (Dehli: Motilal Banarsidass, 2003), xiv.

The Mystery of the Most Holy Trinity

We can come to the knowledge of the existence of God through sheer reason and deduce His main attributes, by analogy, from Creation: omniscience, omnipotence, omnipresence, love, goodness, and so forth. In fact, creation is a mirror that reflects God. Psalm 18:2 reads, "The heavens shew forth the glory of God, and the firmament declareth the work of his hands."

However, the fact that this *one* creator God is a God in *three distinct persons* is a mystery that we can only learn through divine revelation. For example:

> I am the Lord, and there is none else: there is no God besides me (Isa. 45:5).
> Grace to you, and peace from God our Father, and

from the Lord Jesus Christ (1 Cor. 1:3).

Know you not, that you are the temple of God, and that the Spirit of God dwelleth in you? (1 Cor. 3:16).

In the beginning was the Word, and the Word was with God, and the Word was God (John 1:1).

Going therefore, teach ye all nations; baptizing them in the name of the Father, and of the Son, and of the Holy Ghost (Matt. 28:19).

Once the intimate nature of God in His Most Holy Trinity is revealed, theologians try to show how this unfathomable mystery is not contrary to human reason, even though it surpasses human comprehension.[220]

Now, the Koran states that it is a "Book, confirming what went before it; and He sent down the Law (of Moses) and the Gospel (of Jesus) before this, as a guide to mankind, and He sent down the criterion (of judgment between right and wrong)" (3:3).

Nevertheless, it rejects the Incarnation of the Word and His redemptive work foretold by the prophets.[221]

"Allah, He Is Self-Sufficient!"

The Koran's main argument against the Most Holy Trinity is that God, being almighty and sufficient unto Himself, does not need a son: "They say: '(Allah) hath begotten a son!'—Glory be to Him! He is self-sufficient!" (10:68). "They say: 'Allah hath begotten a son!' Glory be to Him! Nay, to Him belongs all that is in the heavens and on earth: everything renders worship to Him" (2:116).

The above argument of the Koran against the Holy Trinity assumes that Christians believe in the absurd notion of a *tritheism*, that is to say, three gods associated together. It is true that God is "self-sufficient" because He is the supreme perfection. However, because He is supremely perfect, He is Triune. This is God's very essence.[222]

---

220. See St. Thomas Aquinas, *On Reasons for Our Faith Against the Muslims* (New Bedford, Mass.: Franciscans of the Immaculate, 2002).

221. For example, Isa. 7:14; 59:20.

222. "The whole perfection of the Godhead is contained in the one infinite Divine Essence. The Father is that Essence as it eternally regards the Son and the Spirit; the Son is that Essence as it eternally regards the Father and the Spirit; the Holy Spirit is that Essence as it eternally regards the Father and the Son. But the eternal regard by which each of the Three Persons is constituted is not an addition to the infinite perfection of the Godhead." Joyce, "The Blessed Trinity."

"Allah Has Taken Neither a Wife nor a Son"

Another argument, which shows the Koran's carnal and anthropomorphic conception of God, is that to have a Son, God needs a wife: "How can He have a son when He hath no consort?" (6:101). "He has taken neither a wife nor a son" (72:3).

Saint Thomas Aquinas responds to this absurdity as follows:

> First of all we must observe that Muslims are silly in ridiculing us for holding that Christ is the Son of the living God, as if God had a wife. Since they are carnal, they can think only of what is flesh and blood. For any wise man can observe that the mode of generation is not the same for everything, but generation applies to each thing according to the special manner of its nature. . . .
>
> God, however, is not of a fleshly nature, requiring a woman to copulate with to generate offspring, but he is of a spiritual or intellectual nature, much higher than every intellectual nature. So generation should be understood of God as it applies to an intellectual nature.[223]

Mary in the Most Holy Trinity?

The current Muslim interpretation of *ayat* 5:116–117 is that Christians understand the Most Holy Trinity as being the Father, the Mother (Mary), and the Son (Jesus): "And behold! Allah will say, 'O Jesus the son of Mary! Didst thou say unto men, worship me and my mother as gods in derogation of Allah?' He will say, 'Glory to Thee! Never could I say what I had no right (to say)'" (5:116).

In fact, here the Koran is most likely repeating an affirmation from the apocryphal *Gospel of the Hebrews*. In a confused way, this apocryphal gospel presents the Holy Spirit—who would be the same as Saint Michael or the Virgin Mary—as the mother of Jesus. This false gospel is lost, but Fathers of the Church and other early Christian writers quoted or summarized passages from it. Here are some quotations:

■ Saint Cyril of Jerusalem (315–386): "It is written in the [Gospel] to the Hebrews that when Christ wished to come upon the earth to men, the Good Father summoned a mighty 'power' in heaven,

223. St. Thomas Aquinas, *Reasons for the Faith Against Muslim Objections (And One Objection from the Greeks and Armenians) to the Cantor of Antioch,* trans. Joseph Kenny, OP, ch. 3, accessed Apr. 11, 2018, *http://www.catholicapologetics.info/apologetics/islam/rationes.htm.*

which was called 'Michael,' and committed Christ to the care thereof. And the 'power' came into the world, and it was called Mary, and Christ was in her womb for seven months."[224]

■ Origen (185–232): "If anyone should lend credence to the Gospel according to the Hebrews, where the Savior Himself says, 'My mother, the Holy Spirit, took me just now by one of my hairs and carried me off to the great Mount Tabor.'"[225]

■ Saint Jerome (ca. 347–420): "In the Gospel according to the Hebrews, which the Nazarenes like to read as Scripture, the Lord says, 'My mother, the Holy Spirit, recently bore me.'"[226]

If the Koran was the divine word itself, God could not fail to know that the Church never accepted such an aberration, and that the dogma of the Most Holy Trinity—Father, Son, and Holy Spirit—is both in the Gospels (Matt. 28:19) and in the Church's most ancient confessions of Faith.[227]

The practical consequence of Muslim denial of the Holy Trinity is the persecution of Christians, on the charge of idolatry.

The Koranic Concept of God: A Denial of the Trinity

Let us now see what the Koran's conception of God is. Rejecting the Trinitarian God, the Koran preaches a God who is Creator and omnipotent, but not a loving and paternal God, whose love for Himself, being absolute and perfect, is diffusive, that is, extends to the creatures He brought forth from nothing.[228]

In his Gospel, Saint John attests to this divine love: "For God so loved the world, as to give His only begotten Son; that whosoever believeth in Him, may not perish, but may have life everlasting" (John 3:16).

---

224. St. Cyril of Jerusalem (attributed), *Discourse on the* Theotokos.
225. Origen, *Commentary on the Gospel of John*, bk. 2, no. 6.
226. St. Jerome, *Commentary on Isaiah* 68:539.
227. See *Most Ancient Forms of the Apostolic Creed*, in Denzinger, *Enchiridion symbolorum*, 1–40, http://patristica.net/denzinger/.
228. St. Thomas Aquinas says, "Just as all things participate in God's goodness not in identity but in likeness thereto so also do they participate in a likeness of God's being. But there is a difference: for goodness implies the relationship of cause, since good is self-diffusive: whereas being connotes mere existence and quiescence." St. Thomas Aquinas, *Quaestiones disputatae de Potentia Dei–On The Power Of God*, trans. English Dominican Fathers (Westminster, Maryland: The Newman Press, 1952), q.7, a.5, ad 7, 1932 reprint, html ed. Joseph Kenny, O.P, http://dhspriory.org/thomas/QDdePotentia.htm.

Moreover, as the same Gospel attests in its introduction, God has given us the possibility of becoming His adopted children through grace: "[The Word Incarnate] gave them power to be made the sons of God, to them that believe in His name" (John 1:12).

However, Islam does not accept this.

A God Unrelated to Creatures

The Muslim conception is similar to that of the Deists of the eighteenth century, who, like Voltaire, conceived of God like a clockmaker Who, having made the clock, wound it up, and left it to itself. Similarly, after creating the Universe, God supposedly ceased having any relation to it. This is a purely utilitarian conception of God.

In his 2006 lecture in Regensburg, Pope Benedict XVI described the Islamic concept of God. Quoting Professor Fr. Theodore Khoury, the Pontiff stated:

> For Muslim teaching, God is absolutely transcendent. His will is not bound up with any of our categories, even that of rationality. Here Khoury quotes a work of the noted French Islamist [*sic*] R. Arnaldez, who points out that Ibn Hazm went so far as to state that God is not bound even by his own word, and that nothing would oblige him to reveal the truth to us. Were it God's will, we would even have to practice idolatry.[229]

Another consequence of this misconception of God's complete transcendence is that the acts of men, whether good or bad, neither please nor offend Him.

Though Muslims adopted the Christian formula "merciful God" and use it when referring to Allah,[230] they do not have a right notion of God's mercy. This is because they do not see God as the supreme Wisdom but pure will, and thus, arbitrary.

Roger Arnaldez, a noted Islamicist, cited, as we have seen, by Benedict XVI, comments:

> Koranic *rahma* [mercy] is nothing but an arbitrary decision that God makes either to succor or not to succor,

---

229. Benedict XVI, "Speech at the University of Regensburg," Sept. 12, 2006, http://w2.vatican.va/content/benedict-xvi/en/speeches/2006/september/documents/hf_ben -xvi_spe_20060912_university-regensburg.html.

230. As mentioned, 'Allah' was the name Arab Christians used for God.

to forgive or not to forgive. . . . He exercises his mercy when he wants and toward whom he wants. The Koranic verses are perfectly clear on this point: "He punishes whom *He pleases*, and He grants mercy to whom He pleases" (29:21). "He forgiveth whom He pleaseth, and He punisheth whom He pleaseth" (5:18). "Again will Allah, after this, turn (in mercy) to whom He will" (9:27).[231]

Thus, rewards and punishments are not distributed according to the good or bad acts of men, but according to the arbitrary will of God: "Whom he pleases."

"Deep down," says Arnaldez, "in Islam there is no sin in the Christian sense of the word. There are only disobediences that do not touch God and could not offend him, and which furthermore do not affect the human being profoundly."[232]

However, the sin of idolatry (which Muslims say includes adoring the Most Holy Trinity) is the only one that Allah does not forgive (4:48, 116; 39:53).

The practical consequence of considering Christians as idolaters for "associating" the Son and the Holy Spirit with the Eternal Father is the implacable persecution that Islam has waged against Christians from its earliest days until today.

An Anti-Trinitarian Book That Mentions the Holy Trinity?

However, despite everything just said, there are passages in the Koran that seem to indicate that the Muslim book accepts the dogma of the Trinity. In fact, we find in different verses apparent references to the Three Persons of the Holy Trinity.

For example, there is a seemingly indirect reference to the Holy Spirit, when the Angel explains to Mary that Allah will blow His Spirit upon her: "And (remember) her who guarded her chastity: We breathed into her of Our spirit, and We made her and her son a sign for all peoples" (21:91).

In 4:171, which denies the Holy Trinity, mention is seemingly made, however, of the Second Person, the Word of God, and likewise

231. Roger Arnaldez, "Réflexion sur le Dieu du Coran, du point de vue de la logique formelle," in *Vivre avec l'Islam? Reflections chrétiennes sur la religion de Mahomet*, ed. Annie Laurent (Versailles, France: Saint-Paul, 1996), 135–6.
232. Ibid.

of the Third, the Holy Spirit: "Christ Jesus the son of Mary was (no more than) a messenger of Allah, and His Word, which He bestowed on Mary, and a spirit proceeding from Him." But immediately the *ayah* concludes, "so believe in Allah and His messengers. Say not 'Trinity.'"

Is the "Word of Allah" in the Koran, Christianity's Second Person of the Blessed Trinity? Is the "Spirit proceeding from Allah" the Holy Spirit? Would the book of Islam be describing the Trinity as the Catholic Church teaches, even as it rejects it? How can we reconcile these passages with the context of the Koran and Islamic practice?

The answer seems to be: This is yet another of the contradictions of this very contradictory and confusing book. This is to be expected from a book which—though self-proclaimed divine revelation—borrows from multiple sources, such as the Scriptures and the Apocrypha.

Stone statue of Our Lord at the entrance of the Sainte Chapelle, Paris, France.

CHAPTER 16

The Koran's 'Îsâ Is Not the Jesus of the Gospels

Those who strive to view Islam as a religion akin to Christianity insist that the Koran speaks of Jesus, "the son of Mary," with great respect, and even presents him as a prophet and the Messias. The truth that we shall see in this chapter is that the Muslim Jesus and the true One are radically different.

Our Lord Jesus Christ: Either He Is God or an Impostor

To knowingly deny the divinity of Jesus, the Word Incarnate (see John 1:14) and Redeemer of fallen humanity, and contumaciously insist that He is a mere prophet, as Muhammad and Islam do, is *blasphemy*.

Just as God is either Trinitarian or He is not God—for this is how He revealed Himself to us—so also, either Jesus Christ is the God-Man, or He is an impostor, not a prophet, for the divinity of Jesus is revealed to us repeatedly in the Gospels. Not only did Jesus declare Himself God, but He proved His divinity with miracles, finishing them with His triumphant Resurrection and Ascension into Heaven.

In innumerable passages of the Gospels, Jesus presents Himself as equal to the Eternal Father. For example, "If you knew me, you would know my Father also" (NA John 8:19), and "I and the Father are one" (John 10:30).

Before the Sanhedrin, when the High Priest Caiphas adjured Him to say, in the name of God, whether He was the Son of God, Jesus did not back down. He proclaimed His divinity: "Thou hast said it. Nevertheless I say to you, hereafter you shall see the Son of man sitting on the right hand of the power of God, and coming in the clouds of heaven. Then the high priest rent his garments, saying: He hath blasphemed; what further need have we of witnesses? Behold, now you have heard the blasphemy" (Matt. 26:64–5).

Thus, by His words, the sublimity of His doctrine, and His miracles in raising the dead, healing the lame, making the blind see, and casting out demons, it is impossible to deny the divinity of Jesus without denying Divine Revelation.

Jesus Is Not the Koran's 'Îsâ/Esau

The Koran's "Jesus" has nothing in common with Our Lord, starting with His name.

Abandoning the way Christian Arabs referred to Jesus—*Yasu*, from the Hebrew Yechua (or *Yeshua*), meaning *He will save*—the Koran called him *'Îsâ*. But Fr. Antoine Moussali stresses that "*'Îsâ* does not mean anything in Arabic unless it is connected to *'Icho,'* *Esau*. In that case, Jesus would be from the lineage of the unfortunate Esau, who sold his birthright for a dish of lentils (See Gen. 25:29–34). Jesus ('Îsâ) would thus have no right to present himself as the Son of David."[233]

For the Koran, Jesus Is Not the Son of Mary

The Koran refers to Jesus as "son of Mary" 23 times, but, in fact, it denies this filiation. It holds that Mary Most Holy did *not* conceive Jesus, but that he was created directly by God in her womb from the dust, just like Adam in the Garden of Eden. We read in 3:59: "The similitude of Jesus before Allah is as that of Adam; He created him from dust, then said to him: 'Be.' And he was" (3:59).

Father Moussali comments: "Be that as it may, 'Îsâ, the object of divine benevolence, since he has been made of a word from his mouth, is the Word of God. Not in the sense Saint John uses the term, but as having been created in the womb of Mary, of a word uttered by God who, when he says 'be,' what is created becomes. 'Îsâ is created and not begotten: 'Îsâ is like Adam, he was made of dust, he says to him, 'Be,' and he is (3:59). . . . Mary should never be called *Theotokos*, the mother of God." [234]

The Koran's purpose in insistently calling Jesus the "son of Mary" is to deny His divinity more emphatically. For example, Sadullah Khan, on the Muslim website IslamiCity, points out: "However, the Qur'an presents Jesus as the son of Mary and not as the Son of God, a significant point particularly emphasized.

---

233. Moussali, *La croix et le croissant*, 58.
234. Moussali, "Ce qu'un Chrétien doit savoir," 3–4.

Like Adam (pbuh)—Though the unique birth of Jesus with one parent is no indication of divinity just as Adam's creation was without any parentage [3:59]."[235]

Jesus as Muhammad's Precursor?

The Koran recognizes the miracles of Jesus and even calls him Messias, but not in the sense of the Redeemer of humanity since Islam rejects the doctrine of Original Sin. He is a prophet, a messenger, who comes to confirm the previous prophets and bring a new message, a new book, which is a single gospel and not four.

Above all, he was a precursor. He came to prepare the coming of the last of the prophets who, according to Islam, is Muhammad: "And remember, Jesus, the son of Mary, said: 'O Children of Israel! I am the messenger of Allah (sent) to you, confirming the Law (which came) before me, and giving Glad Tidings of a Messenger to come after me, whose name shall be Ahmad'" (61:6).

Were we to give any credence to this falsehood, we would need to scour the Gospels looking for some mention by Our Lord of a prophet who was to come after Him. The only future prophets Jesus mentions are false ones: "And many false prophets shall rise, and shall seduce many" (Matt. 24:11). "Beware of false prophets, who come to you in the clothing of sheep, but inwardly they are ravening wolves" (Matt. 7:15). "For there shall arise false Christs and false prophets, and shall shew great signs and wonders, insomuch as to deceive (if possible) even the elect. Behold I have told it to you, beforehand" (Matt. 24:24–25).

The rebuttal Islam found to the Gospel truth was to say that when Jesus Christ said he would send the Paraclete, that is the Holy Spirit, the Comforter (see John 15:26; 14:16–26, 16:7), he was referring to Ahmad, using an epithet for Muhammad.

Since the Greek term *Parakletos* in the Gospel means *lawyer, defender, comforter*, and *Ahmad* means *much praised*, Islamic apologists claim there was an error in the Gospel of Saint John and that, instead of *Parakletos* it should have been *Periklitus*, which can be roughly understood as much praised.[236]

235. Sadullah Khan, "Jesus in Islam," *IslamiCity*, Jan 3, 2017, http://www.islamicity.org/5797/jesus-in-islam/.

236. See Gallez, *Le messie et son prophète*, 2:341–44.

Jesus Will Return to Destroy Crosses?

According to the Koran, Jesus was not crucified, nor did He die on the cross, but was taken to Heaven, and only a mirage in the shape of His body was on the cross. Building on this, according to the *hadith*, Jesus will return at the end of the world to condemn Christianity and destroy all crosses.[237] Bukhari comments, "Allah's Messenger said, 'The Hour will not be established until the son of Mary (i.e., Jesus) descends amongst you as a just ruler, he will break the cross, kill the pigs, and abolish the Jizya tax. Money will be in abundance so that nobody will accept it (as charitable gifts)'" (SB 2476).

Also, Jesus Christ's divinity is continually denied in the Koran, even by Our Lord Himself:

> In blasphemy indeed are those that say that Allah is Christ the son of Mary. Say: 'Who then hath the least power against Allah, if His will were to destroy Christ the son of Mary, his mother, and all every one that is on the earth? (5:17).
>
> They do blaspheme who say: "(Allah) is Christ the son of Mary." But said Christ: "O Children of Israel! Worship Allah, my Lord and your Lord (5:72).
>
> Christ the son of Mary was no more than a messenger; many were the messengers that passed away before him (5:75).
>
> And behold! Allah will say: "O Jesus the son of Mary! Didst thou say unto men, worship me and my mother as gods in derogation of Allah?" He will say: "Glory to Thee! never could I say what I had no right (to say)" (5:116).

Marie-Thérèse Urvoy, professor of Islamic Studies and Medieval History of Islam and Arabic language at the Catholic University of Toulouse, aptly sums up the Koran's Christology:

> Koranic Christology, therefore, consists essentially of four values, presented in the form of absolute negations for fear of associationism: *Jesus is not God* (5:72, 116) because he took food (5:75); *Jesus is not the son of God* (9:30; 19:34-35); *Jesus is not the third of a triad*, as the Trinity is assimilated to polytheism (4:171; 5: 73); finally, *Jesus was not crucified* (4:157), for this would have been unworthy of a great prophet like him. With this, the Koran attacks

---

237. For Shia Twelver Muslims, this will be done by the Mahdi, the Hidden Imam.

three essential mysteries of Christianity directly connected with Jesus: the *Trinity*, in the name of absolute divine oneness; the *Incarnation*, in the name of God's exclusive transcendence; the Redemption, since there was no sacrifice.[238]

Thus, the Koran and Islamic traditions vilify and blaspheme Our Lord Jesus Christ, the Word Incarnate and our Redeemer. There is nothing in common between what our Faith teaches us about Him and His grotesque and sacrilegious caricature as presented by Islam.

In fact, this is what the saints and the entire Christian tradition have always thought. Only at a time when the Faith is moribund, and relativism reigns even in ecclesiastical circles is it possible to establish equivalency between the Gospels' Jesus and the Koran's 'Îsâ.

Muslim Veneration for the Mother of God?

As they do with Jesus, those stubbornly trying to see common ground between Islam and Christianity point to references to the Virgin Mary in the Koran and Islamic tradition. They even speak of Muslim veneration for Mary. At best, this is the result of superficial readings of Islamic texts, or mere wishful thinking, for the reality is quite the opposite.

First of all, any apparent praise of the Virgin in the Koran is meaningless because its text rejects her status as the *Theotokos*, the Mother of God. As we have just seen, it denies the divinity of Jesus, reducing Him to a simple prophet, and does not consider Our Lady to be His True Mother. Also, the references to her are confusing, contradictory, and some are even blasphemous.

Although it is true that the Muslim book speaks of the miraculous maternity of the Virgin Mary, saying that she remained a virgin (see 21:91; 66:12), it contradictorily presents the birth of her Son as a normal and painful delivery. Worse yet, it depicts the Blessed Virgin as revolting against her pain: "And the pains of childbirth drove her to the trunk of a palm-tree: She cried (in her anguish): 'Ah! Would that I had died before this! Would that I had been a thing forgotten and out of sight!'" (19:23).

If God operated the greater miracle—the virginal and divine con-

---

238. Marie-Thérèse Urvoy, "Jésus," in *Dictionnaire du Coran*, ed. Mohammad Ali Amir-Moezzi (Paris: Robert Laffont, 2007), 440.

ception—how could He fail to work the lesser but consistent miracle of granting her a miraculous delivery whereby the Divine Word would leave the maternal cloister as light passes through a crystal, without breaking it, to employ a classical metaphor?[239]

In brutal terms, the Koran presents the birth of the Child Jesus as having been a scandal to the relatives of Mary Most Holy, completely ignoring her marriage to Saint Joseph. Islamic traditions portray Saint Joseph as a cousin of Mary Most Holy without mentioning their wedding.[240] The terms of the Koran are blasphemous: "At length she brought the (babe) to her people, carrying him (in her arms). They said: 'O Mary! Truly an amazing thing hast thou brought! 'O sister of Aaron! Thy father was not a man of evil, nor thy mother a woman unchaste!'" (19:27–28).

Calling the Virgin Mary a "sister of Aaron" is another of the Koran's aberrations. Aaron and Moses, in fact, had a sister named Mary (or *Myriam*), but 1,400 years separated her from the Virgin Mary.

What "Mary" is the Koran talking about? The Mother of the Savior? The sister of Moses? An unspecified third woman? It is all very confusing.

Rather than revering Mary or Jesus, the Koran's seemingly respectful verses about Our Lady are intended to paint as blasphemous the Christian doctrine that Jesus is the Son of God.

---

239. See Alexis Henri Marie Lépicier, *The Fairest Flower of Paradise: Considerations on the Litany of the Blessed Virgin* (New York: Benziger Brothers, 1922), 29.

240. See Masud Masihiyyen, "Joseph the Carpenter in Islam [Part 1]," *AnsweringIslam: A Christian–Muslim Dialog*, accessed Mar. 5, 2018, http://www.answering-islam.org/authors/masihiyyen/joseph_carpenter1.html.

Cross of Christ, Venerated by Christians, Hated by Islam

The cross is the symbol of our Redemption, of the Son of God's immolation to save us. That is why the Apostle of the Gentiles, Saint Paul, only gloried in the Cross of Christ and preached only Christ crucified:

> But God forbid that I should glory, save in the cross of our Lord Jesus Christ; by whom the world is crucified to me, and I to the world (Gal. 6:14).
>
> But we preach Christ crucified, unto the Jews indeed a stumbling block, and unto the Gentiles foolishness: But unto them that are called, both Jews and Greeks, Christ the power of God, and the wisdom of God (1 Cor. 1:23–4).

Muhammad, on the contrary, hated this symbol of our redemption to the point of saying that Our Lord Jesus Christ Himself would return in the future to break all crosses.

Islam is a ritualistic but naturalistic religion. Its vision of heaven is entirely natural and sensual; what the Koran gives to understand is that heavenly delights are an extension of earthly pleasures. It is a vision with nothing to do with the Christian supernatural beatific vision where saved souls will contemplate God face-to-face.

Chapter 17
A Naturalistic Religion

Islam is a purely natural religion. While it talks of angels and Paradise, it rejects grace and the supernatural. Its Paradise is a garden of sensible delights and sensuality. Its vision of God is no different than our gazing at the moon, with our bodily eyes.

Rejection of the Supernatural

Father Jomier writes:

> Islam. . . . admits the dogma of the resurrection of the body and retribution according to works and to the observance of a revealed law. It should be noted that we remain at the level of an essentially natural religion, for Islam definitely rejects everything supernatural, any participation through grace in God's own life. . . . The eternal bliss promised to the elect will be purely natural. It is announced as an earthly paradise with natural enjoyments and higher, more subtle joys of knowledge, but still purely human.[241]

Cardinal Pietro Palazzini also highlights the absence of the supernatural in Islam: "The religion of the Koran is a religion of dogma and precepts; these exist without a trace of the supernatural."[242]

A Strictly Natural Vision of God

According to the *hadith*, not everyone in Paradise will see God face-to-face, only the highest-placed:

> Thuwair narrated from Ibn Umar, saying:
> The Messenger of Allah (s.a.w) said: "Indeed the least of the people of Paradise in rank is the one who shall look at his gardens, his wives, his bounties, his servants and his beds for the distance of a thousand years, and the noblest of them with Allah is the one who shall look at His Face morning and night." Then the Messenger of Allah (s.a.w) recited: Some faces on that day shall be radiant.

---

241. Jomier, *The Bible and the Qur'an*, 35–6.
242. Pietro Palazzini, "Islamism," in Francesco Roberti and Pietro Palazzini, *Dictonary of Moral Theology*, trans. Henry J. Yannone (Westminster, Md.: Newman, 1962), 656.

They shall be looking at their Lord (JT 2750).

Those who do see God face-to-face will have only a natural vision of Him, as in this life we look at physical things. It is not the Christian concept of the supernatural beatific vision. Ibn Majah recounts in *The Book of the Sunna*:

> It was narrated that Jarir bin 'Abdullah said:
> We were sitting with the Messenger of Allah. He looked at the moon, which was full, and said, "Indeed, you will see your Lord as you see this moon. You will not feel the slightest inconvenience and overcrowding in seeing Him. If you have the power not to be overcome and to say this prayer before the sun rises and before it sets, then do that." Then he recited: "And glorify the praises of your Lord, before the rising of the sun and before (its) setting" (SIM 182).

Supernatural Happiness

Heaven is the place of perfect happiness, of which, as Saint Paul says, "Eye hath not seen, nor ear heard, neither hath it entered into the heart of man, what things God hath prepared for them that love him" (1 Cor. 2:9).

However, to have a correct understanding of the heavenly Paradise, we must also have a right notion of happiness on this earth.

For a Christian, true happiness on this earth presupposes love of God and participation in the divine life through sanctifying grace. For this reason, the joy a Christian expects to have in heaven is above all the fullness of sanctifying grace, the light of glory (*lumen gloriae*), that gives us the supreme happiness, of being able to see God "face-to-face" (1 Cor. 13:12) through the beatific vision.

It is true that Heaven is a marvelous place and that this unspeakable happiness of contemplating God in His infinite perfections is enhanced by the joy of the society of the blessed—the angels and saints—the perfection of the resurrected body, tranquility, and peace of soul.

To the Sadducees, who sought to embarrass Our Lord by asking Him which husband a woman who had been married seven times would keep in heaven, He answered, "You err, not knowing the Scriptures, nor the power of God. For in the resurrection they shall neither marry nor be married; but shall be as the angels of God in heaven" (Matt. 22:29–30).

Heaven in Islam, a Place of Sensible Pleasures

Naturalists and hedonists understand earthly happiness only as sensible pleasures with no link to the supernatural. Consequently, their views of Heaven are that it is merely a continuation of the enjoyment of these sensible, and especially carnal, pleasures on earth.

This naturalistic conception is prevalent, for example, in the mythological religion of the Greeks and Romans. For them, heavenly delights would be the same as the pleasures of this earth, even those gained through the practice of vices. That is why Saint Augustine said the Greeks turned vices into gods: "These are, indeed, his fictions, but he [Homer] attributed divine attributes to sinful men, that crimes might not be accounted crimes, and that whosoever committed any might appear to imitate the celestial gods and not abandoned men."[243]

Saint Alphonsus Liguori (1696–1797), Doctor of the Church, in his book *History of Heresies and Their Refutation*, gives the following judgment of the Islamic conception of Heaven: "The Mahometan Paradise, however, is only fit for beasts; for filthy sensual pleasure is all the believer has to expect there."[244]

Beautiful Celestial Young Men and Women

The Muslim heaven resembles very much that of ancient mythology, where its inhabitants would indulge in sensible pleasures, especially those of the flesh.

According to the Koran and the *hadith*, the elect will spend time in tents of precious cloths, seated on comfortable cushions, enjoying tasty fruits, and delicious wines, in spectacular gardens, and by rivers of crystal-clear water. They will be served by handsome, heavenly young men and virgins (called *houris*), with whom they will have conjugal relations.

Here are some quotations from the Koran:

> Indeed, the righteous will be in a secure place; within gardens and springs, wearing [garments of] fine silk and brocade, facing each other. Thus. And We [Allah] will

---

243. St. Augustine, *Confessions*, bk. 1, ch. 16, no. 26.
244. St. Alphonsus Marie de Liguori, *The History of Heresies, and Their Refutation; Or, The Triumph of the Church*, trans. Rev. John T. Mullock (Dublin: James Duffy, 1847), 1:188, https://archive.org/stream/thehistoryofhere01liguuoft/thehistoryofhere01liguuoft_djvu.txt.

marry them to fair women with large, [beautiful] eyes.
They will call therein for every [kind of] fruit – safe and
secure. (SI 44:51–55).

They will be reclining on thrones lined up, and We will
marry them to fair women with large, [beautiful] eyes. (SI
52:20).

"[They are] reclining on beds whose linings are of silk
brocade, and the fruit of the two gardens is hanging low.
. . . In them are women limiting [their] glances, untouched
before them by man or jinni. . . . As if they were rubies and
coral. . . . In them are good and beautiful women. . . . Fair
ones reserved in pavilions. . . . Untouched before them by
man or jinni. . . . Reclining on green cushions and beautiful fine carpets (SI 55:54, 56, 58, 70, 72, 74, 76).

Besides the beautiful women who men will marry in Heaven,
handsome young men will serve them: "There will circulate among
them [servant] boys [especially] for them, as if they were pearls well-
protected" (SI 52:24). "There will circulate among them young boys
made eternal. When you see them, you would think them [as beautiful as] scattered pearls" (SI 76:19).

72 Virgins, Not Just for Martyrs

The *hadith* speak more directly of Paradise's carnal pleasures than
the Koran.

Abu 'Isa Muhammad al-Tirmidhi (b. 824) is the author of one of
the most respected collections of *hadith* held as canonical by the
Sunnis, the *Jami' at-Tirmidhi*. He deals with Heaven at length, tran-
scribing what Muhammad purportedly said and was handed down
to posterity. He cites the famous 72 virgins to whom martyrs are
said to be entitled in the Muslim heaven. However, he claims that
this prize would belong to all devout Muslims, not just the martyrs.
Here are some of his statements: "Abu Sa'eed Al-Khudri narrated
that the Messenger of Allah (Peace be upon him) said: 'The least of
the people of Paradise in position is the one with eighty thousand
servants and seventy-two wives'" (JT 2760).

Not only will each of the elect have a harem in heaven, but they will
receive extraordinary power to have conjugal relations with all these
women: "Anas narrated that the Prophet (s.a.w) said: 'The believer
shall be given in paradise such and such strength in intercourse.' It

was said: 'O Messenger of Allah! And will he [be] able to do that?' He said: 'He will be given the strength of a hundred'" (JT 2732).

One of the many problems with the Islamic notion of heaven is that it is conceived in terms of man and his carnal pleasures. That is why imams have great difficulty in answering the questions of women—especially Western ones—as to whether they will also have the same pleasure as men, with different heavenly companions. In general, answers evade the topic and say that women will have all possible happiness, but just one husband.[245]

The Muslim conception of Heaven is so naturalistic and carnal that it includes births: "Abu Sa'eed Al-Khudri narrated that the Messenger of Allah (s.a.w) said: 'The believer, when he desires a child in Paradise, he shall be carried (in pregnancy), born, and complete his aging in an hour as he desires'" (JT 2762).

No Need for Faith

Alain Besançon, a French historian and philosopher, stresses another aspect of the Islamic naturalism—there is no need for faith:

> A common feature of natural religions is a sense of God, or of the divine, being everywhere present in nature. For the Greeks and the Romans, it was enough to contemplate the cosmos, the created universe, to be certain, prior to any process of mental reasoning, that God, or the gods, existed. *Not* to believe in them was a sign of insanity, marking off the unbeliever from the realm of the human.
>
> This is not the Christian viewpoint, which holds rather that the existence of God can be grasped only with the help of investigation and reason, with faith coming in as an act of heavenly grace to seal this acquired knowledge. But the Christian perspective is not the Islamic perspective, which in this regard bears a greater resemblance to the classical pagan sense of things. Islam does not suppose that faith is needed to perceive the divine presence; that presence is obvious. Although Islam is, to be sure, a religion of faith, where faith comes in is in acknowledging not God's omnipresence but His oneness.[246]

---

245. Islamweb.net, "Sex life of women in Paradise: Fatwa No. 83922. Fatwa Date: 31/03/2002," accessed Feb. 28, 2018, http://www.islamweb.net/emainpage/PrintFatwa.php?lang=E&Id=83922.

246. Alain Besançon, "L'Islam," *Académie des Sciences morales et politiques*, 7–8, accessed Mar. 2, 2018, https://www.asmp.fr/fiches_academiciens/textacad/besancon/islam.pdf.

There is nothing in common between Abraham, as known to us from Sacred Scripture, to whom God's promise was fulfilled in Jesus Christ, and Islam's Abraham.

CHAPTER 18
Islam, the "Religion of Human Nature"?

It has become common in Christian circles devoted to "interreligious dialogue" to speak of three "Abrahamic" religions: Christianity, Judaism, and Islam.

One of the great exponents of this theory was the aforementioned French Orientalist Fr. Louis Massignon who influenced the Second Vatican Council's references to Islam.[247]

Abraham, the Father of Different Religions?

Father Jourdan asks, "How can Abraham be the father of different religions? ... Under what title is Abraham a father in *the* Faith? How is he father in *our* respective faiths, since they are different?"[248]

He goes on to explain that Islam is more appropriately termed an "Adamic religion," since it considers Adam to have been the first monotheistic prophet: "For Muslims, the first monotheist in history is Adam. But, Shh! Don't say this out loud! Nevertheless, Islam is fundamentally Adamic, 'the religion of always.' It is not Abrahamic."[249]

In his turn, Fr. Antoine Moussali shows that there is nothing in common between Abraham, as known to us from Sacred Scripture, to whom God's promise was fulfilled in Jesus Christ, and Islam's Abraham. The Koran presents Abraham as the defender of the oneness of God.

The only common trait between the Abraham of the promise and that of Islam, Father Moussali explains, is the name itself: "Spiritually and theologically speaking, they are radically different. Indeed, there is a great distance between the character of the covenant and the promise, open to the future [coming of Christ] and the one whose mission was only to re-establish the 'primitive' religion. They are not the bearers of the same message. Understood in this way,

---

247. See Chapter 12.
248. François Jourdan, CMJ, *Dieu des chrétiens, Dieu des musulmans: Des repères pour comprendre* (Paris: l'Œuvre, 2008), 42. (Emphases in the original.)
249. Vulpillières, "Les impasses du dialogue."

the Koranic Abraham . . . is, above all, he who restored the primitive norm and the natural religion, Islam."[250]

Islam, the "Primitive Religion"?

Here we come to Islam's doctrinal core, which is its claim to be not only the "primitive religion" but also the "religion of human nature." For Islam, every child is supposedly born a Muslim, but many are then diverted by their parents to other religions. According to the *Sahih Bukhari*, "Allah's Messenger said, 'No child is born except on Al-Fitra (Islam) and then his parents make him Jewish, Christian or Magian'" (SB 4775).

For Muhammad, not being a Muslim is having one's nature amputated. For him, just as animals have perfect offspring, so also a mother has a normal child, namely, a Muslim: "As an animal produces a perfect young animal: Do you see any part of its body amputated? Then he rec[ited] "The religion of pure Islamic Faith (Hanifa), (i.e., to worship none but Allah)" (SB 4775).

Therefore, in coming into existence, along with his human nature, a child receives "Allah's Islamic nature with which He (Allah) has created mankind. Let there be no change in Allah's religion (i.e., to join none in Allah's worship). That is the straight religion; but most of men know not" (30:30)" (SB 4775).

Islam's founder insists: "The mother of every person gives him birth according to his true nature. It is subsequently his parents who make him a Jew or a Christian or a Magian. Had his parents been Muslim he would have also remained a Muslim" (SM 2659a).

Here Muhammad is commenting on 30:30:

> Muhammad Ali's Urdu translation of this verse reads in English:
> "Remain firm in the nature framed by Allah in which He created people in the original state. There is no altering the state framed by Allah. This is the right religion, but most men know not."
> Muhammad Ali continues his discussion on this verse by noting that Muhammad commented:
> "*Fitra* is Islam. Then he added: The child of every person is born in the state of nature (*fitrat ki halat men*), that

---

250. Moussali, *La croix et le croissant*, 55.

is Islam. His mother and father make him a Jew or a Christian or a Magian." [251]

Therefore, for Muslims, Islam and human nature come together, and, therefore, the difference between a Muslim and a Christian, for example, is *ontological*: They are two distinct human natures.

Fr. Samir Khalil Samir, SJ explains, "As regards inequality between Muslims and non-Muslims, Islam considers the former superior to the latter from the ontological [of the very nature] and juridical point of view."[252] This explains Muslim contempt and cruelty toward Christians.

In this sense, the testimony of Joseph Fadelle, an Iraqi Shi'ite Muslim of high birth who later converted to Catholicism, is very illustrative. During his military service, he was ordered to share a room with a Christian. He describes the horror this caused in him:

> At those words I stopped short, as though hit over the head with a club I felt that I was becoming very pale and listless, and I dropped my things and the mattress that I had under my arm. Then surprise gave way to fear and panic....
>
> Where I come from, Christians are regarded as impure pariahs, as less than nothing, and you must avoid any dealings with them at all cost....
>
> I was afraid of being touched by that Christian, of having to speak to him, or even to share my meal with him. Never in my life had I imagined such a trial.[253]

---

251. Khwaja Kamal Ud-Din, Mawlawi Muhammad Ali, and Sultan Muhammad Khan Paul, "A Summary of The Fall of The Human Race," accessed Feb. 28, 2018, http://www.answering-islam.org/Hahn/fall.html.

252. Samir, *111 Questions*, 91.

253. Joseph Fadelle, *The Price to Pay: A Muslim Risks All to Follow Christ* (San Francisco: Ignatius, 2012), 13–4.

The Koran is full of contradictions. In 2:62 it says that Christians will be saved. But in 9:5 the Koran says they are to be killed, unless they pay the *zakat* tribute.

CHAPTER 19
Islam's Doctrine of Abrogation

The Koran's Contradictions

As stated, the Koran is a very confused book, full of contradictions. Here it affirms one thing, there the opposite. For example, it states that Christians will be saved: "Those who believe (in the Qur'an), and those who follow the Jewish (scriptures), and the Christians and the Sabians, any who believe in Allah and the Last Day, and work righteousness, shall have their reward with their Lord; on them shall be no fear, nor shall they grieve" (2:62).

The Koran says the contrary, however, in the very next *sura*: "If anyone desires a religion other than Islam (submission to Allah), never will it be accepted of him; and in the hereafter he will be in the ranks of those who have lost (all spiritual good) (3:85).

Another blatant contradiction is the Koran's teaching on religious tolerance. Reading this verse, we would conclude that Islam preaches tolerance: "Let there be no compulsion in religion" (2:256).

Seven chapters later, however, the Koran leads us to the opposite conclusion: "And when the sacred months have passed, then kill the polytheists [Christians] wherever you find them and capture them and besiege them and sit in wait for them at every place of ambush. But if they should repent, establish prayer, and give zakah, let them [go] on their way. Indeed, God is Forgiving and Merciful" (SI 9:5).[254]

In chapter 47, the Koran conduces to the same conclusion. It commands the killing of infidels:

> So when you meet those who disbelieve [in battle], strike [their] necks until, when you have inflicted slaughter upon them, then secure their bonds, and either [confer] favor afterwards or ransom [them] until the war lays down its burdens. That [is the command]. And if God had

---

254. *Zakat*(h) "is . . . a tax, or obligatory alms. . . . It is customarily 2.5% . . . of . . . total savings and wealth above a minimum amount known as *nisab*. . . . Today, in most Muslim-majority countries, zakat contributions are voluntary, while in a handful (Libya, Malaysia, Saudi Arabia, Sudan, and Yemen), zakat is mandated and collected by the state." *Wikipedia*, s.v. "Zakat," updated Jun. 7, 2018, 00:51, https://en.wikipedia.org/wiki/Zakat. [Ed.: On Apr. 6, 2018, at 20 dinars (85 grams=3 ounces) of gold, the nisab threshold beyond which the zakat would apply is approximately USD$4,000.]

willed, He could have taken vengeance upon them [Himself], but [He ordered armed struggle] to test some of you by means of others. And those who are killed in the cause of God - never will He waste their deeds (SI 47:4).

So which one is it? Does Islam preach tolerance for other religions or does it command the slaughter of non-Muslims? Faced with these contradictions in the Koran, how does a sincere Muslim know which verse of the Koran to obey?

Koranic Basis for the Abrogation Doctrine

To resolve this prickly question, Muslim scholars early on developed the doctrine of *abrogation* (*naskh*),[255] according to which, verses Muhammad claimed were revealed to him later in life abrogate (supersede) contradicting *ayat* received earlier.

French Islamicists Dominique and Marie-Thérèse Urvoy explain: "This difficulty is solved by Muslim exegetes and theologians, with the system of 'abrogated' verses (*mansukh*) and 'abrogation' (*nasikh*). The general rule is then: When two verses contradict one another, the verse revealed last abrogates (cancels out) the verse revealed earlier."[256]

For her part, in *The Cambridge Companion of The Koran*, Jane Dammen McAuliffe clarifies: "Put very simply, 'abrogation' refers to the exegetical conviction that some verses of the Qur'an restrict, modify or even nullify other verses. The key texts upon which this principle has been built are Q 2:106 and 16:101 but the basic operational concept is the sequential nature of qur'anic revelations."[257]

Indeed, the Koran states: "We do not abrogate a verse or cause it to be forgotten except that We bring forth [one] better than it or similar to it. Do you not know that God is over all things competent?" (SI 2:106).

---

255. "Naskh literally means 'obliteration, cancellation, transfer, suppression, suspension' depending on the context. It is also referred to as *Mansukh* doctrine (or, that which has been abrogated)." *Wikipedia*, s.v. "Naskh (tafsir)," updated Apr. 19, 2018, 09:07, https://en.wikipedia.org/wiki/Naskh_(tafsir).

256. Dominique et Marie-Thérèse Urvoy, "Abrogation - vocabulaire de l'islam 9," Jan. 13, 2018, http://urvoy.blogspot.com/2018/01/abrgation-vocabulaire-de-lislam-9.html.

257. Jane Dammen McAuliffe, "The Tasks and Traditions of Interpretation," in *The Cambridge Companion to the Qur'an*, ed. Jane Dammen McAuliffe (Cambridge: Cambridge University Press, 2006), 187, http://www.almuslih.org/Library/McAuliffe,%20J%20-%20The%20Cambridge%20Companion.pdf.

Jihad: A Practical Consequence of Abrogation

One of the consequences of this doctrine that later verses abrogate contradicting earlier ones, is that all the tolerance-promoting verses are said to have been abrogated by the *sword* and *jihad* verses.

Such is the general opinion of Islamic scholars. According to Dominique and Marie-Thérèse Urvoy: "It is generally accepted that the 124 verses of the Koran, encouraging peace and forgiveness, are abrogated by verse 4 (on *jihad*) of *sura* 47 (Muhammad)."[258]

Alexander Knysh says the same, "The abrogation theory achieved great sophistication at the hands of later legal scholars, who, for instance, argued that the famous 'Sword Verse' enjoining the believers to 'slay the idolaters wherever you find them' (Q 9:5) abrogated no fewer than 124 other verses commanding 'anything less than a total offensive against the non-believers.'"[259]

The Sunna Abrogates the Koran?

David Bukay, in an article in the *Middle East Quarterly*, presents another aspect of the doctrine of abrogation. He states that some Muslim schools of thought hold that the Sunna abrogates the Koran: "Still, there are internal debates about various manners of abrogation. Among Sunni theologians, there are disputes about whether *sunna* . . . can abrogate the Qur'an. The Maliki and Hanafi schools suggest that the *sunna* and the Qur'an can abrogate each other while Shafi'is do not."[260]

Abrogation Derives From Islam's Understanding of God Being Arbitrary, Not Wise

Fr. Claude Gilliot, OP, professor of Islamic Thought at the University of Provence (Aix-en-Provence), shows how the abrogation doctrine derives from the Muslim concept of an arbitrary God rather than a wise one:[261]

---

258. Urvoy, "Abrogation."

259. Alexander Knysh, "Multiple Areas of Influence," in *The Cambridge Companion to the Qur'an*, ed. Jane Dammen McAuliffe, 218. In his footnote 29, Knysh cites D. Powers, "The Exegetical Genre *nasikh al-Quran wamansukhuhu*," in Rippin (ed.), *Approaches to the history of the interpretation of the Qur'an*, 130.

260. David Bukay, "Peace or Jihad? Abrogation in Islam," *Middle East Quarterly* 14, no. 4 (Fall 2007-Sept. 1, 2007), https://www.meforum.org/articles/2007/peace-or-jihad-abrogation-in-islam.

261. See Chapter 20: Islam's Morals.

Another problem concerning the Koran's theological-juridical status is that of abrogation (*naskh*). . . . Changes were found in some of the stipulations contained in the Koran and in the prophetic traditions (*sunna*). That could hardly seem compatible with the divine transcendence not subject to change but would become so when we consider that good is what God ordains and bad is what he forbids without being able to 'ask him to render accounts.' The rule, we would say, is 'arbitrary,' depending only on the divine will. Some people with a more rationalistic tendency opposed, in vain, this abrogation theory, which finally imposed itself.[262]

Ignoring Abrogation Helps Anesthetize the West

As seen, the abrogation doctrine gives Islamic jihadists an authentic Koranic basis to impose Islam by the sword, perpetrating barbarous deeds such as the beheading of non-Muslims.

At the same time, widespread ignorance of the abrogation doctrine in the West allows Islam's propagators and enablers to continue anesthetizing Christian public opinion by repeating the mantra that Islam is a religion of peace, quoting the abrogated 2:256 as proof for their misleading claim: "Let there be no compulsion in religion."

---

262. Claude Gilliot, OP, "A propos du Coran," in *Vivre avec l'Islam?* ed. Annie Laurent, 147.

CHAPTER 20
Islam's Morals

Islam's concept of morals differs from Christianity's. The variance stems from the Koranic conception of a God entirely aloof from His creatures, a God Who is not the Supreme Wisdom but acts capriciously.

Legalistic Morals

Fr. Antoine Moussali, points out that in Islam, "Good and evil are created by God, and it is by the free choice of His will that good is good and evil is evil." Therefore, "There is no intrinsic good or evil: God is the absolute master of truth and sets the standard of the true, the beautiful and the good."[263]

However, if there is no intrinsic good or evil, then blasphemy, apostasy, lying, and so on, can all be done if circumstances or intentions favoring Islam would seem to condone it. This is what Muslims call *taqiya* or deception. It will be discussed in the next chapter.

Another consequence is that, if good and evil are unrelated to the nature of things or the intention of our acts, then human reason is unable to make any objective moral judgment. Thus the natural law—the moral compass that guides human action—collapses and moral life depends exclusively on revelation, an arbitrary law without resonance in the conscience of man.

"For this reason," Father Moussali says, "morality is reduced to a chapter of Muslim legislation, making obedience to God and His decrees the virtue par excellence of the Muslim."[264]

Ultimately, the foundation of Islamic morality is not to "love God above all things," as in Christian teaching,[265] but instead, submit

---

263. Moussali, *La croix et le croissant*, 36.

264. Ibid.

265. Catholic Church, *Catechism of the Catholic Church* (Vatican: Libreria Editrice Vaticana, 1994), nos. 1809, 1822, and 1844, http://www.vatican.va/archive/ccc_css/archive/catechism /p3s1c1a7.htm. St. Thomas Aquinas teaches: "Before His Passion, our Lord, being asked by one of the scribes, a doctor of the law, which was the greatest and first commandment, answered (Mk 22:30), 'Thou shalt love the Lord thy God with thy whole heart, and with thy whole soul, and with thy whole mind, and with thy whole strength.' Among all the commandments this is the most useful, the greatest, and the grandest. That can be seen at once, for in this commandment all the others are fulfilled." St. Thomas Aquinas, *The Two Commandments of Charity and the Ten Commandments of the Law*, trans. Fr. Henry Rawes (London: Burns & Oates, 1880), chap. 4, 44.

blindly to the arbitrary will of God. This concept is encapsulated in the very name of Muhammad's religion, Islam, meaning *submission.*[266]

"An Eye for an Eye, a Tooth for a Tooth"

While Our Lord Jesus Christ commanded us to love our enemies, the Koran restored the primitive *lex talionis*, that is, "an eye for an eye, a tooth for a tooth." "We ordained therein for them: 'Life for life, eye for eye, nose for nose, ear for ear, tooth for tooth and wounds equal for equal.' But if anyone remits the retaliation by way of charity, it is an act of atonement for himself. And if any fail to judge by (the light of) what Allah hath revealed, they are (no better than) wrongdoers" (5:45).

Contempt for Virginity

Nor does Islam show any love of virginity and celibacy "for the sake of the kingdom of heaven" (NA Matt. 19:12). According to Koranic doctrine, as we have seen, one of the prizes in Heaven is 72 spotless virgins for every devout Muslim.

Divine Predestination and Fatalism

Man's predestination to the joys of Heaven or the pains of Hell is the sixth dogma of Islamic belief.[267]

As always, the Koran and *hadith* are confused, sometimes upholding free will, sometimes denying it outright. Analyzing the Koran, A. Palmieri, an Islamicist and Catholic theologian, explains that while some verses defend human freedom and free will, "They are however few in number compared to those that attribute divine predestination [which leads man] to evil or good, to faith or to unbelief."[268]

Palmieri illustrates his point with examples from the Koran:

---

266. "Many people have wrongly attempted to equate the word *Islam* with peace by showing that *Islam*, meaning 'submission,' shares a root word with *Salaam*, meaning 'peace.' However, if such relationships between the meanings of Arabic words can be created then that would imply that there is a relationship between one of the derivations of the infinitive *Salama*, meaning the stinging of the snake or tanning the leather, and *Salam*, meaning peace; a relationship which obviously does not exist." *WikiIslam: The Online Resource on Islam*, s.v. "The Meaning of Islam," updated Feb. 6, 2014, 18:59, https://wikiislam.net/wiki/The_Meaning_of_Islam.

267. Islam's six fundamental beliefs are: a non-Trinitarian God; angels; the Koran; the Prophets; the Day of Judgment; and predestination. See *BBC News*, "Basic Articles of Faith," updated Jul. 19, 2011, http://www.bbc.co.uk/religion/religions/islam/beliefs/beliefs.shtml.

268. A. Palmieri, "Coran (sa théologie)," col. 1810, in *Dictionnaire de théologie Catholique* (Paris: Letouzey et Ané, 1938).

Allah leaves straying those whom He pleases: and guides whom He pleases (14:4).

Many are the Jinns and men we have made for Hell (7:179).

I will fill Hell with jinn and men, all together (11:119).

Allah has, knowing (him as such), left him astray, and sealed his hearing and his heart (and understanding), and put a cover on his sight (45:23).

Of them are some who (pretend to) listen to thee; but We have thrown veils on their hearts, so they understand it not, and deafness in their ears; if they saw every one of the signs, not they will believe in them (6:25).

In this way, Palmieri concludes, "The edifice of Islamic morality rests upon the denial of the foundations of the moral law, which cannot be conceived without admitting that man is responsible for his actions."[269]

Polygamy and Muhammad's Four, Nine, or Eleven Wives

Although the Koran presents principles of natural law enshrined in the Decalogue, Islamic morality as a whole represents a giant step backward from that of the Gospel. For example, the Koran restores polygamy (see 4:3), allowed by God temporarily for the growth of mankind, and authorizes divorce (*sura* 65, *The Divorce*), tolerated by Moses because of the Jews' hardness of heart. However, Our Lord explicitly condemned divorce and abolished polygamy, restoring marriage to its intrinsic perfection (see Matt 19:8).

Although the Koran limits the number of wives to four (plus slaves and concubines) (see 4:3), it made an exception for Muhammad, thereby violating the principle of the universal application of the moral law. Thus, when Muhammad burned with lust for Zaynab,[270] wife of Zayd—his secretary and adopted son (among

---

269. Ibid., col. 1817.

270. Muhammad ibn Jarir al-Tabari (839–923) was a Muslim historian and religious scholar whose annals are the most important source for the early history of Islam. He recorded the following: "One day the Messenger of God went out looking for Zayd. Now there was a covering of haircloth over the doorway, but the wind had lifted the covering so that the doorway was uncovered. Zaynab was in her chamber, undressed, and admiration for her entered the heart of the Prophet. After that happened, she was made unattractive to the other man." Muhammad ibn Jarir al-Tabari, *The History of al-Tabari (Ta'rikh al-rusul wa'l-muluk)*, vol. 8, *The Victory of Islam*, trans. and ann. Michael Fishbein (Albany: State University of New York Press, 1997), 4, http://www.kalamullah.com/Books/The%20History%20Of%20Tabari/Tabari

Arabs, adoption established blood ties)—he already had four wives, and, moreover, it was not licit for him to marry the wife of his adopted son.

However, Allah favored him with a new revelation, which became part of the Koran: "Then when Zaid had dissolved (his marriage) with her, with the necessary (formality), We joined her in marriage to thee: in order that (in future) there may be no difficulty to the Believers in (the matter of) marriage with the wives of their adopted sons, when the latter have dissolved with the necessary (formality) their marriage with them. And Allah's command must be fulfilled" (33:37).

Another revelation gave Muhammad the privilege of having more than four wives, a right that was exclusively his: "O Prophet! We have made lawful to thee thy wives . . . this only for thee, and not for the Believers (at large)" (33:50).

This exception for Muhammad is an inconvenient one for Muslims, who struggle to justify it. For example, Islamic scholar Maududi comments: "This [33:50], in fact, is an answer to the objection of the people who said that Muhammad (peace be upon him) forbade others to keep more than four wives at a time but had himself taken a fifth wife. This objection was raised because at the time the Prophet (peace be upon him) married Zainab, he already had four wives with him."[271]

According to Bukhari, Aisha, Muhammad's favorite wife, found Allah's timing of 33:51 (on Muhammad's wife-rotating practices) somewhat strange and said to her husband: "I feel that your Lord hastens in fulfilling your wishes and desires" (SB 4788).

Muhammad did not restrict himself, however, to just a fifth wife, Zayd's divorced one, plus his concubines and war captives. As Bukhari observes: "Anas bin Malik said, 'The Prophet used to visit all his wives in a round, during the day and night and they were eleven in number.' I asked Anas, 'Had the Prophet the strength for it?' Anas replied, 'We used to say that the Prophet was given the strength of thirty (men).' And Sa'id said on the authority of Qatada that Anas had told him about nine wives only (not eleven)" (SB 268).

_Volume_08.pdf. It may be said that Tabari's narration closely resembles that of David and Bathsheba; with the difference, however, that David was punished by God and did penance for the rest of his life (see 2 Sam. 11–12).

271. Sayyid Abul A'la Maududi, "Tafheem ul Quran: *Sura* 33 Al-Ahzab, Ayat 50," accessed Feb. 28, 2018, http://islamicstudies.info/reference.php?sura=33&verse=50.

However, if according to the Koran Muhammad is "a beautiful pattern (of conduct) for any one whose hope is in Allah and the Final Day" (33:21), then his followers should imitate him. The Koran says, though, that Allah created this special law for him alone, and, therefore, he must not be emulated on this point.

The September 11, 2001 attack on America was a declaration of war by Islamists against the Christian West.

CHAPTER 21
Taqiya: Dissimulation and Deceit

The Islamic site *al-Islam.org* defines *taqiya* as follows: "'Concealing or disguising one's beliefs, convictions, ideas, feelings, opinions, and/or strategies at a time of imminent danger, whether now or later in time, to save oneself from physical and/or mental injury.' A one-word translation would be 'Dissimulation.'"[272]

Taqiya and Islamic Terrorism

With the advent of Islamic terrorism in the West, this Arabic term is being heard more often because the terrorists employ deception while preparing their attacks.

Already in 2013, Anne-Diandra Louarn, a *France24* television network journalist, in an article titled "Taqiya, or the terrorist 'art of deception'" reported that "French counterterrorism experts are monitoring the practice of 'taqiya'—or deceiving society by concealing one's faith—and its uses in jihadist circles."[273]

According to *The Religion of Peace* website, in the United States,

> The 9/11 hijackers practiced deception by going into bars and drinking alcohol, thus throwing off potential suspicion that they were fundamentalists plotting jihad. This effort worked so well that John Walsh, the host of a popular American television show, claimed well after the fact that their bar trips were evidence of "hypocrisy."
>
> The transmission from Flight 93 records the hijackers telling their doomed passengers that there is "a bomb on board" but that everyone will "be safe" as long as "their demands are met." Obviously none of this was true, but these men, who were so intensely devoted to Islam that they were willing to "slay and be slain for the cause of Allah" (as the Quran puts it), saw nothing wrong with employing *taqiya* to facilitate their mission of mass murder.[274]

272. "Al-Taqiyya, Dissimulation Part 1, Introduction," *Al-Islam.org*, accessed Apr. 2, 2018, https://www.al-islam.org/shiite-encyclopedia-ahlul-bayt-dilp-team/al-taqiyya-dissimulation-part-1.

273. Anne-Diandra Louarn, "Taqiyya, or the Terrorist 'Art of Deception,'" *France24.com*, Mar. 13, 2013, http://www.france24.com/en/20130313-taqiya-france-islam-deception-favoured-terrorists-jihad.

274. "Deception, Lying and Taqiyya: Does Islam Permit Muslims to Lie?" *TheReligionofPeace.com*,

An Ancient Islamic Practice

As can be seen in the example given by French Islamicist Annie Laurent, this strategy of dissimulation is far from being new. Islam has long made use of it: "Taqiya was legitimately observed by the Moriscos living under Christian rule in Andalusia. Thus, in 1504, the mufti Ahmed Ibn Jumaïra published a fatwa (legal opinion) giving precise instructions on this subject. If Christians forced Muslims to insult Muhammad they had to do it believing that word was pronounced by Satan. If they were forced to drink wine or eat pork, they could do so but knowing that it was an impure act and mentally condemning it."[275]

Origin in the Koran

A series of Koranic verses seems to authorize this practice, and both the *hadith* and the history of Islam, in addition to the cases cited above, show that *taqiya* is commonplace in Islam.

Take, for example, this *ayah*: "Anyone who, after accepting faith in Allah, utters unbelief—except under compulsion, his heart remaining firm in Faith—but such as open their breast to unbelief, on them is wrath from Allah, and theirs will be a dreadful penalty" (16:106).

The text states that anyone who becomes a Muslim and apostatizes will be the object of a "dreadful penalty." Indeed, in Islam, the penalty for apostasy is death. However, the same verse contains a phrase that is interpreted as justifying taqiya: "except under compulsion, his heart remaining firm in Faith."

That is, a Muslim can resort to dissimulation if under pressure. He can pretend to have apostatized by acting *externally* as if he had abandoned Islam while remaining faithful *interiorly*.

According to Ali ibn Ahmad al-Wahidi (d. 1075) in his *Book of Occasions of Revelation*, this is how this verse of the Koran was revealed to Muhammad: A certain Ammar saw his father and mother being tortured to death to abandon Islam. To avoid the same fate, he reneged on his Muslim belief. "Ammar then went to see the Messenger of Allah,

accessed Apr. 4, 2018, https://www.thereligionofpeace.com/pages/quran/taqiyya.aspx. (Reprinted with permission.)

275. Annie Laurent, "La Taqiya ou le concept coranique qui permet aux musulmans radicaux de dissimuler leurs véritables croyances," *Atlantico.fr*, Nov. 19, 2015, http://www.atlantico.fr/decryptage/taqiya-ou-concept-coranique-qui-permet-aux-musulmans-radicaux-dissimuler-veritables-croyances-annie-laurent-2445946.html.

Allah bless him and give him peace, crying. The Messenger of Allah, Allah bless him and give him peace, wiped his tears with his own hand and said: 'if they return to you, let them hear again what you told them.' Then, Allah, exalted is he, revealed this verse [16:106]."[276]

In other words, Muhammad authorized him to continue his dissimulation, and a Koranic revelation immediately confirmed his decision. With that, it became part of Islamic doctrine and practice, since Muhammad's attitude is recorded in the Koran, and he is the model to be imitated in all things.

This *hadith* makes clear the meaning of this Koranic verse which serves as the basis for *taqiya*, namely, that it is licit to affirm one thing with our lips while believing another in our heart.

Although *taqiya* saw wide use by Shia Muslims living in Sunni-dominated lands, it became common to all Muslim sects. For instance Jarīr al-Ṭabarī (d. 923), "who made a distinct contribution to the consolidation of Sunni thought during the 9th century,"[277] commented: "If anyone is compelled and professes unbelief with his tongue, while his heart contradicts him, to escape his enemies, no blame falls on him, because God takes his servants as their hearts believe."[278]

Ismail ibn Kathir (1300–1373), also a Sunni scholar, commented on the same verse (16:106):

> **Allah's Wrath Against the Apostate, Except for the One Who Is Forced Into Disbelief. . . .**
>
> This is an exception in the case of one who utters statements of disbelief and verbally agrees with the Mushrikin [idolaters] because he is forced to do so by the beatings and abuse to which he is subjected, but his heart refuses to accept what he is saying, and he is, in reality, at peace with his faith in Allah and His Messenger. The scholars agreed that if a person is forced into disbelief, it is permissible for him to either go along with them in the interests of self-preservation, or to refuse.[279]

---

276. Ali ibn Ahmad al-Wahidi, *Kitab Asbab al-Nuzul*, trans. Mokrane Guezzou, *AlTafsir.com*, accessed Apr. 3, 2018, http://altafsir.com/Tafasir.asp?tMadhNo=0&tTafsirNo=86&tSoraNo=16&tAyahNo=106&tDisplay=yes&UserProfile=0&LanguageId=2.

277. David Waines, s.v. "Al-Ṭabarī, Muslim scholar," *Encyclopedia Britannica*, accessed Apr. 3, 2018, https://www.britannica.com/biography/al-Tabari.

278. Jarīr al-Ṭabarī comment on 16:108. In *Tafsir*, Bulak 1323, xxiv, 122, quoted in R. Strothman, s.v. "Taqiya," in *E.J. Brill's First Encyclopedia of Islam 1913–1936*, ed. M. Th. Houtsma et al. (New York: E.J. Brill, 1993), 3:628.

279. Ismail ibn Kathir, *Quran Tafsir*, accessed Apr. 6, 2018, http://www.qtafsir.com/index.php?option=com_content&task=view&id=2933.

Other Koran verses cited to justify *taqiya* are these from the third *sura*: "Let not the believers take for friends or helpers unbelievers rather than believers: if any do that, in nothing will there be help from Allah, except by way of precaution, that ye may guard yourselves from them. But Allah cautions you (to remember) Himself; for the final goal is to Allah. Say: Whether ye hide what is in your hearts or reveal it, Allah knows it all" (3:28–29).

Al-Ṭabarī comments: "If you [Muslims] are under their [infidels'] authority, fearing for yourselves, behave loyally to them, with your tongue, while harboring inner animosity for them."[280]

A School of Amorality

While we could cite other passages on *taqiya* from the Koran (for example, 2:225; 8:30; 9:3; 10:21; 40:28; and 66:2) and from the *hadith*, those quoted suffice to show that this practice is based on principles contrary to revealed morals and natural law, namely, that the end justifies the means, and that external acts (words, attitudes, commitments, oaths, etc.) can be separated from internal acts of the intellect and will.

In short, since what we believe and accept as good and true ceases to be the guide to our action, this practice leads to complete amorality, even cynicism. There is no longer a correlation between what we think and desire, and what we say and do. This is the very definition of a lie.

Indeed, deception and lying are in keeping with the purely legalistic principles of Islamic morality, whereby what determines the goodness or wickedness of an act is not its nature but rather the arbitrary will of God. Thus, if the Koran and *hadith* allow dissimulation and deception, *taqiya*, this is the will of Allah, and, therefore, good, even though lying is intrinsically evil under the natural moral law—the law which Saint Paul teaches was inscribed by God on the hearts of all men (see Rom. 2:15), including Muslims.

---

280. Raymond Ibrahim, "Islam's doctrines of deception," *MEForum.org*, Oct. 1, 2008, https://www .meforum.org/articles/2009/islam-s-doctrines-of-deception.

No One Is Dispensed From
Obeying Natural Law

Man performs free acts in his capacity as a rational being endowed with intellect and will. As such, he has the power to do or not do these actions as he so chooses.

Nevertheless, these acts are also subject to rules of behavior established by the Creator. This supreme ordering of human conduct, this *moral blueprint* inscribed by the Creator in man's very nature, is called *natural law.*

This natural law reflects in man the eternal law, which is simply the Divine Wisdom ruling the universe and establishing a supreme order and governance of all things, visible and invisible, living and inanimate.

As its name indicates, natural law flows from human nature. It is that law which man can know with the light of reason without the aid of Divine Revelation, since God inscribed it in the depths of all hearts as Saint Paul teaches. ("For when the Gentiles who do not have the law by nature observe the prescriptions of the law, they are a law for themselves even though they do not have the law. They show that the demands of the law are written in their hearts, while their conscience also bears witness and their conflicting thoughts accuse or even defend them" [Rom. 2:14–15]). Since it is inscribed on the hearts of all men, it is the same for everyone, everywhere and throughout time. Thus, natural law is *universal.* It is also *immutable*; time does not affect it. Moreover, there is *no dispensation* from natural law. All men must observe it. Lastly, it is *perceptible* and *knowable* by all men who have reached the age of reason.

Man's conscience assures him of the existence of this law when it declares certain actions good and others bad. Its existence is further attested to by the common witness of all peoples, for they are unanimous in making the distinction between good and evil.

TFP Committee on American Issues, *Defending a Higher Law* (Spring Grove, Penn.: The American TFP, 2004), 142.

Islam is fundamentally egalitarian. It has no ordained priesthood, sacraments, or sacrifice. It has no magisterium.

CHAPTER 22

Islam and Egalitarianism

An Egalitarian Religion

Islam is an egalitarian religion. The conception of a hierarchy and governing authority like that of the Catholic Church—with its teaching, ministerial, and ruling authorities—is irreconcilable with Allah's imprescriptible rights and absolute dominion over men.

In Islam, every believer communicates directly with Allah and is taught directly by him through the Koran or the words and deeds of Muhammad as shown in the *Sunna*. Consequently, there is no central authority with magisterial power, such as the pope in Catholicism, to resolve doubts and make dogmas explicit.

No Priesthood, Sacraments, or Sacrifice

As already mentioned, Islam is a naturalistic religion that "rejects everything supernatural, any participation through grace in God's own life."[281] Consequently, Islam has no priesthood, since it knows neither sacrifice nor sacraments.

Thus, knowing nothing of sacramental life, sanctifying grace, and the Christian dogma of atonement, Islam has no need for a priestly ministry. Furthermore, a clergy especially ordained to direct divine worship is meaningless to a faith without a liturgy or religious ceremonies.

As for the spiritual and pastoral care of souls, Islam denies its necessity since everything comes directly from Allah.

The imams who direct the prayers and preach at mosques have nothing similar to the sacramental character a priest receives at his ordination. Accordingly, they do not differ substantially from other believers except in their degree of Koranic learning, which anyone can acquire.[282]

Is the Caliph a "Pope"?

Western politicians and Orientalists, especially in the nineteenth

---

281. Jomier, *The Bible and the Qur'an*, 35.
282. See Lammens, *Islam Beliefs*, 103–5.

century, sought to present the caliph (a dignity abolished in 1924 by Mustapha Kemal Ataturk), as a kind of Muslim pope, a religious leader with final doctrinal and disciplinary authority, which facilitated political maneuvers and compromises. However, the idea of a pope contradicts the Muslim notion of God's absolute omnipotence.

In *The Oxford Dictionary of Islam*, John L. Esposito confirms this fact in his definition of caliph and caliphate as a "Term adopted by dynastic rulers of the Muslim world, referring to the successor to the Prophet Muhammad as the political-military ruler of Muslim community. . . . It is not a spiritual office, but the institution was imbued with political and religious symbolism, particularly regarding the unity of the Muslim community."[283]

Father Lammens points out that the caliph is "not a Pontiff, but the lay defender of the *Sharia*. . . . He is *Vicar* of the Prophet, but in temporal matters alone."[284]

---

283. Esposito, "Caliph/Caliphate," *Oxford Dictionary of Islam*, 49.
284. Lammens, *Islam Beliefs,* 108. (Emphasis in the original.)

CHAPTER 23

Islam's Origins in a Judeo-Christian Heretical Sect

Influences of Anti-Trinitarian Heresies

From its earliest days, Islam was seen to have been influenced by the anti-Trinitarian heresies that exploded in the Middle East between the third and fifth centuries: Nestorianism, Arianism, Monophysitism, Ebionism, Modalism, and others.[285]

Speaking about these heresies, the distinguished theologian Fr. Reginald Garrigou-Lagrange, OP includes the doctrines of Muhammad among them:

> In the third century Sabellius proposed his Modalism, so called because in God he did not admit distinct persons but only accidental modes....
>
> In the seventh century Modalism was revived by the Mohammedans. Mohammed admitted the existence of only God the Creator, Allah, who alone was to be adored, excluding the Trinity of persons. The Islamic formula of prayer, "There is no God but Allah, and Mohammed is His prophet," was in Mohammed's mind a negation of the Trinity and contained within it the total apostasy from the Christian faith, denying at the same time the dogmas of the incarnation and redemption by Christ, who was no more than one of the prophets. Those who now write about the mysticism of Islam, should note this essential difference between Islam and Christianity.[286]

The Testimony of a Church Father

Saint John Damascene (ca. 676–749), a Church Father who lived in a Muslim environment and knew Koranic doctrine well, deals with Islam at length in his book, *On Heresies*. We highlight this essential section:

---

285. In one way or the other, these heresies denied the Holy Trinity and that Jesus Christ is true God and true man, and, as God, He is of the same essence of the Father and consubstantial with Him.

286. Reginald Garrigou-Lagrange, OP, *The Trinity and God the Creator*, trans. Rev. Frederic C. Eckhoff, OP (St. Louis: B. Herder, 1952), intro., no. 3, 18, https://www.ewtn.com /library/theology/trinity.htm.

101. There is also the superstition of the *Ishmaelites* [Arabs] which to this day prevails and keeps people in error, being a forerunner of the Antichrist. . . . From that time to the present a false prophet named Mohammed has appeared in their midst. This man, after having chanced upon the Old and New Testaments and likewise, it seems, having conversed with an Arian monk, devised his own heresy.[287]

Later, the saint deals with the charge that Christians "associate" other gods with Allah: "Moreover, they call us *Hetaeriasts*, or *Associators*, because, they say, we introduce an associate with God by declaring Christ to be the Son of God and God."[288]

The saint adroitly answers this argument:

We say to them in rejoinder: The Prophets and the Scriptures have delivered this to us, and you, as you persistently maintain, accept the prophets. So, if we wrongly declare Christ to be the Son of God, it is they who taught this and handed it on to us. But some of them say that it is by misinterpretation that we have represented the Prophets as saying such things, while others say that the Hebrews hated us and deceived us by writing in the name of the Prophets so that we might be lost.[289]

Saint John Damascene again refutes the falsehood:

And again we say to them: "As long as you say that Christ is the Word of God and Spirit [see 4:171], why do you accuse us of being Hetaeriasts [Associators]? For the word, and the spirit, is inseparable from that in which it naturally has existence. Therefore, if the Word of God is in God, then it is obvious that He is God. If, however, He is outside of God, then, according to you, God is without word and without spirit. Consequently, by avoiding the introduction of an associate with God you have mutilated Him. It would be far better for you to say that He has an associate than to mutilate Him, as if you were dealing with a stone or a piece of wood or some other inanimate object. Thus, you speak untruly when you call us Hetaeri-

---

287. St. John Damascene, *On Heresies*, 153.
288. Ibid., 155.
289. Ibid., 155–6.

asts; we retort by calling you Mutilators of God." [290]

Elements From Judaism and Christianity in the Koran

While many later authors insisted on the Koran's similarities with heresies, especially Arianism, others emphasized the influence that Judaism had on it.

From the mid-nineteenth century to the present, a large number of scholars have concluded that Islam is a Judeo-Christian heresy, which would explain the presence of unconventional elements of Christianity and Judaism in the Koran.[291]

For example, the Koran invokes the witness of a Jew to convince the unbelievers that the message of Muhammad comes from God:

> "See ye? If (this teaching) be from Allah, and ye reject it, and a witness from among the Children of Israel testifies to its similarity (with earlier scripture), and has believed while ye are arrogant, (how unjust ye are!) truly, Allah guides not a people unjust" (46:10).
>
> "If thou wert in doubt as to what We have revealed unto thee, then ask those who have been reading the Book from before thee: the Truth hath indeed come to thee from thy Lord: so be in no wise of those in doubt" (10:94).

At the same time, the Koran accuses other Jews of perverting the Scriptures, being unfaithful to Moses, rejecting the Gospel, and trying to kill Jesus (for Muslims, Our Lord did not die on the cross):

> Of the Jews there are those who displace words from their (right) places, and say: "We hear and we disobey"; and "hear what is not heard"; and "ra'ina" [an insult]; with a twist of their tongues and a slander to Faith. . . . Allah hath cursed them for their unbelief; and but few of them will believe (4:46).
>
> But because of their breach of their covenant, We cursed them, and made their hearts grow hard; they change the words from their (right) places and forget a good part of the message that was sent them, nor wilt

---

290. Ibid, 156.

291. Patricia Crone writes, "[M]any scholars have come away from the Qur'ān with the impression that Jewish Christianity must have played a role in its formation." She then mentions the names of ten scholars that upheld this thesis. Crone, "Jewish Christianity and the Qur'ān," 227.

thou cease to find them barring a few (5.13).

That they said (in boast), "We killed Christ Jesus the son of Mary, the Messenger of Allah; but they killed him not, nor crucified him, but so it was made to appear to them (4:157).

Say O People of the Scripture! Ye have naught (of guidance) till ye observe the Torah and the Gospel and that which was revealed unto you from your Lord (MP 5:68).

Then will Allah say: "O Jesus the son of Mary!...I did restrain the Children of Israel from (violence to) thee" (5:110).

It would seem that, for the Koran, there are two types of Jews: the good, who were to be consulted, and the bad, who were cursed by God. Two verses that seem to show this follow. The first, concerns the bad faction: "O ye who believe! If ye listen to a faction among the People of the Book, they would (indeed) render you apostates after ye have believed!" (3:100). Whereas the verse related to the good group reads: "Of the people of Moses there is a section who guide and do justice in the light of truth" (7:159).

Accusation Against Christians: Divinization of Jesus

Regarding Christians, the Koran accuses them of having divinized Our Lord Jesus Christ and the Blessed Mother. This accusation results from Islam's fundamental dogma, which is a negative one: its rejection of the Blessed Trinity.[292]

Neither True Jews nor Christians, but *Judeo-Nazarenes*

Therefore, the Koran condemns some Jews for hiding or covering up part of the truth. It also accuses them of rejecting the Gospel and Jesus, the Messias (the Koran uses "Messias" eleven times, although not in the Christian meaning).

We suggest that those Jews condemned by the Koran are the ones who did not accept the role of Our Lord Jesus Christ and the Gospel; for although the Koran does not accept Jesus' divinity, it does recognize Him as a Prophet, Messenger, and Messias.

On the other hand, the Jews whom the Koran praises as being a

---

292. See Chapter 15: The Koran, an Anti-Trinitarian Book.

"guide in the light of Truth," are those who accepted Jesus and His Gospel. In other words, they were both Jews and Christians at the same time:

    a) Like the other Jews, they accepted the Torah (Pentateuch) and the rabbinic tradition (Talmud);

    b) But, unlike rabbinic Jews, they also accepted the Gospel and Jesus Christ;

    c) However, in contradiction with faithful Christians, they denied the Trinity and the divinity of Christ, accepting him only as a Messenger;

    d) Therefore, they were a special category of "Christians" belonging to a heretical Judeo-Christian sect.

This heretical sect, scattered throughout the Arabian Peninsula and existing in Mecca during Muhammad's time, is known as the *Judeo-Nazarenes*.

CHAPTER 24
The Judeo-Nazarenes or Ebionites

To understand the appearance of the Judeo-Christian sect known as the *Nazarenes*, we must look back to the second century before Christ. Then, the Maccabees resisted to the Temple's profanation by Antiochus Epiphanes and part of the Jewish people, including the High Priest Alcimus, during the Hellenization of the Faith of Abraham (see 1 Macc., especially 1:21–4; 7:2–25).

Messianic Mysticism
A faction of the Jews, who opposed both Hellenization and the unfaithful High Priest Alcimus, fell into a Messianic mysticism, ever further removed from orthodoxy.[293] They began believing in the coming of a "kingdom of God" on earth, after the "sons of light" would absolutely defeat the "sons of darkness." This was recorded in the books found in the Qumran caves.

For them, two Messias would come: a political chief from the house of David and a religious one from that of Aaron. Salvation would be collective rather than individual, coming to the whole Jewish people as a group.

Father Gallez points out, "All the essential features of Messianism are there. Later they converged and developed the image of the implacable warrior king and conqueror of the earth; David's kingship is then taken as the image of the universal Kingdom to come: God's Anointed One will extend his dominion over the world and dye the earth with the blood of the wicked."[294]

To them, the future Messias would be a temporal king who would not only restore Israel but also extend its dominion over the world.

Also, they promoted Jewish liberation from the Roman yoke in Palestine, and, thus, actively participated in the revolts.

---

293. In this section we follow closely Father Gallez's monumental work, *Le Messie et son prophète*. Our use of the word messianic is that seen in Jewish messianism throughout the centuries. It is not that of today's Messianic Judaism which accepts the Blessed Trinity and tries to bridge the gap between Jews and Christians.
294. Gallez, *Le Messie et son prophète*, 1:130.

A Great Battle, a Rude Slaughter

After the coming of Christ, they accepted Jesus, but only as a prophet, not as God. To avoid confusion, we will refer to this sect as the *Judeo-Nazarenes*.[295]

Contrary to the Gospel, in which Jesus commanded us to love our enemies (see Matt. 5:43–4), they preached that not only should one's enemies be defeated, but also hated and physically destroyed.

The War Scroll is an example of Messianic Judeo-Nazarene literature. Found in the Qumran Caves, it showcases their thinking: "Then at the time appointed by God, His great excellence shall shine for all the times of e[ternity;] for peace and blessing, glory and joy, and long life for all Sons of Light. On the day when the Kittim [the Sons of Darkness] fall there shall be a battle and horrible carnage before the God of Israel, for it is a day appointed by Him from ancient times as a battle of annihilation for the Sons of Darkness."[296]

Commenting on the prophecies of Isaiah at 11:1–5, another Dead Sea Scroll (1Q161, col. 3, frags. 8–10) gives us the Nazarene concept of the Messias: "[This saying refers to the Branch of] David, who will appear in the Las[t Days, . . .] [. . .] his [ene]mies; and God will support him with [a spirit of] strength [. . . and God will give him] a glorious [th]rone, [a sacred] crown, and elegan[t] garments. [. . . He will put a scepter] in his hand, and he will rule over all the G[ent]iles, even Magog [and his army . . . al]l the peoples his sword will control."[297]

The Witness of Church Fathers

Fathers of the Church and ancient ecclesiastical writers made numerous references to this sect but often confused its name, sometimes calling its adherents *Ebionites*, other times calling them *Nazarenes*.

Ebionite comes from the Hebrew *ébionîm*, from *ébyôn*, meaning poor. The Judeo-Nazarenes called themselves poor. Therefore, when the Fathers of the Church refer to Ebionites or to Nazarenes, they

---

295. See Pritz, *Nazarene Jewish Christianity*.

296. Michael O. Wise, Martin G. Abegg, Jr., and Edward M. Cook, *The Dead Sea Scrolls: A New Translation*, rev. ed. (New York: Harper Collins, 2005), 148. [Ed. After 2,000 years, fragments are all that remain of the Dead Sea Scrolls. Scholars piece them together and interpret where letters or words are missing. These interpretations are shown in brackets.]

297. Ibid., 238.

are usually talking about the same heretical movement.[298]

We know the main doctrines and practices of this movement through the writings of the Church Fathers and ancient writers.

■ Saint Irenaeus (d. ca. 202):

> Those who are called Ebionites. . . . they practice circumcision, persevere in the observance of those customs which are enjoined by the law, and are so Judaic in their style of life, that they even adore Jerusalem as if it were the house of God.[299]

■ Eusebius of Caesarea (263–339):

> The ancients quite properly called these men Ebionites [poor], because they held poor and mean opinions concerning Christ. For they considered him a plain and common man. . . . In their opinion the observance of the ceremonial law [of Moses] was altogether necessary, on the ground that they could not be saved by faith in Christ alone and by a corresponding life.[300]

■ Saint Jerome writes of the Judeo-Nazarenes:

a) Neither Christians nor Jews

> Why do I speak of the Ebionites, who make pretensions to the name of Christian? In our own day, there exists a sect among the Jews. . . . The adherents to this sect are known commonly as Nazarenes; they believe in Christ the Son of God, born of the Virgin Mary. . . . But while they desire to be both Jews and Christians, they are neither the one nor the other.[301]

b) Gospel of the Hebrews

> The Gospel that the Nazarenes and Ebionites use . . . and which many call the authentic Gospel of Matthew [the Gospel of the Hebrews].[302]

---

298. Indeed, Father Gallez explains, "'Ebionites' is an adjective that means 'poor.' That is how the Nazarenes called themselves. But certain Greek-Latin Fathers of Church turned this adjective into a name. And at times they spoke of certain Gnostic groups as being 'Nazarenes' (which some of them indeed became, with the passing of time)." Édouard-Marie Gallez, correspondence with author, Mar. 25, 2011.

299. St. Irenaeus, *Adversus Haeresis*, bk. 1, ch. 26, no. 2.

300. Eusebius, *Church History*, bk. 3, ch. 27, nos. 1–2.

301. St. Jerome, *Letter 112 to Augustine*, ch. 4, no. 13.

302. St. Jerome, *Commentary on St. Matthew*, 12:13.

- Saint Augustine writes of them:

> 9. The Nazarenes, although they confess that Christ is the Son of God, they nevertheless observe the precepts of the Old Law, which the Christians learned by apostolic tradition to consider no longer in a material sense, but in a spiritual one.

> 10. The Ebionites even say Christ is nothing but a man. They observe the Commandments of the law in a material sense, that is to say, the circumcision and the other burdens which the New Testament abrogated.[303]

The Ebionites are also mentioned by Saint Epiphanius (d. 403), Tertullian (d. 220), Origen (d. 254), and others.

Summarizing Judeo-Nazarene or Ebionite Doctrine

In short, the Judeo-Nazarenes or Ebionites had a Messianic conception of salvation. They believed in the collective salvation of the entire Jewish people, not a salvation that needed to be worked out by each individual on his own, through personal effort, in the steady practice of virtue.

They considered themselves instruments of God to destroy the "Sons of Darkness" by violent means, physically annihilating them. They wanted a Messianic Kingdom in which they would dominate the whole world.

They accepted the Old Testament and rabbinical commentaries (Talmud) and continued to follow the Old Law. Nevertheless, at the same time, they called themselves Christians, although they did not accept Christ's divinity.

They followed the apocryphal Gospel of the Hebrews while borrowing elements from other apocryphal gospels.

Nasârâ: Are They Judeo-Nazarenes or Christians?

The Koran's reference to Judeo-Nazarenes is obscured by the fact that many translators and commentators consider its fourteen references to *Nasârâ* to mean Christians. However, Fr. Maurice Borrmans, Professor of the Pontifical Institute for Arabic and Islamic Studies of Rome, states that, "Arab Christians have always been

---

303. St. Augustine, *Letter on the heresies to Quodvultdeus*, nos. 9–10.

called *Masîhiyyûn*, which translates as 'Christians' or 'Messianists.'"[304]

Nasârâ refers more appropriately to the Christian Jews known as Nazarene Jews or Ebionites. It does not mean true Christians. Were *Nasârâ* to mean faithful Christians, it would lead to glaring contradictions in the Koran.

For example, in 5:51, the Koran warns Muslims not to be friends with Jews and Christians: "O you who have believed, do not take the Jews and the Christians as allies. They are [in fact] allies of one another." (SI 5:51).

Further down, in 5:82, the Koran says that Christians are Muslims' best friends: "And you will find the nearest of them in affection to the believers those who say, 'We are Christians.' That is because they are priests and monks and because they are not arrogant (SI 5:82).

This contradiction is only resolved if the statement "We are Christians," is substituted by "We are Nazarenes," as some Koran translations do, such as Qaribullah and Darwish: "You will find that the most people in enmity to the believers are the Jews and idolaters [Christians], and that the nearest in affection to the believers are those who say: 'We are Nazarenes.' That is because amongst them there are priests and monks; and because they are not proud" (QD 5:82).

304. Maurice Borrmans, "Regards coraniques sur les chrétiens," *Études* 401 (2004/12): 646, https://www.cairn.info/revue-etudes-2004-12-page-645.htm.

CHAPTER 25

Muhammad's Mission Confirmed by a Judeo-Nazarene

According to Islamic tradition, Muhammad's prophetism began in the cave of Hira. It was his custom to go there to fast and pray, and it was there that he supposedly had his first extraordinary experience. Aisha, his favorite wife, describes it in vivid language, in a narrative found in the *Sahih Bukhari*.

The Angel Subjugates Muhammad

"He [Muhammad] used to go in seclusion in the cave of Hira where he used to worship (Allah alone). . . . Suddenly the Truth descended upon him while he was in the cave of Hira. The angel [Gabriel] came to him and asked him to read. The Prophet replied, 'I do not know how to read'" (SB 3).

Then the founder of Islam struggled with the angel, which is similar to the story of Jacob (Gen. 32:22–32). However, unlike Jacob, Muhammad lost his fight.

Aisha continues: "The Prophet added, 'The angel caught me (forcefully) and pressed me so hard that I could not bear it anymore. He then released me and again asked me to read and I replied, 'I do not know how to read'" (SB 3).

Then the angel seized him a second and third time, always asking him to read in the name of Allah. When the extraordinary phenomenon ceased, Muhammad was very disturbed and, returning home, went to Khadija, his first wife, saying: "'Cover me! Cover me!' They covered him till his fear was over and after that he told her everything that had happened and said, 'I fear that something may happen to me.' Khadija replied, 'Never! By Allah, Allah will never disgrace you. You keep good relations with your kith and kin, help the poor and the destitute, serve your guests generously and assist the deserving, calamity-afflicted ones'" (SB 3).

Consulting a Judeo-Nazarene Priest

To reassure him, his wife took him to consult their common relative, Waraqa bin Naufal.[305] Why did they place such confidence in the opinion of that relative?

Aisha's narrative continues: "Khadija then accompanied him to her cousin Waraqa bin Naufal bin Asad bin 'Abdul 'Uzza, who, during the pre-Islamic Period became a Christian and used to write the writing with Hebrew letters. He would write from the Gospel in Hebrew. . . . He [Waraqa] was an old man who had lost his eyesight. Khadija said to Waraqa, 'Listen to the story of your nephew, O my cousin!' Waraqa asked, 'O my nephew! What have you seen?' Allah's Messenger described whatever he had seen" (SB 3).

The Christian Priest Likens Muhammad to Moses

Apprised of what had happened, Waraqa gives his assessment: "Waraqa said, 'This is the same one who keeps the secrets (angel Gabriel) whom Allah had sent to Moses. I wish I were young and could live up to the time when your people would turn you out'" (SB 3).

Now Moses is the prophet par excellence. God spoke to him "face-to-face" (Exod. 33:11) and established His covenant with the Chosen People through him (see Exod. 19:24). By saying that the angel whom God sent to Moses was the same one who spoke to Muhammad, Waraqa was suggesting that Muhammad's prophetism was in the same line as that of Moses, who delivered the Hebrew people.

Aisha's text continues: "Allah's Messenger asked, 'Will they drive me out?' Waraqa replied in the affirmative and said, 'Anyone (man) who came with something similar to what you have brought was treated with hostility; and if I should remain alive till the day when you will be turned out then I would support you strongly.' But after a few days, Waraqa died and the Divine Inspiration was also paused for a while" (SB 3).

Judeo-Nazarenes in Mecca

Fr. Joseph Azzi, a Lebanese Catholic priest and an expert on Islam's origins, studied the ancient Muslim historians and chroniclers for many years to answer this question: Who was Waraqa, the

---

305. See Muhammad's genealogy in Joseph Azzi, *Le prêtre et le prophète, aux sources du coran*, trans. Maurice S. Garnier (Paris: Maisonneuve et Larose, 2001), ch. 1.

"Christian priest" and relative of both Muhammad and his first wife Khadija, who played such a vital role in the emergence of Islam?

Using a pseudonym, in 1979, Father Azzi published the results of his research, in Arabic. They were reprinted thirteen times. Twenty years later, his book was translated into French and English, and published with the author's name.[306]

Father Azzi explains that according to Ibn Ishaq (d. 768), who wrote the first biography of the founder of Islam, Muhammad, his first wife, Khadija, and Waraqa were descendants of Qussayy ibn Kilāb ibn Murrah. In the middle of the fifth century, this tribal chieftain emigrated to Mecca and imposed the dominion of his Quraysh clan on the city. He was a monotheist and fought idolatry.

The branch from which Khadija and Waraqa descended remained rich and powerful, while the branch from which Muhammad was born had fallen into poverty. However, both family branches were connected to the Judeo-Nazarenes.

Judeo-Nazarenes in Arabia: Ancient Historians

Ancient Islamic historians attest to the presence of Judeo-Nazarenes in Arabia and even in the Quraysh tribe. Waraqa was one of them.

Father Azzi writes:

> The historical records on Islam reveal that in this Hijaz area [Mecca region] of central Arabia there were several groups of Arabs who embraced the Nosrania faith [the Judeo-Nazarene faith]. Included among the individual converts were some members of the Quraysh tribe. Standing out on this list is Abd al-Uzzah, son of Qussayy [ancestor of Muhammad, Khadija, and Waraqa]. The historian al-Yaʿqubi alludes to this fact by writing, "Among Arabs converted to Nosrania, there a group of Quraysh, of Banu-Assad son of Abd al-Uzzah, and Waraqa, son of Nawfal, son of Assad."[307]

So Waraqa was a Judeo-Nazarene scholar who translated the Gospel of the Hebrews—the only one accepted by Judeo-Nazarenes—into Arabic. According to the *hadith* compiler Muslim ibn al-Hajjaj (d. 875), "[H]e used to write books in Arabic and, therefore, wrote Injil

---

306. See Azzi, *Le prêtre et le prophète*.

307. Joseph Azzi, *The Priest and the Prophet*, trans. Maurice Saliba, ed. David Bentley (Los Angeles: Pen, 2005), 4.

[the Gospel] in Arabic" (SM 160a). Similarly, ninth century historian Abu al-Faraj al-Isfahani wrote, "Waraqa wrote from the Hebrew Gospel. He wrote in Hebrew what he wanted from the Gospel."[308]

How would a Judeo-Christian Arab have learned Hebrew so well? In fact, Islamic tradition presents him as a Christian priest.[309] So it was a Judeo-Nazarene (Ebionite) priest, who confirmed the mission of Muhammad as, indeed, two other heretical Christian priests had done before him, the monk Bahira and Father Nestorius.[310]

Now if both Khadija and Muhammad had so much confidence in the priest Waraqa, it is highly probable that they shared his Judeo-Nazarene beliefs. Even the Koran itself suggests this.

The Koran's whole view of Christianity and classical Judaism fits into the Judeo-Nazarene doctrine we described earlier. Significantly, like the Judeo-Nazarenes, the Koran never refers to "Gospels" in the plural form, but always in the singular, "Gospel" (Injil), as if there were only one. For example, the Koran says, "We sent after them Jesus the son of Mary, and bestowed on him *the Gospel*" (57:27).

Another indication that both Muhammad and Khadija were Judeo-Nazarenes is that the founder of Islam remained married to Khadija for 25 years, in spite of the fact that she was already mature when she married him, having been married and widowed twice before.[311] Muhammad only adopted polygamy and divorce, after Khadija's death. This suggests that his first marriage had been a Christian one, monogamous and indissoluble.

To gauge the fundamental role Waraqa played in Muhammad's mission, let us consider this significant quote from Bukhari:

> But after a few days Waraqa died and the Divine Inspiration was also paused for a while and the Prophet became so sad as we have heard that he intended several times to throw himself from the tops of high mountains and every time he went up the top of a mountain in order

---

308. Abu al-Faraj al-Isfahani, *Kitab al-Aghani* (*The Book of Songs*), 3:114, quoted in Azzi, *Le prêtre et le prophète*, 40, note 79.

309. As to Waraqa being a Christian priest, in addition to Azzi above, one Islamic site states: "Waraqa bin Nufail who was a pious Christian Priest." *Ilm ul Qur'an (Introduction to Holy Qur'an)*, updated Aug. 29, 2006, http://www.al-adaab.org/Quran_Majid/ilm_ul_quran.html .

310. See Muslimpath.com, "Muhammad(s). The Prophet Meets the Christian Priests!!" accessed Mar. 1, 2018, http://www.muslimpath.com/english/index.php?page=meeladdet23.

311. See Yasin T. al-Jibouri, "Khadijah, Daughter of Khuwaylid, Wife of Prophet Muhammad," *Al-Islam.org*, accessed Feb. 28, 2018, https://www.al-islam.org/articles/khadijah-daughter -khuwaylid-wife-prophet-muhammad-yasin-t-al-jibouri.

to throw himself down, Gabriel would appear before him and say, "O Muhammad! You are indeed Allah's Messenger in truth" whereupon his heart would become quiet and he would calm down and would return home. And whenever the period of the coming of the inspiration used to become long, he would do as before, but when he used to reach the top of a mountain, Gabriel would appear before him and say to him what he had said before (SB 6982).

In summary, the hypothesis of Muhammad's connection with the Judeo-Nazarenes makes the Koran more intelligible, especially regarding its references to the Blessed Trinity, Jesus Christ, the Virgin Mary, and the conquering Islamic Messianism.

Waraqa, Chief of the Nazarenes

Father Gallez states:

> "Waraqa . . . the sources are not clear if he was an Arab or not. . . . Moreover, being related to Muhammad as well as the rich widow merchant Khadija, he officiated at their marriage. What explains best the situation is that Waraqa was of Jewish (Nazarene) origin on his mother's side, and Arab on his father's—thus the lack of precision in the traditions on how to classify him."

Gallez, *Le Messie et son prophète*, 2:132–3.

As to Waraqa being a Nazarene, Fr. Joseph Azzi quotes Ibn Hisham: "The biographer Ibn Hisham said of the priest Waraqa that 'he belonged to the religion of Moses, before embracing that of Jesus.' In other words, that he was a Jew, and then became a Nazarene.

Ibn Hisham, Al-Sira al Nabawiya, [Life of the Prophet] 1:203, quoted in *Le prêtre et le prophète*, 28.

Father Azzi adds, "According to Ibn Hisham, 'Waraqa ibn Nawfal was the priest and chief of the Nazarenes. . . . Waraqa was the head of the Nazarene Church in Mecca during the days of Abd al Muttalib [Muhammad's grandfather] and for a short period during those of Muhammad.'"

Ibid., 43, note 94.

Non-Islamic Contemporary Documents

In 1977, Patricia Crone and Michael Cook published a scholarly study on the beginnings of Islam which had enormous repercussions. In it, they cite contemporary documents of non-Islamic origin which shed light on how contemporaries saw the origin and progress of the new religion.

The first document they quote was written around 634, probably in Palestine, and is titled *Doctrina Iacobi*. It claims that Muhammad preached the coming of the Messias: "A false prophet has appeared among the Saracens . . . They say that the prophet has appeared coming with the Saracens, and is proclaiming the advent of the anointed one who is to come."[312]

Another telling document is the *Secrets of Rabbi Simon ben Yohay*, a Jewish apocalypse of a mystical nature written in the mid-eighth century. This apocalypse presents a messianic vision of the advancing conquests of Islam. Addressing the Muslim conquest of Palestine it states: "Do not fear, son of man, for the Holy One, blessed be He, only brings the kingdom of Ishmael in order to save you from this wickedness. He raises up over them a Prophet according to His will and will conquer the land for them and they will come and restore it in greatness, and there will be great terror between them and the sons of Esau."[313]

This text confirms what is said in the *Doctrina Iacobi*, that the Islamic prophet Muhammad preached the coming of the Jewish Messias. It is also evidence that in Islam's early days there were Jews who viewed it favorably.

Crone and Cook cite another document that is the first articulated narrative of Muhammad's career and perhaps the first non-Islamic source to mention his name. It was written ca. 660 and is attributed to the Armenian Bishop Sebeos:

> They [Jews] set out into the desert and came to Arabia, among the children of Ishmael; they sought their help, and explained to them that they were kinsmen ac-

---

312. Patricia Crone and Michael Cook, *Hagarism: The Making of the Islamic World* (Cambridge: Cambridge University Press, 1977), 3, https://archive.org/stream/Hagarism/Hagarism;%20The%20Making%20of%20the%20Islamic%20World-Crone,%20Cook_djvu.txt.

313. Ibid., 4. Regarding this document, see also John C. Reeves, "Nistarot (Secrets of) R. Shimon b. Yohai," accessed Mar. 1, 2018, https://clas-pages.uncc.edu/john-reeves/research-projects/trajectories-in-near-eastern-apocalyptic/nistarot-secrets-of-r-shimon-b-yohai-2/.

cording to the Bible. Although they [the Ishmaelites] were ready to accept this close kinship, they [the Jews] nevertheless could not convince the mass of the people, because their cults were different. At this time there was an Ishmaelite called *Mahmet, a merchant*; he presented himself to them as though at God's command, as a preacher, as the way of truth, and taught them to know the God of Abraham, for he was very well informed, and very well-acquainted with the story of Moses. As the command came from on high, they all united under the authority of a single man, under a single law, and, abandoning vain cults, returned to the living God who had revealed Himself to their father Abraham. Mahmet forbade them to eat the flesh of any dead animal, to drink wine, to lie or to fornicate. He added: 'God has promised this land to Abraham and his posterity after him forever; he acted according to His promise while he loved Israel. Now you, you are the sons of Abraham and God fulfills in you the promise made to Abraham and his posterity. Only love the God of Abraham, go and take possession of your country which God gave to your father Abraham, and none will be able to resist you in the struggle, for God is with you.'[314]

The authors note that, in spite of historical anachronisms,[315] Sebeos' description correctly presents the doctrine of the Judeo-Christians who allied themselves with the Arabs at the time of Muhammad.

A study by Fr. René Dagorn confirms the opinion that the Jews taught the Arabs that they descended from Abraham through Ishmael. The book's conclusion states: "This examination, almost exclusively based on the meticulous analysis of Arabian genealogical works and the oldest Muslim tradition, leads us to formally conclude the absolute and radical non-existence of Ishmael, Hagar, his mother, and even Abraham in the pre-Islamic Arab tradition."[316]

Additionally, Father Dagorn insists that there is no basis for af-

---

314. Crone and Cook, *Hagarism*, 6–7.

315. Sebeos says the narrative is about the exodus of Jews from Edessa after its recovery by Heraclius (628), but Crone and Cook suggest that it more likely describes their flight from Persian-occupied Palestine (ca. 617).

316. René Dagorn, *La geste d'Ismael d'après l'onommastique et la tradition arabes* (Geneva: Librairie Droz, 1981), 377.

firming that, before the appearance of Islam, "the Arabs would have preserved the historical memory of a carnal and even spiritual attachment to Abraham through his Ishmaelite lineage. Even less can we start from such a basis, which in fact does not exist at all, for pseudo-theological or mystical deductions concerning the origins of Islam."[317]

---

317. Ibid.

CHAPTER 26
Islam: a Gnostic Religion?

Gnosis (Greek for *knowledge*) refers to numerous philosophical-religious systems or sects which seek perfection not by the help of Divine Grace and good works, but from the acquisition of an intuitive, non-rational knowledge of things. This intuitive Gnostic knowledge supposedly opens a new, non-sensorial reality to the perfection-seeker.

Gnostics also explain the creation of man and the Universe not as a free and sovereign act of God, but as stemming from an accident in the Godhead which caused emanations of divine particles. These divine particles, they claim, were imprisoned in matter (which for them is eternal) by the Demiurge, a bad being who some Gnostics equate with the God of the Bible.[318]

Pre-Christian Gnosticism

Gnosticism precedes Christianity and is found in Greek philosophy, especially in neo-Platonism, pagan religions of antiquity, and esoteric movements.

It also made inroads into Jewish circles. According to Jakob Josef Petuchowski (1925–1991), who taught at the Hebrew Union College, in Cincinnati, Ohio: "For some time now, the old view of Gnosticism, that it was a specifically Christian heresy, has been given up in favor of the assumption of a pre-Christian Gnosticism. It has even been claimed that the oldest documents of Christian Gnosticism *presuppose* a Jewish Gnosis in which the figure of the Redeemer has not yet acquired a central place."[319]

---

318. See TFP Committee on American Issues, *Rejecting the Da Vinci Code* (Spring Grove, Penn.: The American Society for the Defense of Tradition, Family, and Property, 2005); See also, Joseph Jacobs and Ludwig Blau, s.v. "Gnosticism," in *The Jewish Encyclopedia*, vol. 5 (New York: Funk & Wagnalls, 1903), http://www.jewishencyclopedia.com/articles/6723-gnosticism; John Arendzen, s.v. "Gnosticism," in *The Catholic Encyclopedia*, vol. 6 (New York: Robert Appleton, 1908), New Advent online edition, http://www.newadvent.org/cathen/06592a.htm; Hans Jonas, *The Gnostic Religion* (Boston: Beacon Press, 2001).

319. Jakob Josef Petuchowski, review of *Jewish Gnosticism, Merkabah Mysticism, and Talmudic Tradition*, by Gershom G. Scholem, *Commentary Magazine*, Feb. 1, 1961, https://www.commentarymagazine.com/articles/jewish-gnosticism-merkabah-mysticism-and-talmudic-tradition-by-gershom-g-scholem/.

Already in an article in the 1903 edition of *The Jewish Encyclopedia*, Joseph Jacobs and Ludwig Blau had remarked:

> There is, in general, no circle of ideas to which elements of gnosticism have been traced, and with which the Jews were not acquainted. It is a noteworthy fact that heads of gnostic schools and founders of gnostic systems are designated as Jews by the Church Fathers. Some derive all heresies, including those of gnosticism, from Judaism (Hegesippus in Eusebius, "Hist. Eccl." iv. 22; comp. Harnack, "Dogmengesch." 3d ed. i. 232, note 1). It must furthermore be noted that Hebrew words and names of God provide the skeleton for several gnostic systems.[320]

As mentioned, Gnostic systems promote a new dimension of reality that is off limits to mortal senses and is known only to those who receive the illuminations of Gnosis. It is a magic knowledge distinct from knowledge through reason. It transforms its possessor into what Gnostics call a different, perfect, or spiritual (*pneumatic*) being.

Like everything based on falsehood, Gnostic myths and theories are full of internal contradictions and veiled in obscure and complicated language. They involve a dizzying array of beings and names. The resulting confusion is at times mistaken for profundity.

Gnostic-Christian Heresies

With the advent of Christianity, Gnosticism sought to penetrate the nascent Church. Its doctrines are best known and denounced in the writings of Fathers of the Church such as Saints Irenaeus of Lyon and Epiphanius of Salamis (d. 403), and writers like Tertullian (d. 220), Hippolytus of Rome (d. ca. 235), and others.

Among the Gnostic heresies of the early Church are those of Valentinus, Basilides and Marcion, and the Docetists. The latter affirmed that Our Lord was not true God and true man, that His body was a mere appearance (*dokesis*, appearance or semblance in Greek).

Unlike the Christian doctrine that presents Original Sin as being at the origin of moral evil, the Gnostics maintained that evil comes from matter. They claim that matter imprisons the spirit, which is a divine particle that emanated from God.

---

320. Jacobs-Blau, *Gnosticism.*

In this way, the Gnostic-Christian heresies did not accept the need for redemption to satisfy divine justice offended by the sin of our first parents. Instead, they claimed that Our Lord came as a heavenly Messenger to promote Gnostic knowledge. Also, unlike Christianity, Gnostic heresies held that man's perfection and salvation did not depend on faith and good works, but on magical practices and the illumination of Gnosis.

These heresies denied that Our Lord Jesus Christ died on the cross, upholding either that He was replaced by Simon of Cyrene or that his crucifixion was only apparent, an illusion, and that Jesus was taken to Heaven and is waiting to return to earth.

Elements of Gnosticism in the Koran

The Koran does not accept Original Sin. Although it narrates the fall of Adam and Eve more or less along the lines of the third chapter of Genesis (see 2:25–36), it affirms that Allah forgave the fault of our first parents: "Then Adam received from his Lord [some] words, and He accepted his repentance. Indeed, it is He who is the Accepting of repentance, the Merciful" (SI 2:37).

In 20:117–123, the Koran speaks again of the absence of Original Sin, presenting it only as a fault provoked by the deceit of Satan that was forgiven by Allah. Verse 121 concludes: "thus did Adam disobey his Lord, and allow himself [2645] to be seduced."

Yusuf Ali comments: "2645. Adam had been given the will to choose, and he chose wrongly, and was about to be lost in the throng of the evil ones, when Allah's Grace came to his aid. His repentance was accepted, and Allah chose him for His Mercy, as stated in the next verse."[321] "But his Lord chose him (for His Grace): He turned to him, and gave him Guidance" (20:122).

Therefore, according to Islam, Adam and Eve, although they committed a fault and were expelled from the earthly Paradise, were forgiven by Allah, and, thus, no Original Sin was transmitted to their descendants. Divine forgiveness was given without need for reparation to Divine Justice, offended by sin. Muslims also believe that Adam was the first of the prophets.[322]

---

321. Yusuf Ali, *Meaning of the Noble Qur'an* (20:121), comment 2645, 213.
322. See Hadith Of The Day, "Prophet Adam (AS) – Part I," HOTD, Dec. 1, 2012, http://hadithoftheday .com/adam-part1/.

Regarding the crucifixion and death of Our Lord, the Koran agrees with the position of the Gnostic sects, especially Docetism, which taught that Jesus did not die on the cross, it only appeared that He had.

Thus we read in 4:157: "That they [the Jews] said (in boast), 'We killed Christ Jesus the son of Mary, the Messenger of Allah;' but they killed him not, nor crucified him [663], but so it was made to appear to them, and those who differ therein are full of doubts, with no (certain) knowledge, but only conjecture to follow, for of a surety they killed him not."

Yusuf Ali, in his commentary on this *ayah*, acknowledges that this was the position of the Gnostic-Christian sects:

> "663 ... The Orthodox-Christian Churches make it a cardinal point of their doctrine that his [of Jesus] life was taken on the Cross, that he died and was buried, that on the third day he rose in the body with his wounds intact, and walked about and conversed, and ate with his disciples, and was afterwards taken up bodily to heaven. This is necessary for the theological doctrine of blood sacrifice and vicarious atonement for sins, which is rejected by Islam. But some of the early Christian sects did not believe that Christ was killed on the Cross. The Basilidans believed that someone else was substituted for him. The Docetae held that Christ never had a real physical or natural body, but only an apparent or phantom body, and that his Crucifixion was only apparent, not real. The Marcionite Gospel (about A.C. 138) denied that Jesus was born, and merely said that he appeared in human form. The [Gnostic] Gospel of St. Barnabas supported the theory of substitution on the Cross. The Qur'anic teaching is that Christ was not crucified nor killed by the Jews, notwithstanding certain apparent circumstances which produced that illusion in the minds of some of his enemies; that disputations, doubts, and conjectures on such matters are vain; and that he was taken up to Allah (see 4:158 and 3:55).[323]

It seems evident that early Christian Gnosticism influenced both the Koran and Judeo-Nazarenes who appear to have influ-

---

323. Yusuf Ali, *Meaning of the Noble Qur'an* (4:157), comment 663, 65.

enced its origin.[324]

Such was the opinion of Adolph von Harnack (1851–1930), a German Lutheran theologian, historian, and specialist on Gnosis. He observed, "Islam is a transformation of the Jewish religion, itself already transformed by Judeo-Christian Gnosticism, grafted on to Arab culture."[325]

Similarly, Fr. François Jourdan characterized Islam as a "Gnostic prophetism reshaped out of real history with Mani, the 'seal of prophets.'"[326]

---

324. See Gallez, *Le Messie et son prophète*, 1:352–56; Guy G. Stroumsa, "Jewish Christianity and Islamic Origins," in *Islamic Culture, Islamic Context: Essays in Honor of Professor Patricia Crone*, ed. Behnam Sadeghi, et al. (Leiden: Brill, 2015), 72–96, https://www.academia.edu /9997797/Jewish_Christianity_and_Islamic_Origins; Mustafa Akyol, *The Islamic Jesus: How the King of the Jews Became a Prophet of the Muslims* (New York: St. Martin's, 2017) 81–103. [Kindle Edition].

325. Adolph von Harnack, *Lehrbuch der Dogmengeschichte* (Tübingen: Verlag Von J. C. B. Mohr [Paul Siebeck], 1909), 2:537. Although Harnack was a liberal theologian, he is respected as a specialist on Gnosis. We only cite him as such.

326. Vulpillières, "Les impasses du dialogue"; Mani (ca. 216–274) was the founder of Manichaeism. "Mani . . . he becomes a *gnosticus*, someone with divine knowledge and a liberating insight into things. He claimed to be the *Paraclete of the Truth*, as promised in the New Testament: the Last Prophet and Seal of the Prophets that finalized a succession of men guided by God and included figures such as Zoroaster, Hermes, Plato, Buddha, and Jesus." (*Theopedia*, s.v. "Manicheanism," accessed Mar. 20, 2018, https://www.theopedia.com/manicheanism).

Saint Thomas Aquinas, Doctor of the Church says of Muhammad: "He seduced the people by promises of carnal pleasure to which the concupiscence of the flesh goads us. His teaching also contained precepts that were in conformity with his promises, and he gave free rein to carnal pleasure."

WHAT DID THE SAINTS SAY
ABOUT ISLAM?

Saint Thomas Aquinas (1225–1274): "Those Who Place Any Faith in Muhammad's Words Believe Foolishly"

On the other hand, those who founded sects committed to erroneous doctrines proceeded in a way that is opposite to this [the way the Apostles acted]. The point is clear in the case of Muhammad. He seduced the people by promises of carnal pleasure to which the concupiscence of the flesh goads us. His teaching also contained precepts that were in conformity with his promises, and he gave free rein to carnal pleasure. In all this, as is not unexpected, he was obeyed by carnal men. As for proofs of the truth of his doctrine, he brought forward only such as could be grasped by the natural ability of anyone with a very modest wisdom. Indeed, the truths that he taught he mingled with many fables and with doctrines of the greatest falsity. He did not bring forth any signs produced in a supernatural way, which alone fittingly gives witness to divine inspiration; for a visible action that can be only divine reveals an invisibly inspired teacher of truth. On the contrary, Muhammad said that he was sent in the power of his arms—which are signs not lacking even to robbers and tyrants. What is more, no wise men, men trained in things divine and human, believed in him from the beginning. Those who believed in him were brutal men and desert wanderers, utterly ignorant of all divine teaching, through whose numbers Muhammad forced others to become his followers by the violence of his arms. Nor do divine pronouncements on the part of preceding prophets offer him any witness. On the contrary, he perverts almost all the testimonies of the Old and New Testaments by making them into fabrications of his own, as can be seen by anyone who examines his law. It was, therefore, a shrewd decision on his part to forbid his followers to read the Old and New Testaments, lest these books convict him of falsity. It is thus clear that those who place any faith in his words believe foolishly.

St. Thomas Aquinas, *Contra Gentiles*, bk. 1, ch. 6, no. 4.

Saint John Bosco (1815–1888): "Muhammad Incited People's Passions; Jesus Christ Commanded Self-Denial"

He writes in the form of a dialog between a father (F) and a son (S):

> F. Islam is a collection of maxims drawn from various religions, which, if practiced, brings about the destruction of every moral principle.
>
> S. Why did Muhammad put together this blend of various religions?
>
> F. The peoples of Arabia being in part Jews, Christians and Pagans, to obtain their adhesion he picked a part of each of their religions, and particularly those points that most favor sensual pleasures.
>
> S. What difference is there between the Catholic Church and Islam?
>
> F. The difference is huge. Muhammad established his religion with violence and weapons; Jesus Christ founded His Church with words of peace using His poor disciples. Muhammad incited people's passions; Jesus Christ commanded self-denial. Muhammad worked no miracle; Jesus Christ worked countless miracles in broad daylight and in the presence of numerous multitudes. Muhammad's doctrines are ridiculous, immoral, and corrupt; those of Jesus Christ are august, sublime and most pure. Not even one prophecy was fulfilled in Muhammad; all prophecies were fulfilled in Jesus Christ.

In short, in a certain way, the Christian Religion makes man happy in this world to later raise him to the enjoyment of heaven; Muhammad degrades and vilifies human nature, and placing all happiness in sensual pleasures, reduces man to the level of filthy animals.

St. John Bosco, *Il Cattolico istruito nella sua religione: Trattenimenti di un padre di famiglia co' suoi figliuoli secondo i besogni del tempo* (Turin: Tipografia Dir. da P. de- Agostini, 1853), vol. 2, conv. 23, 50–1, 53-6, http://www.donboscosanto.eu/download_orig/ Don_Bosco-Il_Cattolico_istruito_nella_sua_Religione-i.pdf.

Saint Alphonsus Liguori: "The Mahometan Paradise Is Only Fit for Beasts"

He [Muhammad] professes that there is but one God; but in his Alcoran he relates many trivialities unworthy of the Supreme Being, and the whole work is, in fact, filled with contradictions, as I have shown in my book on the "Truth of the Faith." Jews or Christians, he says, may be saved by the observance of their respective laws, and it is indifferent if they exchange one for the other; but hell will be forever the portion of the infidels; those who believe in one God alone will be sent there for a period not exceeding, at most, a thousand years, and then all will be received into the House of Peace, or Paradise. The Mahometan Paradise, however, is only fit for beasts; for filthy sensual pleasure is all the believer has to expect there. I pass over all the other extravagancies of the Koran, having already, in the "Truth of the Faith," treated the subject more fully.

St. Alphonsus M. Liguori, *The History of Heresies, and Their Refutation; Or, The Triumph of the Church*, trans. Rev. John T. Mullock (Dublin: James Duffy, 1847), 1:188, https://archive.org /stream/thehistoryofhere01liguuoft/thehistoryofhere01liguuoft_djvu.txt.

Saint Francis de Sales (1567–1622): "The Sect of This Great Impostor, Mohammed"

Ah! That the French are brave when they have God on their side! How valiant they are when they are devout! How happy they are to fight the infidels! . . . O France that will strike the last destructive blow "upon the sect of this great impostor, Mohammed."

Saint Francis de Sales, *Œuvres Complètes de Saint François de Sales* (Paris: Bethune, 1836), 2:412.

Saint Juan de Ribera (1532–1611): Islam Does Not Deserve to Be Called a Religion

What has been said suffices to close this article, which is so essential to your salvation; to wit, the destruction of this perverse sect of Muhammad. Because if we have proved that the end that it sets is all beastly and unworthy of man's authority; that its author was an adulterer, perjurer, robber, murderer, blasphemer, and most ignorant in human and divine letters; that the things

contained in his law are all fables in philosophy and errors in theology even for those with just a glimmer of reason; that what it teaches in terms of customs is a school
of bestial vices; that he failed to produce any proof, supernatural with miracles, or natural with reasoning to
prove his new sect but established it only with the force
of arms, violence, fiction, lies, and carnal license, then all
that remains is the fact that it is an impious, blasphemous, and vicious sect, an invention of the devil that
leads straight to hell, and does not deserve, therefore, to
be called a religion.

Francisco Pons Fuster, "El patriarca Juan de Ribera y el Catechismo para instrucción de los nuevamente convertidos de moros," *Studia Philologica Valentina*, vol. 15, n.s. 12 (2013), 209–10,
https://www.uv.es/SPhV/15/10_pons15.pdf.

Hope in the Message of Fatima

The bulk of this study was written during the centennial of the apparitions of Our Lady in Fatima, Portugal (1917–2017). Reference to these famous Marian apparitions might seem out of place in a book about Islam. However, this is not the case. The very name of the site where the apparitions occurred, *Fatima*, attests to the propriety of their inclusion in this work, since Fatima was also the name of Muhammad's favored daughter by Khadija.

One could argue that this is merely a coincidence. However, seriousness obliges us to ponder if Our Lady had something more profound in mind when choosing this remote village to deliver her message for our time.

How did this hamlet in a mountainous region of Portugal receive a name of evident Muslim origin?

Conversion of a Moorish Princess

What we know comes from a legend which, like all legends, has been embellished over the generations. However, many legends are based remotely on true history.

The tale harkens back to the twelfth century when the Portuguese were fighting to liberate their territory from the Moorish invaders who had conquered the Iberian Peninsula in the eighth century.

This story was handed down from father to son over the centuries and written down by Fr. Bernardino de Brito in his *Chronicle of the Order of Cister* (1602). It recounts that a Moorish princess named Fatima lived in Portuguese lands. She was the daughter of a mighty emir.

In 1158, a Portuguese knight named Gonçalo Hermingues, nicknamed "Traga-Mouros" (the Moor-Swallower) for his epic deeds against the Muslims, defeated her father in battle and took Princess Fatima as his prisoner. He then asked the Portuguese King, Dom Afonso Henriques, for permission to marry her. The king gave his consent on two conditions, that she freely convert to Catholicism, and that she agree to marry him.

At baptism, the princess received the name Oriana or Oureana.

As a wedding gift, the king gave her a city which she named Oure-ana, after her new Christian name. Over time it became known as Ourém. Meanwhile, the mountainous lands nearby, where the princess lived for some time, became known by her original Muslim name: Fatima.[327]

Coincidence or Design of Providence?

Whatever we think about the legend of the Moorish princess, the apparition of Mary for our times, happened precisely at a place which shares the name of Muhammad's daughter, Fatima.

The Mother of God could have appeared in any other village or country. However, she chose a town that calls to mind Islam as a podium from which she would address the world and Divine Providence does nothing by chance. While the message of Our Lady of Fatima explicitly speaks of the conversion of Russia, could it be revealing a Providential design for Islam as well? Did the Blessed Mother want to establish a connection between these apparitions and the religion of Muhammad?

Serious minds will ponder these questions. So are there elements in the Fatima message that support such conjectures?

Mary Most Holy appeared in Fatima six times, from May to October 1917, to three little shepherds, Lucia, Francisco, and Jacinta, 10, 9, and 7 years old respectively.

The authenticity of these apparitions was confirmed on October 13 by a miracle of biblical proportions, perhaps the most striking event in Church history since apostolic times: the phenomenon of the sun "dancing" in the sky, seen by tens of thousands of people at the place of the apparition and within a radius of 25 miles. This was reported prominently by the anti-clerical newspaper *O Século*.[328] Later, after due canonical investigation, the apparitions were officially approved by the Church.

The Message of Fatima was given at the July apparition. Our Lady showed Hell to the children, saying: "You have seen hell, where the souls of poor sinners go." She continued,

---

327. See Gentil Marques, *Lendas de Portugal, Lendas dos nomes das terras* (Lisbon: Âncora, 1962, 1999), 1:13–18; *Wikipedia*, s.v. "Fátima, Portugal," updated Jun. 22, 2018, 03:24, https://en .wikipedia.org/wiki/Fátima,_Portugal; *Wikipedia*, s.v. "Ourém," updated Jun. 26, 2018, 15:47, https://en.wikipedia.org/wiki/Ourém.

328. See Appendix I – The Great Miracle of the Sun.

In order to save them, God wants to establish devotion to my Immaculate Heart in the world. If they do what I tell you, many souls will be saved and there will be peace. The war [World War I] will come to an end. But if they do not stop offending God, in the reign of Pius XI a worse war will begin. When you see a night illuminated by an unknown light, know that it is the great sign that God gives you that He will punish the world for its crimes by means of war, hunger and persecutions against the Church and the Holy Father.

To prevent it I will come to ask the consecration of Russia to my Immaculate Heart and the Communion of reparation on the first Saturdays. If my requests are fulfilled, Russia will convert and there will be peace; if not, she will spread her errors throughout the world, promoting wars and persecutions of the Church. The good will be martyred, the Holy Father will have much to suffer and many nations will be annihilated. Finally, my Immaculate Heart will triumph. The Holy Father will consecrate Russia to me and she will be converted and the world will be given a certain period of peace. In Portugal the dogma of the Faith will always be preserved, etc.[329]

Triumph of Mary's Immaculate Heart

In this part of the Message, a few points must be stressed:

1. The expansion of Communism (the "errors of Russia") and its consequences: wars and persecution of the Church;

2. The punishment for sin and humanity's unresponsiveness: Several nations will be annihilated;

3) Finally, the triumph of the Immaculate Heart of Mary.

It is the third point, the triumph of the Immaculate Heart that is the most relevant for our reflection.[330]

Plinio Corrêa de Oliveira draws attention to the expression Our Lady employed, triumph.

[In Fatima] Our Lady could have said "My Immaculate Heart will win." She did not. Instead, she used an ex-

---

329. Luiz Sérgio Solimeo, *Fatima: A Message More Urgent Than Ever*, 3rd Printing (Spring Grove, Penn.: The American Society for the Defense of Tradition, Family and Property—TFP, 2008), 49–50.

330. See Luiz Sérgio Solimeo, *The Immaculate Heart of Mary and God's Plan for America* (Hanover, Penn.: America Needs Fatima, 2017), 59–80.

pression with a sharply different nuance. There is a difference between a victory and a triumph. A triumph is not just any win. It is a great victory, a remarkable victory! Our Lady announces her triumph, that is, a glorious victory in which she will completely master the situation and the Reign of Mary will come, for one cannot understand that she would win without becoming Queen.[331]

This great victory, this triumph of the Immaculate Heart of Mary, will only be possible if not just Communism is eliminated in all its forms, but also that power today which, like Communism, represents such an imminent threat and danger for Christendom: Islam.

Hence, the Message of Fatima implies a great conversion of Muslims and a complete victory of the Cross over the Crescent.

Only in this way can we hope that "the world will be given some time of peace," as Mary Most Holy promised.

Therefore, devotion to Our Lady of Fatima and the Immaculate Heart of Mary and faithful obedience to her requests are the most effective means to counter the growing threat Islam presents for the Christian West.

---

331. Plinio Corrêa de Oliveira, Lecture at Fifth SEFAC, Jul. 14, 1971 (unpublished).

The Great Miracle of the Sun: An Event of Biblical Proportions

The miracle that happened at Cova da Iria on October 13, 1917, when the sun "danced" in the sky (to use the expression of a newspaper at the time) was an extraordinary event of biblical dimensions. It is comparable to Joshua's making the sun stop during his battle with the Amorites, or to Moses opening the Red Sea so that the Jews could escape from Pharaoh and his pursuing army.

A Miracle That Was Foretold

If the event itself is stupendous, perhaps no less extraordinary is the fact that it was foretold three months in advance as proof that the children were telling the truth: That they had seen Our Lady and received a message from her.

After the apparitions of August and September, the seers confirmed that in October Our Lady would work a miracle that would be seen by everyone.

That announcement of a spectacular supernatural event at a time when the world had supposedly freed itself from the supernatural thanks to science sounded like a far-fetched challenge. It could not happen because it would negate all the official ideology of the time—pretentious scientism, high-sounding but empty liberalism, and gross materialism.

Campaigns of Hatred

All over the country, newspapers began a bitter campaign of mockery to discredit the apparitions. Lisbon's leading daily, *O Século*, published a cartoon showing a peasant in a state of revolt facing a skeleton half enveloped in a death shroud with "Hunger" written on it and the phrase: "Hunger is the one true, palpable, real apparition."

Although the multitudes of believers increased by the day, real but incomplete threats could be heard: "If the children have lied and nothing happens. . . ."

Among the tens of thousands who flocked to Fatima that October 13 the majority believed they would see the promised miracle, but a minority of impious people thought they would have some fun, ridiculing Catholics' gullibility. However, as the Psalmist says, God would laugh at them (see Psalms 2:4).

The Miracle of the Sun in the Words of an Agnostic Journalist

Among others who described what happened is Avelino de Almeida, an agnostic journalist from the anti-clerical newspaper *O Século*. He was there to report on everything with skeptical but keenly observant eyes. Here is his description of the miracle of the sun published by his Lisbon newspaper two days later.[332]

> The point of the low land of Fatima where the Virgin is said to have appeared to the little shepherds of the village of Aljustrel can be seen from a long stretch of the road to Leiria, where the vehicles that brought the pilgrims and curiosity seekers were parked. Someone counted more than one hundred automobiles and more than one hundred bicycles, and it would be impossible to count the innumerable vehicles cluttering the road, one of them a bus from Torres Novas with people from all layers of society.
>
> But the bulk of the pilgrims, thousands of creatures who had come from many miles away to join the faithful of various provinces such as Além Tejo, Algarves, Minho and Beira, congregated around the small holm oak which, as the little shepherds put it, the vision had chosen as its pedestal; it could be considered the center of an ample circle around whose borders other spectators and devotees assembled. Seen from the road, the ensemble is simply fantastic. Many of the prudent peasants, protected by enormous hats, accompany the spiritual hymns and decades of the rosary while nibbling on their poor fare.
>
> No one fears to walk through this mushy clay to see up close the holm oak over which was built a rude portal on which two lanterns flicker. . . . As groups singing praise

---

332. Avelino de Almeida, "Coisas espantosas! Como o sol bailou ao meio dia em Fátima," *O Século*, Oct. 15, 1917, (edição da manhã), http://www.santuariofatima.org.br/downloads/oseculo.pdf.

of the Virgin take turns, a frightened rabbit sprinting out of the woods barely manages to get the attention of a half-dozen youngsters who catch up with it and bludgeon it unconscious. . . .

And what about the little shepherds? Lucia, 10, the seer, and her small companions Francisco, 9 and Jacinta, 7 still have not arrived. Their presence is noticed a half-hour before the time set for the apparition. The little girls, crowned with garlands of flowers, are led to the place where the portal stands. The rain falls incessantly but no one despairs. Cars with late comers arrive on the road. Groups of faithful kneel down on the mud and Lucia asks and orders them to close their umbrellas. The order is passed on and obeyed immediately without the least reluctance. Many people find themselves, as it were, in ecstasies; many are touched, prayer has paralyzed their dry lips; many seem dazed, with their hands together and eyes wide open; people seem to feel and touch the supernatural. . . .

The child says that the Lady spoke to her once again and the sky, still dark, begins to clear up on high; the rain stops and one feels the sun will flood with light that landscape which the wintry morning had made even sadder . . . .

The "old time" [because of daylight savings time, their clocks had advanced one hour] is the one that matters for this crowd, which impartial and cultured people completely alien to mystical influences calculate in about thirty or forty thousand creatures. . . . Many pilgrims say the miraculous manifestation, the visible sign announced, is about to happen. . . . And then one witnesses a spectacle unique and unbelievable for someone not there to see it. From the top of the road, where cars are parked and hundreds of people gather who do not want to brave the mud, one sees the huge crowd turn toward the sun, now freed from the clouds, at its zenith. The sun resembles a plate of opaque silver and one can look at it without any strain. It does not burn or blind. One would say an eclipse is taking place. Then a huge roar comes from the crowd and those closer to the place cry out:

"—Miracle, miracle! Marvel, marvel!"

As the peasants typically put it, the sun "danced," shook and made abrupt movements outside all cosmic laws as those people filled with awe, with an attitude that recalls biblical times, heads uncovered, looked up into the blue with their fascinated eyes. . . . It is close to three o'clock pm.[333]

333. Solimeo, *Fatima: A Message More Urgent*, 77–84.

Christmas 2017 Open Letter:
From Former Muslims Who Became Catholics, and Their Friends, to His Holiness Pope Francis, About His Attitude Towards Islam

On December 25, 2017, a group of Muslim converts to Catholicism and their friends made public an Open Letter to Pope Francis.[334] Due to the importance of the initiative and its argumentation, we publish it below.

Most Holy Father,

Many of us have tried to contact you, on many occasions and for several years, and we have never received the slightest acknowledgement of our letters or requests for meetings. You do not like to beat around the bush, and neither do we, so allow us to say frankly that we do not understand your teaching about Islam, as we read in paragraphs 252 and 253 of *Evangelii Gaudium*,[335] because it does not account for the fact that Islam came AFTER Christ,[336] and so is, and can only be, an Antichrist (see 1 Jn 2:22), and one of the most dangerous because it presents itself as the fulfillment of Revelation (of which Jesus would have been only a prophet). If Islam is a good religion in itself, as you seem to teach, why did we become Catholic? Do not your words question the soundness of the choice we made at the risk of our lives? Islam prescribes death for apostates (Quran 4.89, 8.7–11), do you know? How is it possible to compare Islamic violence with so-called

---

334. "From Former Muslims Who Became Catholics, and Their Friends, to His Holiness Pope Francis, About His Attitude Towards Islam," accessed Mar. 21, 2018, http://exmusulmanschretiens.fr/351-2/.

335. http://w2.vatican.va/content/francesco/en/apost_exhortations/documents/papa-francesco_esortazione-ap_20131124_evangelii-gaudium.html. [Ed.: The Open Letter's live links were converted to footnotes.]

336. https://www.islam-et-verite.com/deuxieme-lettre-ouverte-au-pape-francois/.

Christian violence?[337] *"What is the relationship between Christ and Satan? What union is there between light and darkness? What association between the faithful and the unfaithful?"* (2 Cor 6:14–17) In accordance with His teaching (Lk 14:26), we preferred Him, the Christ, to our own life. Are we not in a good position to talk to you about Islam?

In fact, as long as Islam wants us to be its enemy, we are, and all our protestations of friendship cannot change anything. As a proper Antichrist, Islam exists only as an enemy of all: "Between us and you there is enmity and hatred forever, until you believe in Allah alone!"(Quran 60.4) For the Quran, Christians "are only impurity" (Quran 9.28), "the worst of Creation" (Quran 98.6), condemned to Hell (Quran 4.48), so Allah must exterminate them (Quran 9.30). We must not be deceived by the Quranic verses deemed tolerant, because they have all been repealed by the verse of the Sword (Quran 9.5). Where the Gospel proclaims the good news of Jesus' death and resurrection for the salvation of all, and the fulfillment of the Covenant initiated with the Hebrews, Allah has nothing to offer but war and murder of the "infidels" in exchange for his paradise: *"They fight on the way of Allah, they kill and are killed."* (Quran 9.11) We do not confuse Islam with Muslims, but if for you "dialogue" means the voice of peace, for Islam it's only another way to make war. Also, as it was in the face of Nazism and communism, naiveté in the face of Islam is suicidal and very dangerous. How can you speak of peace and endorse Islam, as you seem to do: "To wring from our hearts the disease that plagues our lives (. . .) Let those who are Christians do it with the Bible and those who are Muslims do it with the Quran. (Rome, January 20, 2014)?[338] That the Pope seems to propose the Quran as a way of salvation, is that not cause for worry? Should we return to Islam?

We beg you not to seek in Islam an ally in your fight against the powers that want to dominate and enslave the world, since they share the same totalitarian logic based on the rejection of the kingship of Christ (Lk 4:7). We know that the Beast of the Apocalypse, seeking to devour the Woman and her Child, has many heads. Allah

---

337. http://www.lefigaro.fr/actualite-france/2016/07/31/01016-20160731ARTFIG00176-pape-francois-si-je-parle-de-violence-islamique-je-dois-parler-de-violence-catholique.php?redirect_premium.

338. http://laportelatine.org/insolites/francois_appelle_les_musulmans_a_lire_le_coran_140101/francois_appelle_les_musulmans_a_lire_le_coran_140120.php.

defends such alliances by the way (Quran 5.51)! Moreover, the prophets have always reproached Israel for its willingness to ally with foreign powers, to the detriment of the complete confidence they should've had in God. Certainly, the temptation is strong to think that speaking in an Islamophilic tone will prevent more suffering for Christians in those countries that have become Muslim, but apart from the fact that Jesus has never indicated any other way than that of the Cross, so that we must find our joy therein and not flee with all the damned, we do not doubt that only the proclamation of the Truth brings with it not only salvation, but freedom as well (John 8:32). Our duty is to bear witness to the truth "in season and out of season" (2 Timothy 4:2), and our glory is to be able to say with St. Paul: "*I did not want to know anything among you except Jesus Christ, and Him crucified.*" (1 Corinthians 2:2)

As to Your Holiness's stance on Islam: even as President Erdoğan, among others, asks his countrymen not to integrate into their host countries, and while Saudi Arabia and all the petrol monarchies do not welcome any refugee, expressions (among others) of the project of conquest and Islamization of Europe,[339] officially proclaimed by the OIC[340] and other Islamic organizations[341] for decades; you, Most Holy Father, preach the welcoming of migrants regardless of the fact that they are Muslims, something forbidden by Apostolic command: "*If anyone comes to you but refuses this Gospel, do not receive him among you nor greet him. Whoever greets him participates in his evil works.*" (2 John 1:10–11); "*If anyone preaches to you a different Gospel, let him be accursed!*" (Galatians 1:8–9)

Just as "*For I was hungry, and you gave me no food.*" (Mt 25:42) cannot mean that Jesus would have liked to be a parasite, so "*I was a stranger and you welcomed Me*" cannot mean "*I was an invader and you welcomed Me*", but rather "*I needed your hospitality for a while, and you granted it to me*". The word ξένος (*xenos*) in the New Testament does not only have the meaning of *stranger* but of *guest* as well (Rm 16:23; 1 Co 16:5–6, Col 4:10; 3 Jn 1:5). And when YHWH in the Old Testament commands to treat foreigners well because the He-

---

339. https://www.alexandredelvalle.com/single-post/2016/10/21/La-strat%C3%A9gie-de-conqu%C3%AAte-des-Fr%C3%A8res-musulmans.

340. https://www.isesco.org.ma/.

341. Wikipedia, s.v. "Muslim World League," https://en.wikipedia.org/wiki/Muslim_World_League.

brews have themselves been foreigners in Egypt, it is on the condition that the foreigner assimilates so well to the chosen people that
he accepts their religion and practices their cult... Never is there
mention of welcoming a foreigner who would keep his religion and
its customs! Also, we do not understand that you are pleading for
Muslims to practice their religion in Europe. The meaning of Scripture should not be supplied by the proponents of globalism, but in
fidelity to Tradition. The Good Shepherd hunts the wolf, He does
not let it enter the sheepfold.

The pro-Islam speech of Your Holiness leads us to deplore the fact
that Muslims are not invited to leave Islam, and that many ex-Muslims, such as Magdi Allam,[342] are even leaving the Church, disgusted
by her cowardice, wounded by equivocal gestures, confused by the
lack of evangelization, scandalized by the praise given to Islam . . .
Thus ignorant souls are misled, and Christians are not preparing for
a confrontation with Islam, to which St. John Paul II has called them
(*Ecclesia in Europa*, no. 57).[343] We are under the impression that you
do not take your brother Bishop Nona Amel, Chaldean-Catholic
Archbishop of Mosul in exile, seriously, when he tells us: "*Our present
sufferings are the prelude to those that you, Europeans and Western
Christians, will suffer in the near future. I have lost my diocese. The headquarters of my archdiocese and my apostolate have been occupied by
radical Islamists who want us to convert or die. (...) You are welcoming
into your country an ever increasing number of Muslims. You are in danger as well. You must make strong and courageous decisions (. . .). You
think that all men are equal, but Islam does not say that all men are
equal. (. . .) If you do not understand this very quickly, you will become
the victims of the enemy that you have invited into your home.*" (August
9, 2014)[344] This is a matter of life and death,[345] and any complacency
towards Islam is treasonous. We do not wish the West to continue
with Islamization, nor that your actions contribute to it. Where then
would we go to seek refuge?

Allow us to ask Your Holiness to quickly convene a synod on the

---

342. http://www.postedeveille.ca/2013/03/pourquoi-je-quitte-leglise-catholique-trop-faible-avec
-lislam-magdi-allam.html.

343. http://w2.vatican.va/content/john-paul-ii/en/apost_exhortations/documents/hf_jp-ii_exh
_20030628_ecclesia-in-europa.html.

344. https://www.catholicnewsagency.com/news/iraqi-bishop-warns-that-west-will-suffer-from
-islamism-19159.

345. https://www.islam-et-verite.com/sils-mont-persecute-persecuteront-jn-15-20/.

dangers of Islam. What remains of the Church where Islam has installed itself? If she still has civil rights, it is in dhimmitude, on the condition that she does not evangelize, thus denying her very essence. In the interest of justice and truth, the Church must bring to light why the arguments put forward by Islam to blaspheme the Christian faith are false. If the Church had the courage to do that, we do not doubt that millions, Muslims as well as other men and women seeking the true God, would convert. As you said: "*He who does not pray to Christ, prays to the Devil.*" (14.03.13) If people knew they were going to Hell, they would give their lives to Christ. (see Quran 3.55)

With the deepest love for Christ who, through you, leads His Church, we, converts from Islam, supported by many of our brothers in the Faith, especially the Christians of the East, and by our friends, ask Your Holiness to confirm our conversion to Jesus Christ, true God and true man, the only Savior, with a frank and right discourse on Islam, and, assuring you of our prayers in the heart of the Immaculate, we ask your apostolic blessing.

List of names of signatories and their email (certainly not all ex-Muslims will sign this Letter for fear of possible reprisals).

Bibliography

I. English Translations of the Koran

Dukes, Kais, ed. "The Quranic Arabic Corpus." Language Research Group-University of Leeds. Accessed Feb. 28, 2018. http://corpus.quran.com/.

Hilali, Muhammad Taqi-ud-Din al- and Muhammad Muhsin Khan. *Interpretation of the Meanings of The Noble Quran.* Dar-us-Salam Publications. Accessed Feb. 28, 2018. http://noblequran.com/translation/.

Mehri, A.B. al-, ed. *The Qur'an: With Sura Introductions and Appendices.* Translated by Saheeh International. Birmingham, UK: Maktabah Booksellers and Publishers, 2010. https://archive.org/details/Quran-SaheehInternationalTranslationEnglish.

Pickthall, Mohammed Marmaduke. *The Meaning of the Glorious Quran.* Hyderabad-Deccan: Government Central Press, 1938. http://www.sacred-texts.com/isl/pick/.

Qaribullah, Hasan and Ahmad Darwish, trans. *The Holy Koran*, (2001), accessed Jun. 6, 2018, https://ia600308.us.archive.org/9/items/HolyQuran_prof.hasanQaribullah_sudan/HolyQuran_prof.hasanQaribullah_sudan.pdf.

Quranwow.com. "Quran Multilingual." Accessed Feb. 28, 2018. http://www.quranwow.com.

Sarwar, Muhammad. *The Holy Quran: Arabic Text With English Translation.* Singapore: The Islamic Seminary, 2011. Online Edition. http://www.theislamicseminary.org/wp/TheHolyQuran.pdf.

Yusuf Ali, Abdullah. *The Holy Qur'an: English Translation.* Accessed Feb. 28, 2018.

http://www.wright-house.com/religions/islam/Quran.html.

———. *The Meaning of the Holy Qur'an: Explanatory English Translation, Commentary and Comprehensive Index.* Beltsville, MD: Amana Publications, 2016.

———. *The Meaning of the Noble Qur'an: The English Qur'an With Commentaries.* Accessed Feb. 28, 2018. https://ia802500.us.archive.org/23/items/English-quran-with-commentariesyusuf-ali/english-quran-with-commentaries%28yusuf-ali%29.pdf.

———. *Translation of the Qur'aan: Old Testament for Jews, New Testament for Christian, Final Testament for Humanity.* Mt. Holly, N.J.: Islamic Educational Service, 1998.

* Translations of the Koran into other languages, especially French, were also consulted.

II. Islamic Sources

al-adaab.org. "'Ilm ul Qur'an (*Introduction to Holy Qur'an*)." Accessed Feb. 28, 2018. http://www.al-adaab.org/Quran_Majid/ilm_ul_quran.html.

Al-Islam.org. Ahlul Bayt Digital Islamic Library Project (DILP). Accessed Apr. 2, 2018. https://www.al-islam.org.

AlIslam.org. "Al Islam: The Official Website of the Ahmadiyya Muslim Community." Accessed Feb. 28, 2018. https://www.alislam.org/.

Bukhari, Muhammad al-. *Sahih Bukhari*. Accessed Mar. 1, 2018. https://sun nah.com/bukhari.

———. *Sahih Bukhari*. Accessed Mar. 1, 2018. https://www.sahih-bukhari.com.

———. *Sahih Bukhari*. Accessed Mar. 1, 2018. https://www.thereligionofpeace .com/quran/bukhari/060-sbt.htm.

Dabiq [online ISIS magazine]. "In the Words of the Enemy." *Dabiq*, 1437 Shawwal, Issue 15:74–76. Accessed Feb. 28, 2018. https://clarionproject.org /factsheets-files/islamic-state-magazine-dabiq-fifteen-breaking-the-cross.pdf.

Elias, Abu Amina. "Sharia, Fiqh, and Islamic Law Explained." *Faith in Allah*, Apr. 18, 2013. https://abuaminaelias.com/is-the-sharia-a-single-code-of-law -an-explanation-of-sharia-fiqh-and-islamic-law/.

Hajjaj al-Naysaburi, Muslim ibn al-. *Sahih Muslim*. Translated by Abdul Hamid Siddiqui. Accessed Feb. 28, 2018. https://Sunnah.com/muslim.

Hamidullah, Muhammad. *Islam and Communism: A Study in Comparative Thought*. Accessed May 7, 2018. http://ebooks.rahnuma.org/religion /Dr.Hamidullah/Dr.HamidUllah-Islam-and-Communism.pdf.

HOTD. "Prophet Adam (AS) – Part I." HOTD, Dec. 1, 2012. Accessed Mar. 2, 2018. http://hadithoftheday.com/adam-part1/.

Ibn Hisham. *The Life of Muhammad*. Villach, Austria: Light of Life, 1997.

Ibn Ishaq, Muhammad. *Sirat Rasoul Allah: The Earliest Biography of Muhammad. An Abridged Version*. Accessed Feb. 28, 2018. http://www.usislam .org/pdf/sirat-RasulAllah-Ibn-Ishaq.PDF.

———. *The Life of Muhammad: A Translation of Ibn Ishaq's Sirat Rasul Allah. With Introduction and Notes by A. Guillaume*. Translated by A. Guillaume. Karachi: Oxford University Press, 2010.

Ibn Majah al-Qazvini, Muhammad bin Yazid. *Sunan ibn Majah*. Accessed Mar. 5, 2018. https://sunnah.com/ibnmajah.

Ibn Khaldun, Abd ar Rahman bin Muhammed. *The Muqaddimah*. Translated by Franz Rosenthal. Accessed Mar. 24, 2018. https://archive.org/stream/ibn _khaldun-al_muqaddimah_201611/ibn_khaldun-al_muqaddimah_djvu.txt.

Isfahani, Abu al-Faraj al-. *Kitab al-Aghani* (The book of songs). Vol. 3.

Islamweb.net. "Sex life of Women in Paradise: Fatwa no. 83922. Fatwa Date: 31/03/2002." Accessed Feb. 28, 2018. http://www.islamweb.net/emain page/PrintFatwa.php?lang=E&Id=83922.

———. "Slaves Your Right Hands Possess: Fatwa No: 85061. Fatwa Date: 26-10-2002." Accessed Feb. 28, 2018. http://www.islamweb.net/emainpage /index.php?page=showfatwa&Option=FatwaId&Id=85061.

Jibouri, Yasin T al-. "Khadijah, Daughter of Khuwaylid, Wife of Prophet Muhammad." *Al-Islam.org*. Accessed Feb. 28, 2018. https://www.al-islam .org/articles/khadijah-daughter-khuwaylid-wife-prophet-muhammad -yasin-t-al-jibouri.

Kathir, Ismail ibn. *Quran Tafsir*. Accessed Apr. 6, 2018. http://www.qtafsir.com /index.php.

Khan, Muhammad Muhsin. *The Translation of the Meanings of Sahîh Al-Bukhâri Arabic-English*. Riyadh: Darussalam Publishers and Distributors, 1997. Vol. 6. https://futureislam.files.wordpress.com/2012/11/sahih-al-bukhari -volume-6-a*hadith*-4474-5062.pdf.

Khan, Sadullah. "Jesus in Islam." *IslamiCity*, Jan 3, 2017. http://www.islamicity .org/5797/jesus-in-islam/.

Maududi, Sayyid Abul A'la. "Tafheem ul Quran: *Sura* 33 Al-Ahzab, Ayat 50–50." Accessed Feb. 28, 2018. http://islamicstudies.info/reference.php?sura =33&verse=50.

———. *Tafhim al-Qur'an - The Meaning of the Qur'an*. Accessed Mar. 6, 2018. http://www.englishtafsir.com.

———. "An Introduction to The Qur'an." Introduction to *Translation of the Qur'aan: Old Testament for Jews, New Testament for Christian, Final Testament for Humanity*. 5-24. Trans. by Abdullah Yusuf Ali. 3rd US edition. Mt. Holly N.J.: Islamic Educational Service, 1998.

Mufti, Kamil. "Prophets of the Kuran: An Introduction (Part 1 of 2). *The Religion of Islam*, Apr. 22, 2013. https://www.islamreligion.com/articles/10228 /viewall/prophets-of-quran/.

Muslim Brotherhood. "The Principles of the Muslim Brotherhood." Ikhwan-web.com. Feb. 1, 2010. http://www.ikhwanweb.com/article.php?id=813.

Muslimpath.com. "Muhammad(s). The Prophet Meets the Christian Priests!!" Accessed Mar. 1, 2018. http://www.muslimpath.com/english/index.php ?page=meeladdet23.

Qaradâwî, Yûsuf Al-. "Introduction à l'Islam: Section: Les sources primaires de l'islam—La sunna prophétique." *Islamophile.org*. Jul. 17, 2001. http://www .islamophile.org/spip/La-sunna-prophetique.html.

Qutb, Sayyid. *Islam: The Religion of the Future*. Delhi: Markazi Maktaba Islami, 1974.

———. *Milestones: Ma'alim fi'l-tareeq*. Ed. A.B. al-Mehri. Birmingham, U.K.: Mak-tabah Booksellers & Publishers, 2006. PDF edition. https://ia800708.us .archive.org/34/items/SayyidQutb/Milestones%20Special%20Edition.pdf.

———. *Social Justice in Islam*. Trans. John B. Hardie. Intro. and Rev. Trans. Hamid Algar. Kuala Lumpur: Islamic Book Trust, 2000.

———. *This Religion of Islam*. Riyadh: International Islamic Federation of

Students Organizations, 1994.

Tabari, Muḥammad ibn Jarir al-. *The History of al-Ṭabari (Ta'rikh al-rusul wa'l-muluk)*. Vol. 8, *The Victory of Islam*. Translated and annotated by Michael Fishbein. Albany: State University of New York Press, 1997. http://www. kalamullah.com/Books/The%20History%20Of%20Tabari/Tabari_Vol ume_08.pdf.

Tirmidhi, Abu ʿIsa Muhammad al-. *Jami' at-Tirmidhi*. Accessed Feb. 28, 2018. https://sunnah.com/tirmidhi.

Wahidi, Ali ibn Ahmad al-. *Kitab Asbab al-Nuzul*. Trans. Mokrane Guezzou. *AlTafsir.com*. Accessed Apr. 3, 2018. http://altafsir.com/Tafasir.asp ?tMadhNo=0&tTafsirNo=86&tSoraNo=16&tAyahNo=106&tDisplay=yes&U serProfile=0&LanguageId=2.

III. Other Sources

Abrahamian, Ervand. "The Making of the Modern Iranian State." In *Introduction to Politics of the Developing World,* edited by William A. Joseph, Mark Kesselman, and Joel Krieger, 310–327. Fifth edition. Boston: Wadsworth Cengage Learning, 2010.

Akyol, Mustafa. *The Islamic Jesus: How the King of the Jews Became a Prophet of the Muslims.* New York: St. Martin's, 2017. [Kindle Edition].

Arabic Gospel of the Infancy of the Savior, The. Trans. Alexander Walker. In *Ante-Nicene Fathers*, vol. 8. Ed. Alexander Roberts, James Donaldson, and A. Cleveland Coxe. Buffalo, NY: Christian Literature Publishing, 1886. Rev. and ed. Kevin Knight for New Advent. http://www.newadvent.org/fathers /0806.htm.

Arendzen, John. s.v. "Gnosticism." In *The Catholic Encyclopedia*. Vol. 6. New York: Robert Appleton, 1908. New Advent Online edition. http://www .newadvent.org/cathen/06592a.htm.

Arnaldez, Roger. "Réflexion sur le Dieu du Coran, du point de vue de la logique formelle." In *Vivre avec l'Islam? Reflections chrétiennes sur la religion de Mahomet,* edited by Annie Laurent, 130–7. Versailles, France: Éditions Saint-Paul, 1996.

Augustine, Saint. *The City of God.* Trans. Marcus Dods. In *Nicene and Post-Nicene Fathers, 1st Series*, vol. 2. Ed. Philip Schaff. Buffalo, NY: Christian Literature Publishing, 1887. Rev. and ed. Kevin Knight for New Advent. http://www.newadvent.org/fathers/120119.htm.

———. *Confessions.* Trans. J.G. Pilkington. In *Nicene and Post-Nicene Fathers, 1st Series*, vol. 1. Ed. Philip Schaff. Buffalo, NY: Christian Literature Publishing, 1887. Rev. and ed. Kevin Knight for New Advent. http://www. newadvent.org/fathers/110101.htm.

———. *Contra Faustum.* Trans. Richard Stothert. *In Nicene and Post-Nicene Fathers, 1st Series*, vol. 4. Ed. Philip Schaff. Buffalo, NY: Christian Literature Publishing, 1887. Rev. and ed. Kevin Knight for New Advent. http://www. newadvent.org/fathers/140622.htm.

———. *Letter on the heresies to Quodvultdeus.* Accessed Jun. 18, 2018. http://www.augustinus.it/latino/eresie/index2.htm].

———. *Sermo 302.* Accessed Mar. 18, 2018. https://www.augustinus.it/latino/discorsi/discorso_428_testo.htm.

Aylesworth, Gary. s.v. "Postmodernism." In *The Stanford Encyclopedia of Philosophy.* Ed. Edward N. Zalta. (Spring, 2015 Edition). https://plato.stanford.edu/archives/spr2015/entries/postmodernism/.

Azzi, Joseph. *Le prêtre et le prophète, aux sources du coran.* Translated by Maurice S. Garnier. Paris: Maisonneuve et Larose, 2001.

———. *The Priest and The Prophet.* Translated by Maurice Saliba. Edited by David Bentley. Los Angeles: Pen Publishers, 2005. [Since the English version is somewhat summarized, at times we use the French edition.]

Barreau, Jean-Claude. *De l'Islam en général et du monde moderne en particulier.* Belfont: Le Pré aux Clercs, 1991.

Bat Ye'or. *The Dhimmi: Jews and Christians Under Islam.* Translated by David Maisel, Paul Fenton, and David Littman. London, Ont.: Associated University Press, 1985.

Benedict XVI. "Speech at the University of Regensburg," Sept. 12, 2006. http://w2.vatican.va/content/benedict-xvi/en/speeches/2006/september/documents/hf_ben-xvi_spe_20060912_university-regensburg.html.

Bernard of Clairvaux, Saint. *In Praise of the New Knighthood: A Treatise on the Knights Templar and the Holy Places of Jerusalem.* Translated by M. Conrad Greenia, OCSO. Trappist, Ky.: Cistercian Publications, 1977.

Besançon, Alain. "L'Islam." *Académie des Sciences morales et politiques.* Accessed Mar. 2, 2018. https://www.asmp.fr/fiches_academiciens/textacad/besancon/islam.pdf.

Blachere, Régis. *Le problème de Mahomet.* Paris: Presses Universitaires de France, 1952.

Borrmans, Maurice. "Regards coraniques sur les chrétiens." *Études* 2004/12 (vol. 401), 645–55. https://www.cairn.info/revue-etudes-2004-12-page-645.htm.

Brown, L. Carl. *Religion and State: The Muslim Approach to Politics.* New York: Columbia University Press, 2000.

Carré, Olivier. *Mystique et politique: lecture révolutionnaire du Coran par Sayyid Qutb, frère musulman radical.* Paris: Cerf, 1984.

Catholic Church. *Catechism of the Catholic Church.* Vatican City: Libreria Editrice Vaticana, 1994. http://www.vatican.va/archive/ccc_css/archive/catechism/p3s1c1a7.htm.

Cathrein, Victor, SJ. *Philosophia Moralis.* Fribourg: Herder, 1905.

Center for Security Policy. *Sharia: The Threat to America: An Exercise in Competitive Analysis – Report of Team 'B' II.* Washington, D.C.: Center for Security Policy, 2010.

Coghlan, Daniel. s.v. "Dogmatic Facts." In *The Catholic Encyclopedia.* Vol. 5. New

York: Robert Appleton, 1909. New Advent online edition. http://www.newadvent.org/cathen/05092a.htm.

Connor, Phillip. "Number of Refugees to Europe Surges to Record 1.3 Million in 2015." *Pew Research Center*, Aug. 2, 2016. http://www.pewglobal.org/2016 /08/02/number-of-refugees-to-europe-surges-to-record-1-3-million-in-2015/.

Cook, Michael. *Muhammad*. Oxford: Oxford University Press, 1996.

———. *The Koran: A Very Short Introduction*. New York: Oxford University Press, 2000.

Corrêa de Oliveira, Plinio. Lecture at Fifth SEFAC. Jul. 14, 1971. Unpublished.

———. "Mohammed's Rebirth." *The American TFP*. Sept. 1, 2014. http://www.tfp.org/muhammad-s-rebirth/. First published as "Maomé renasce." *Legionário*, no. 775, Jun. 15, 1947. http://www.pliniocorreadeoliveira .info/LEG_470615_MAOME_RENASCE.htm#.Wpccaq6nHcs.

———. *Revolution and Counter-Revolution*. Third Edition. York, Penn.: The American Society for the Defense of Tradition, Family and Property, 1993. First Digital Edition. http://www.tfp.org/revolution-and-counter -revolution/.

———. "Unperceived Ideological Transshipment and Dialogue." *Crusade for a Christian Civilization*. Vol. 12, no. 4 (Oct.–Dec. 1982). Digital edition. http://www.tfp.org/unperceived-ideological-transshipment-and-dialogue.

Crone, Patricia. *God's Rule: Government and Islam*. New York: Columbia University Press, 2004.

———. "Jewish Christianity and the Qurʾān (Part One)." *Journal of Near Eastern Studies* 74, no. 2, (October 2015): 225-53. http://www.journals .uchicago.edu/doi/abs/10.1086/682212.

———. and Michael Cook. *Hagarism: The Making of the Islamic World*. Cambridge: Cambridge University Press, 1977. https://archive.org/stream /Hagarism/Hagarism;%20The%20Making%20of%20the%20 Islamic %20World-Crone,%20Cook_djvu.txt.

Cyril of Jerusalem, Saint. (attributed). *Discourse on the Theotokos*. In Fr. John A. Peck, *Discourse on the Theotokos,* Preachers Institute, Aug. 17, 2017. https://preachersinstitute.com/2017/08/17/discourse-theotokos/.

Dagorn, René. *La geste d'Ismael d'après l'onomastique et la tradition arabes*. Geneva: Librairie Droz, 1981.

Dandrieu, Laurent. *Église et immigration: le grand malaise*. Paris: Renaissance, 2017.

Del Valle, Alexandre. *Verdi/Rossi/Neri: La convergenza degli estremismi antioccidentali: islamismo, comunismo, neonazismo*. Turin: Lindau, 2009.

Denzinger, Heinrich Joseph Dominicus. *Most Ancient Forms of the Apostolic Creed*. In *Enchiridion symbolorum, definitionum et declarationum de rebus fidei et morum*. Accessed Mar. 1, 2018. http://patristica.net/denzinger/.

Dewinter, Filip. *Inch'Allah? The Islamization of Europe*. Brussels: Uitgeverij

Egmont, 2012.

Dillon, Michael R. *Wahhabism: Is It a Factor in the Spread of Global Terrorism?* Monterey, Calif.: Naval Postgraduate School, 2009. http://www.dtic.mil/dtic/tr/fulltext/u2/a509109.pdf.

Djait, Hichem. *Europe and Islam.* Translated by Peter Heinegg. Berkeley: University of California Press, 1985.

Donaghy, Rori and Mary Atkinson. "Crime and Punishment: Islamic State vs Saudi Arabia." *Middle East Eye.* Jan. 20, 2015. http://www.middleeasteye.net/news/crime-and-punishment-islamic-state-vs-saudi-arabia-1588245666.

Driscoll, James F. s.v. "Theocracy." In *The Catholic Encyclopedia.* Vol. 14. New York: Robert Appleton, 1912. New Advent online edition. http://www.newadvent.org/cathen/14568a.htm.

Dhulipala, Venkat. *Creating a New Medina: State Power, Islam, and the Quest for Pakistan in Late Colonial North India.* Cambridge: Cambridge University Press, 2015.

Du Pasquier, Roger. *Le réveil de l'Islam.* Paris: Cerf, 1988.

Engels, Frederick. *The Principles of Communism.* In *Selected Works,* vol. 1. Accessed Mar. 6, 2018. https://www.marxists.org/archive/marx/works/1847/11/prin-com.htm.

Epiphanius, Saint. *The Panarion of Epiphanius of Salamis: A Treatise Against Eighty Sects in Three Books.* Translated by Frank Williams. Published 1987–2009. Book I (Sects 1–46), II. Proem I. 4:8, 5:9. https://archive.is/Cgeja.

Esposito, John L. (Editor in Chief). *The Oxford Dictionary of Islam.* New York: Oxford University Press, 2003. *Oxford Islamic Studies Online.* http://www.oxfordislamicstudies.com.

———. *The Islamic Threat: Myth or Reality?* 3rd ed. New York-Oxford: Oxford University Press, 1999.

———. *Unholy War: Terror in the Name of Islam.* New York: Oxford University Press, 2002.

———. and Dalia Mogahed. *Who Speaks for Islam?: What a Billion Muslims Really Think, Based on Gallup's World Poll—The Largest Study of Its Kind.* New York: Gallup, 2007.

Eulogius of Córdoba, Saint. *Memorial de los santos.* In *Obras completas de San Eulogio de Córdoba.* Ed. Pedro Herrera Roldán. Madrid: Akal, 2005.

Eusebius. *Church History.* Book 3. Translated by Arthur Cushman McGiffert. In *Nicene and Post-Nicene Fathers, 2nd Series,* vol. 1. Edited by Philip Schaff and Henry Wace. Buffalo, NY: Christian Literature Publishing, 1890. Rev. and ed. Kevin Knight for New Advent. http://www.newadvent.org/fathers/250103.htm.

Fadelle, Joseph. *Le prix à payer.* Paris: l'Œuvre, 2010.

———. *The Price to Pay: A Muslim Risks All to Follow Christ.* San Francisco: Ignatius, 2012.

Fernández-Morera, Darío. *The Myth of the Andalusian Paradise: Muslims, Christians and Jews Under Islamic Rule in Medieval Spain.* Wilmington, Del.: ISI Books, 2017.

Francis. *Address of the Holy Father.* "Audience With the National Directors of the Pastoral Care of Migrants, Participating in the Meeting Organized by the Council of Episcopal Conferences of Europe (CCEE) (Rome, 21–23 September 2017)," Sept. 22, 2017. https://press.vatican.va/content/salastampa/en /bollettino/pubblico/2017/09/22/170922d.html.

Francis de Sales, Saint. *Œuvres Complètes de Saint François de Sales.* Paris: Bethune, 1836.

Fregosi, Paul. *Jihad in the West: Muslim Conquests From the 7th to The 21st Centuries.* Amherst, NY: Prometheus, 1998.

Gabriel, Richard A. *Muhammad: Islam's First Great General.* Norman, Okl.: University of Oklahoma Press, 2007.

Gallez, Édouard-Marie. "Aperçus relatifs au supposé polythéisme arabe." Accessed Mar. 28, 2018. http://www.lemessieetsonprophete.com/annexes /onze.htm.

———. Correspondence with the author. Mar. 25, 2011

———. *Le Messie et son prophète: Aux origines de l'Islam.* Versailles: Paris, 2005. http://www.lemessieetsonprophete.com/.

———. "Un islam très normalement expansionniste." Accessed Apr. 14, 2018. http://www.lemessieetsonprophete.com/annexes/Questions-debat.htm #expansionniste.

Garaudy, Roger. *Mi vuelta al siglo en solitario.* Barcelona: Plaza y James, 1991.

———. "Pourquoi je suis musulman." *Revue Proche-orient et Tiers-Monde,* 7, June 1983, 57-65. Republished as "Marx, Jésus et Mohammed." Jun. 25, 2016. http://rogergaraudy.blogspot.com/2016/06/marx-jesus-et-mohammed.html.

Garrigou-Lagrange, OP, Fr. Reginald. *The Trinity and God the Creator.* St. Louis: B. Herder, 1952. https://www.ewtn.com/library/theology/trinity.htm.

Gilliot, Claude, OP. "Un non-musulman cultivé et un chercheur occidental face au Coran." *Lumière et Vie,* no. 255 (Jul.–Sept. 2002), Special Issue—*La bibliothèque de Dieu: Coran, Evangile, Torah*: 29–54.

———. "A propos du Coran." In *Vivre avec l'Islam? Reflections chrétiennes sur la religion de Mahomet,* ed. Annie Laurent, 138–49. Versailles, France: Saint-Paul, 1996.

Hackett, Conrad. "5 Facts About the Muslim Population in Europe." *Pew Research Center,* Jan. 15, 2015. http://pewresearch.tumblr.com/post/ 133355017039/5-facts-about-the-muslim-population-in-europe.

Harnack, Adolph von. *Lehrbuch der dogmengeschichte.* Tübingen: Verlag Von J. C. B. Mohr (Paul Siebeck), 1909.

Haykel, Bernard. "ISIS: A Primer–A Leading Scholar Explains the Beliefs and Goals of the Islamic State." *Princeton Alumni Weekly,* Jun. 3, 2015, 20–3.

https://paw.princeton.edu/article/isis-primer.

Hughes, Thomas Patrick. *A Dictionary of Islam*. London: William H. Allen, 1885.

Ibrahim, Raymond. *Crucified Again: Exposing Islam's New War on Christians*. Washington D.C.: Regnery Publishing, Inc., 2013.

"Infancy Gospel of Thomas." Trans. Harold Attridge and Ronald F. Hock. In *The Complete Gospels*, ed. Robert J. Miller. HarperCollins, 1992. http://www.earlychristianwritings.com/text/infancythomashock.html.

Irenaeus, Saint. *Adversus Haeresis*. Translated by Alexander Roberts and William Rambaut. In *Ante-Nicene Fathers*, vol. 1. Edited by Alexander Roberts, James Donaldson, and A. Cleveland Coxe. Buffalo, NY: Christian Literature Publishing, 1885. Rev. and ed. Kevin Knight for New Advent. http://www.newadvent.org/fathers/0103126.htm.

Jacobs, Joseph and Ludwig Blau. s.v. "Gnosticism." In *The Jewish Encyclopedia*. Vol. 5. New York: Funk & Wagnalls, 1903. http://www.jewishencyclopedia.com/articles/6723-gnosticism.

Jerome, Saint. *Commentary on Isaiah* 40:11. In *St. Jerome: Commentary on Isaiah*, bk. 11, no. 24. Translated by Thomas P. Scheck. Vol. 68 in *Ancient Christian Writers: The Works of the Fathers in Translation*. Mahwah, N.J.: Newman, 2015.

———. *St. Jerome: Commentary on Matthew*. Trans. Thomas P. Scheck. Vol. 117 of *The Fathers of the Church: A New Translation*, ed. by Thomas P. Halton et al. Washington, D.C.: The Catholic University of America Press, 2008.

———. *Letter 112 to Augustine*. Translated by J.G. Cunningham. In *Nicene and Post Nicene Fathers, 1st Series*, vol. 1. Edited by Philip Schaff. Buffalo, NY: Christian Literature Publishing, 1887. Rev. and ed. Kevin Knight for New Advent. http://www.newadvent.org/fathers/1102075.htm.

John Damascene, Saint. *On Heresies*. Translated by Frederic H. Chase, Jr. *In Fathers of the Church: A New Translation*. Vol. 37. New York: Fathers of the Church, 1958. https://ia802609.us.archive.org/8/items/fathersofthechur009511mbp/fathersofthechur009511mbp.pdf.

Jomier, OP, Jacques. *The Bible and the Qur'an*. San Francisco: Ignatius, 2002.

Jonas, Hans. *The Gnostic Religion*. Boston: Beacon Press, 2001.

Jones, Ron. *Matthew's Hebrew Gospel and the Gospel of the Hebrews*. Accessed Mar. 1, 2018. http://hebrewgospel.com/Gospel%20of%20Hebrews.php.

Jourdan, CMJ, François. *Dieu des chrétiens, Dieu des musulmans: Des repères pour comprendre*. Paris: l'Œuvre, 2008.

Journet, Charles. *L'Église du Verbe Incarné*. Vol 1. 3rd edition enlarged. Bruges-Paris: Desclée de Brouwer, 1963.

———. *The Church of the Word Incarnate*. London-New York: Sheed & Ward, 1955.

Joyce, George. s.v. "The Blessed Trinity." In *The Catholic Encyclopedia*. Vol. 15. New York: Robert Appleton 1912. New Advent online edition.

http://www.newadvent.org/cathen/15047a.htm.

Karsh, Efraim. *Islamic Imperialism: A History*. New Haven, Conn.: Yale University Press, 2006.

Knysh, Alexander. "Multiple Areas of Influence." In *The Cambridge Companion to the Qur'an*, edited by Jane Dammen McAuliffe. Accessed Apr. 6, 2018. http://www.almuslih.org/Library/McAuliffe,%20J%20-%20The %20Cambridge%20Companion.pdf.

Krokus, Christian S. "Louis Massignon's Influence on the Teaching of Vatican II on Muslims and Islam." *Islam and Christian–Muslim Relations* 23, 2012– Issue 3: 329–45, Jun. 22, 2012. http://www.tandfonline.com/doi/abs/10 .1080/09596410.2012.686264.

Kull, Steven. *Feeling Betrayed: The Roots of Muslim Anger at America*. Washington, D.C.: Brookings Institution, 2011.

Lambert. "From Liber Lamberti." In "Decrees of Pope Urban II at the Council of Clermont, 1095." Accessed Mar. 11, 2018. http://falcon.arts.cornell.edu /prh3/259/texts/clermont.html.

Lammens, SJ, Henri. *Islam Beliefs and Institutions*. Trans. Sir E. Denison Ross. 2nd ed. New Delhi: Oriental Books Reprint, 1979. (Originally published by Methuen, London, 1929).

———. "Qoran et tradition, comment fut composée la vie de Mahomet." *Recherches de Science Religieuse*, 1910. 1:27-51.

Laurent, Annie, ed. *Vivre avec l'Islam?: Reflections chrétiennes sur la religion de Mahomet.* Versailles, France: Éditions Saint-Paul, 1996.

Leiken, Robert. *Europe's Angry Muslims: The Revolt of the Second Generation.* New York: Oxford University Press, 2012.

———. "Europe's Mujahideen: Where Mass Immigration Meets Global Terrorism." *Center for Immigration Studies*, Apr. 1, 2005. https://cis.org/Europes-Mujahideen.

Leo XIII. Encyclical *Immortale Dei*. On the Christian Constitution of States. Nov. 1, 1885. http://w2.vatican.va/content/leo-xiii/la/encyclicals/documents /hf_l-xiii_enc_01111885_immortale-dei.html.

Lépicier, Alexis Henri Marie. *The Fairest Flower of Paradise: Considerations on the Litany of the Blessed Virgin*. New York: Benziger Brothers, 1922.

Lewis, Bernard. *Islam in History: Ideas, People, and Events in the Middle East.* 2nd edition. Chicago: Open Court, 2002.

Liguori, Alphonsus Marie de, Saint. *The History of Heresies, and Their Refutation; Or, The Triumph of the Church*. Trans. Rev. John T. Mullock. Dublin: James Duffy, 1847. https://archive.org/stream/thehistoryofhere01liguuoft /thehistoryofhere01liguuoft_djvu.txt.

Lopez de Coca Castañer, José E. "Cristianos en Al-Andaluz (Siglos VIII–XII)." In *Cristiandad e Islam en la Edad Media Hispania. XVIII Semana de Estudios Medievales (Nájera, 2007)*. La Rioja: Inst. Est. Riojanos, 2008. http://www .vallenajerilla.com/berceo/lopezcoca/cristianosenal-aldalus.htm.

Lüling, Günter. *A Challenge to Islam for Reformation: the Rediscovery and Reliable Reconstruction of a Comprehensive pre-Islamic Christian Hymnal Hidden in the Koran Under Earliest Islamic Reinterpretations*. 1ˢᵗ English Edition. Delhi: Motilal Banarsidass Publishers, 2003.

Malik, Mustafa. "Muslims Pluralize the West, Resist Assimilation." *Middle East Policy Council*, vol. 11, no. 1 (Spring 2004). http://www.mepc.org/journal /muslims-pluralize-west-resist-assimilation.

Marques, Gentil. *Lendas de Portugal*. Vol. 1, *Lendas dos nomes das terras*. Lisbon: Âncora, 1962, 1999.

McAuliffe, Jane Dammen. "The Tasks and Traditions of Interpretation." In *The Cambridge Companion to the Qur'an*, edited by Jane Dammen McAuliffe. Accessed Apr. 6, 2018. http://www.almuslih.org/Library/McAuliffe,%20J %20-%20The%20Cambridge%20Companion.pdf.

Marx, Karl and Frederick Engels. *Manifesto of the Communist Party*. Accessed Mar. 1, 2018. https://www.marxists.org/archive/marx/works/download /pdf/Manifesto.pdf.

Mervin, Sabrina. *Histoire de l'islam: Fondements et doctrines*. Paris: Flammarion, 2000.

Mitchell, Richard P. *The Society of the Muslim Brothers*. New York: Oxford University Press, (1969) 1993.

Monnot, Guy. "Notes Bibliographiques." *Revue de l'Histoire des Religions,* 4/1983. http://www.persee.fr/docAsPDF/rhr_0035-1423_1983_num_200_4_4440.pdf.

Moussali, Antoine, C.M. "Ce qu'un Chrétien doit savoir sur l'Islam." Accessed Mar. 1, 2018. http://henry.quinson.pagesperso-orange.fr /AntoineMoussali.pdf.

———. *La croix et le croissant – Le Christianisme face à l'Islam,* Versailles: 1998.

Moussalli, Ahmad S. *Radical Islamic Fundamentalism: The Ideological and Political Discourse of Sayyid Qutb*. Beirut: American University of Beirut, 1992.

Murray, Douglas. *The Strange Death of Europe: Immigration, Identity, Islam*. New York: Bloomsbury, 2017.

Origen, *Commentary on the Gospel of John*. Translated by Allan Menzies. In *Ante-Nicene Fathers* vol. 9. Edited by Allan Menzies. Buffalo, NY: Christian Literature Publishing, 1896. Rev. and ed. Kevin Knight for New Advent. http://www.newadvent .org/fathers/101502.htm.

Oxford Islamic Studies Online. Oxford University Press. Accessed Mar. 1, 2018. http://www.oxfordislamicstudies.com/article/opr/t125/e758.

Palmieri, A. "Coran (sa théologie)." Cols. 1779–1835. In *Dictionnaire de Théologie Catholique*. Paris: Letouzey et Ané, 1938.

Perrone, Lorenzo. "'Abraham, père de tous les croyants' Louis Massignon et l'apostolat de la prière," *Proche-Orient Chrétien* 60, 2010: 110–133. http://www .academia.edu/1287868.

Peters, F. E. *Muhammad and the Origins of Islam.* Albany, NY: State University of New York Press, 1994.

Petuchowski, Jakob Josef. Review of *Jewish Gnosticism, Merkabah Mysticism, and Talmudic Tradition*, by Gershom G. Scholem. *Commentary Magazine*, Feb. 1, 1961. https://www.commentarymagazine.com/articles/jewish-gnosticism -merkabah-mysticism-and-talmudic-tradition-by-gershom-g-scholem/.

Pew Research Center. "Europe's Growing Muslim Population." Nov. 29, 2017. http: //www.pewforum.org/2017/11/29/europes-growing-muslim-population/.

Pohle, Msgr. Joseph. Grace, *Actual and Habitual: A Dogmatic Treatise.* Adapted and edited by Arthur Preuss. 3rd, Rev. Edition. Toronto: W. E. Blake & Son, 1919. http://biblehub.com/library/pohle/grace_actual_and_habitual /title_page.htm.

Pons Fuster, Francisco. "El patriarca Juan de Ribera y el catechismo para instrucción de los nuevamente convertidos de moros." *Studia Philologica Valentina*, Vol. 15, n.s. 12 (2013), 209–10. https://www.uv.es/SPhV/15/10_pons15.pdf.

Pontifical Council for Interreligious Dialogue. *Dialogue in Truth and Charity: Pastoral Orientations for Interreligious Dialogue.* May 19, 2014. Vatican City: Libreria Editrice Vaticana, 2014. http://www.pcinterreligious.org/ uploads/pdfs/DIALOGUE_IN_TRUTH_AND_CHARITY_website-1.pdf.

Popular Front for the Liberation of Palestine. *Strategy for the Liberation of Palestine.* Chap. 13—"No Revolutionary Party Without Revolutionary Theory." Accessed Mar. 1, 2018. http://pflp.ps/english/strategy-for-the-liberation -of-palestine-no-revolutionary-party-without-revolutionary-theory/.

Pressburg, Norbert G. *What the Modern Martyr Should Know: Seventy-two Grapes and Not a Single Virgin.* Germany: Books on Demand GmbH, 2012.

Pritz, Ray A. *Nazarene Jewish Christianity, From the End of the New Testament Period Until Its Disappearance in the Fourth Century.* Leiden: E.J. Brill.

Protoevangelium of James, The. Ed. by Peter Kirby. "Historical Jesus Theories." *Early Christian Writings.* Accessed Mar. 1, 2018. http://www .earlychristianwritings.com/text/infancyjames-roberts.html

Ramírez Sánchez (Carlos), Ilich. *L'Islam révolutionnaire: Texte et propos recueillis, rassemblés, et presentés par Jean-Michel Vernochet.* Monaco: éditions du Rocher, 2003.

Reeves, John C. "Nistarot (Secrets of) R. Shimon b. Yohai." Accessed Mar. 1, 2018. https://clas-pages.uncc.edu/john-reeves/research-projects/trajectories-in -near-eastern-apocalyptic/nistarot-secrets-of-r-shimon-b-yohai-2/.

Reilly, Robert R. *The Closing of the Muslim Mind: How Intellectual Suicide Created the Modern Islamist Crisis.* Wilmington, Del.: ISI, 2010.

Riedel, Bruce. *The Search for Al Qaeda: Its Leadership, Ideology and Future.* Washington, D.C.: Brookings Institution, 2008.

Roberti, Francesco and Pietro Palazzini. *Dictionary of Moral Theology.* Translated Henry J. Yannone. Westminster, Md.: Newman, 1962.

Robinson, Neal. "Massignon, Vatican II and Islam as an Abrahamic Religion."

Islam and Christian–Muslim Relations, Vol. 2, 1991, Issue 2, 182–205. http://www.tandfonline.com/doi/abs/10.1080/09596419108720957?src=recsys.

Samir, SJ, Samir Khalil. *111 Questions on Islam*. Edited and translated by Wafik Nasry, SJ and Claudia Castellani. San Francisco: Ignatius, 2008.

Second Vatican Council. *Lumen Gentium* (Dogmatic Constitution on the Church). Nov. 21, 1964. http://www.vatican.va/archive/hist_councils/ii_vatican_council/documents/vat-ii_const_19641121_lumen-gentium_en.html.

———. *Nostra Ætate* (Declaration on the Relation of the Church to Non-Christian Religions). Oct. 28, 1965. http://www.vatican.va/archive/hist_councils/ii_vatican_council/documents/vat-ii_decl_19651028_nostra-aetate_en.html.

Simon, Marcel. *Verus Israel: A Study of the Relations Between Christians and Jews in the Roman Empire AD 135–425*. Trans. H. McKeating. London: The Littman Library of Jewish Civilization, 1986, 1996.

Simonet, Francisco Javier. *Historia de los Mozárabes en España*. Madrid: Real Academia de la Historia, n.d.

Solimeo, Luiz Sérgio. *Fatima: A Message More Urgent Than Ever*. Third Printing. Spring Grove, Penn.: The American Society for the Defense of Tradition, Family and Property—TFP, 2017.

———. *The Immaculate Heart of Mary and God's Plan for America*. Hanover, Penn.: America Needs Fatima, 2017.

Song, Sarah. s.v. "Multiculturalism." In *The Stanford Encyclopedia of Philosophy* (Spring 2017 Edition). Ed. Edward N. Zalta. https://plato.stanford.edu/archives/spr2017/entries/multiculturalism.

Speer, Albert. *Inside The Third Reich: Memoirs*. Translated by Richard and Clara Winston. New York: The Macmillan Company, 1970.

Spencer, Robert. *Did Muhammad Exist? An Inquiry Into Islam's Obscure Origin*. Wilmington, Del.: ISI, 2012.

———. *Stealth Jihad: How Radical Islam Is Subverting America Without Guns or Bombs*. Washington, D.C.: Regnery, 2008.

———. *The Complete Infidel's Guide to ISIS*. Washington, D.C.: Regnery. 2016.

———. *The Truth about Muhammad*. Washington D.C.: Regnery, 2006.

———. (Ed.). *The Myth of Islamic Tolerance: How Islamic Law Treats Non-Muslims*. Amherst, New York: Prometheus, 2005.

Stark, Rodney. *God's Battalions: The Case for the Crusades*. New York, HarperOne, 2009.

Strothman, R. s.v. "Taqiya." In *E.J. Brill's First Encyclopedia of Islam 1913-1936*. Ed. M. Th. Houtsma et al. New York: E.J. Brill, 1993.

Stroumsa, Guy G. "Jewish Christianity and Islamic Origins." In *Islamic Culture, Islamic Context: Essays in Honor of Professor Patricia Crone*, ed. Behnam Sadeghi, et al., 72–96. Leiden: Brill, 2015. https://www.academia.edu

/9997797/Jewish_Christianity_and_Islamic_Origins.

TFP Committee on American Issues. *Rejecting the Da Vinci Code.* Spring Grove, Penn.: The American Society for the Defense of Tradition, Family and Property, 2005.

Thomas Aquinas, Saint. *Summa Contra Gentiles, Book One: God.* Translated by Anton C. Pegis. New York: Hanover House, 1955. http://dhspriory.org /thomas/ContraGentiles1.htm.

———. *On Reasons for Our Faith Against the Muslims* (New Bedford, Mass.: Franciscans of the Immaculate, 2002).

———. *Quaestiones disputatae de Potentia Dei–On The Power Of God.* Trans. the English Dominican Fathers. Westminster, Maryland: Newman, 1952. Reprint of 1932. Html edition ed. Joseph Kenny, OP. http://dhspriory .org/thomas/QDdePotentia.htm.

———. *Reasons for the Faith Against Muslim Objections (and one objection of the Greeks and Armenians) to the Cantor of Antioch.* Trans. Joseph Kenny, OP. Accessed Mar. 1, 2018. http://www.catholicapologetics.info /apologetics/islam/rationes.htm.

———. *Summa Theologiae.* Translated by Fathers of the English Dominican Province. 2nd rev. ed., 1920. Rev. and ed. Kevin Knight for New Advent. http://newadvent.org/summa/.

———. *The Two Commandments of Charity and the Ten Commandments of the Law.* Translated by Fr. Henry Rawes. London: Burns & Oates, 1880.

Trifkovic, Serge. *The Sword of the Prophet: Islam History, Theology, Impact on the World.* Boston: Regina Orthodox, 2002.

Urvoy, Dominique et Marie-Thérèse. *Les mots de l'Islam.* Toulouse: Presses Universitaires du Mirail, 2004.

Urvoy, Marie-Thérèse. "Jésus." In *Dictionnaire du Coran.* Edited by Mohammad Ali Amir-Moezzi. Paris: *Robert Laffont,* 2007), 438–441.

Waines, David. s.v. "Al-Ṭabarī, Muslim scholar." *Encyclopedia Britannica.* Accessed Apr. 3, 2018. https://www.britannica.com/biography/al-Tabari.

Watt, William Montgomery. *Muhammad: Prophet and Statesman.* London: Oxford University Press, 1961.

WikiIslam: The Online Resource on Islam. s.v. "The Meaning of Islam." Accessed Feb. 28, 2018. https://wikiislam.net/wiki/The_Meaning_of_Islam.

Wise, Michael O., Martin G. Abegg, Jr., and Edward M. Cook. *The Dead Sea Scrolls: A New Translation.* Rev. Ed. New York: Harper Collins 2005.

Zalba, Marcellino, SJ. *Theologiae Moralis Summa.* Madrid: Biblioteca de Auctores Christianos, 1957.

INDEX